K.I.S.S.

DK

The Only Guides You'll Ever Need!

THIS SERIES IS YOUR TRUSTED GUIDE through all of life's stages and situations. Want to learn how to surf the Internet or care for your new dog? Or maybe you'd like to become a wine connoisseur or an expert gardener? The solution is simple: just pick up a K.I.S.S. Guide and turn to the first page.

Expert authors will walk you through the subject from start to finish, using simple blocks of knowledge to build your skills one step at a time. Build upon these learning blocks and by the end of the book, you'll be an expert yourself! Or, if you are familiar with the topic but want to learn more, it's easy to dive in and pick up where you left off.

The K.I.S.S. Guides deliver what they promise: simple access to all the information you'll need on one subject. Other titles you might want to check out include: Yoga, Photography, Sex, Organizing Your Life, the Internet, Gardening, Gambling, and many more.

K·I·S·S

GUIDE TO

The Unexplained

JOEL LEVY
Foreword by Lionel Fanthorpe
President of the Association for the Scientific Study of Anomalous Phenomena

DK
A Dorling Kindersley Book

LONDON, NEW YORK,
MUNICH, MELBOURNE, DELHI

Dorling Kindersley Limited
Senior Editor Caroline Hunt
Project Editors Julian Gray, Jane Sarluis
Designers Martin Dieguez, Kelly Meyer, Rebecca Studd

Managing Editor Maxine Lewis
Managing Art Editor Heather McCarry

Picture Research Sarah Duncan
Production Rita Sinha
Category Publisher Mary Thompson

DK Publishing, Inc.
Senior Editor Jennifer Williams
Editorial Director Chuck Wills
Publisher Chuck Lang

First published in 2002 by
Dorling Kindersley Limited
80 Strand, London, WC2R 0RL

A Penguin Company

2 4 6 8 10 9 7 5 3 1

A CIP catalogue record for this book is available from the British Library.

ISBN: 0 7513 3688 2

Colour reproduction by Colourscan, Singapore
Printed and bound by MOHN media and Mohndruck GmbH, Germany

See our complete catalogue at

www.dk.com

Contents at a Glance

Part One

Mind

Part Two

Spirit

Part Three

Natural Mysteries

Part Four

Aliens and UFOs

Appendices

Foreword

"BEHOLD, I SHOW YOU A MYSTERY!" wrote Paul to the Corinthians. That captured his readers' attention, as any good mystery still does. My wife Patricia and I have spent years researching and investigating the unknown: it still fascinates us. Some mysteries evaporate in the light and heat of science. Some have natural explanations more probable than any paranormal hypothesis. Other mysteries stubbornly refuse to surrender – and perhaps they always will.

We definitely share the same rational perspective as Joel Levy as far as investigating mysteries is concerned: research should be done carefully, accurately, scientifically, open-mindedly, and objectively. We enjoyed every page: Joel's keen, perceptive, analytical mind produces sound ideas, and expresses clearly and fluently – he brings the subject vividly to life. His work is also very well organized: categorization and taxonomy of the paranormal are never easy – but Joel's system is crisply efficient and brings everything sharply into focus. As we admired Joel's clarification of paranormal data, Patricia and I were reminded of our own research adventures. We were actually cheering audibly for Joel and murmuring "Hear! Hear!" as we read on.

Memory took us back to Oak Island, Nova Scotia, and gazing down 70 metres into the cavern under Borehole 10X with intrepid Dan Blankenship, who was then in charge on Oak Island. Dan came within seconds of death as the steel tubing lining 10X collapsed – while his son winched him to safety. The Oak Island Money Pit mystery still remains defiantly unsolved. We recalled standing in the sinister tomb in Oistins, Barbados, where massive lead-lined coffins had supposedly moved around – even though the vault had been checked by a stonemason and sealed. Memory transported us back to our investigations at Croglin Grange in Cumbria, where the account of the "vampire" that attacked the occupants has been recounted in the village for more than three centuries.

While filming The Real Nostradamus *for Channel 4, we had technical problems with the camera in the side chapel of the old church of St Laurent, in Salon, Provence, where Nostradamus lies in his wall tomb. As visitors enter that side chapel, a spotlight near the ceiling comes on automatically and shines directly on his memorial stone. The light goes off as visitors leave. As we set up ready to shoot my presenter's piece beside Nostradamus' memorial, that automatic spotlight began to flash on and off stroboscopically. The camera could compensate for either on or off – but not for that rapid flickering! We tried everything – unplugging whatever we could reach in the hope that one of those cables led to the flickering lamp above: nothing worked.*

Our cameraman had an idea: "Father, you are a real Priest, as well as an actor, aren't you?" (I'm an ordained Anglican Priest, as well as being Magistral Chaplain General to the Knights Templar Priory of St Mary Magdalene.) "Do you think it's Nostradamus fiddling with that light?" continued the cameraman thoughtfully. "Could you say a prayer for him?" I blessed Nostradamus' memorial stone, and said a short Latin prayer concluding with: "Nostradamus, requiescat in pace." *As I pronounced the "Amen", the spotlight went out, and we filmed our piece with no problems. There's a 0.9 probability that it was simply coincidence – whatever coincidence really is! But I still don't know why it happened exactly when it did – even after reading Joel's first rate book, which I commend enthusiastically and unreservedly to the reader.*

Lionel Fanthorpe

LIONEL FANTHORPE
President of ASSAP
(the Association for the Scientific Study of Anomalous Phenomena)

Introduction

THE WORLD OF THE UNEXPLAINED produces two, equally strong responses from all of us. The first response is fascination, because we all love stories of incredible feats and marvellous powers, strange creatures, and odd happenings. The second response is curiosity, because we want to know if it's true, how it's done, whether it really exists. We want to explain the unexplained.

That's supposed to be my job in this book – to describe the incredible range of mysteries and wonders that make up the world of the unexplained, and to explain them to you. Hopefully you'll agree that the K.I.S.S. Guide to the Unexplained *does a good job of the first bit. It certainly covers a lot of ground, moving from inner mysteries of the mind and spirit to alien mysteries that are out of this world. But although I can present the evidence and discuss the theories, I cannot ultimately tell you what is true and what is not – you have to decide what you believe for yourself, and more often than not there won't be a simple answer.*

The first chapter in each section is intended to be a handy guide to help you better understand what follows. These chapters provide a concise overview of the material covered in each section, and the basic tools that you need to interpret that material. Armed with this knowledge, you should be better equipped to make up your mind about the mysteries that follow.

When you've read the evidence and heard the theories, and you're drawing your own conclusions, there are a few things you might like to bear in mind. The first is a principle called Occam's Razor. William of Occam was a medieval philosopher who came up with a simple principle to help people decide between alternative explanations. In extremely simplified form, Occam's Razor says that firstly, the simplest explanation is usually right; and secondly, you shouldn't add unnecessary complications when you're trying to explain something. In the world of weird phenomena you are often called upon to decide which explanation is most likely – Occam's Razor can help you.

The second and perhaps most important thing is to keep an open mind. This is often harder than it sounds. Some people have trouble with facts that challenge their assumptions; other people want to believe something so badly that they ignore the evidence altogether. In order to be properly open-minded you need to start without preconceptions and then listen to all the evidence.

This doesn't mean you can't be sceptical – a true sceptic is open-minded, with no assumptions about whether something can or can't exist. Someone who insists that UFOs are figments of the imagination or that ghosts cannot be real, without first considering the evidence, is just as dogmatic as someone who insists that secret powers control our every move or that aliens assassinated JFK.

In a book like this it is important for the author to lay his cards on the table, and say what he believes. Having read all the stories, reports, explanations, and theories that you are about to read, I have definitely come to a sceptical conclusion about most (but not all) of the phenomena covered here. Whichever conclusion you come to, I hope that you enjoy reaching it.

JOEL LEVY

What's Inside?

THE INFORMATION in the K.I.S.S. Guide to the Unexplained *has been divided into four separate sections: the power of the mind; the supernatural; mysterious phenomena from the natural world; and UFOs.*

Part One

Do you believe that some people possess strange powers of the mind, powers beyond the limits of nature and science? In this section we'll look at evidence that suggests this might be true, hearing incredible stories and meeting some unusual people along the way. I'll do my best to explain the complicated background and the experts' opinions, but in the end it's up to you to decide what you think.

Part Two

In Part Two we turn to the realm of the spirit, and look at phenomena that are connected, in one way or another, to the existence of powers beyond the human mind, beyond even the natural world. Among the many supernatural phenomena covered in this section, you'll encounter haunted houses, séances, table turning, poltergeists, angels and demons, and witchcraft.

Part Three

This section of the book deals with an amazing range of mysterious phenomena from the natural world that can't be explained by science. You'll discover the real origin of crop circles, unravel the mystery of ley lines, and learn about the strange objects (and animals) that fall from the sky. Decide for yourself what may be simply folklore and what is one of nature's true anomalies.

Part Four

For over fifty years people have reported seeing strange lights and saucer-shaped objects cavorting in the skies. What lies behind these stories? Can there really be aliens among us? In Part Four you'll find out the answers, but they may not be what you expected. I'll explain how the UFO phenomenon became the biggest mystery of them all, and explode a few myths along the way.

The Extras

THROUGHOUT THE BOOK, you'll notice a number of boxes and symbols. They are there to emphasize certain points I want you to pay special attention to, because they are important to your understanding and improvement. You'll find:

Very Important Point

This symbol points out a topic I believe deserves careful attention.

Complete No-No

This is a warning, something I want to advise you not to do or to be aware of.

Getting Technical

When the information is about to get a bit technical, I'll let you know so that you can read carefully.

Inside Scoop

Little-known or "inside" information that you might not normally be told.

You'll also find some little boxes that include information I think is important, useful, or just plain fun.

Trivia...

These are simply fun facts that will give you a new or even amusing angle on some of the subjects I'll be discussing.

DEFINITION

Here I'll **define** *words and terms for you in an easy-to-understand style. You'll also find a glossary at the back of the book with all the paranormal lingo.*

INTERNET

www.dk.com

The Internet is a great resource for anyone interested in mysterious phenomena, so I've scouted out some web sites that I think are worth checking out.

Part One

The Mind

Do some people possess strange powers of the mind, powers beyond the limits of nature? There is a lot of evidence that this is true – there's even evidence that we might all have mental powers! In Part One we'll look at that evidence in detail.

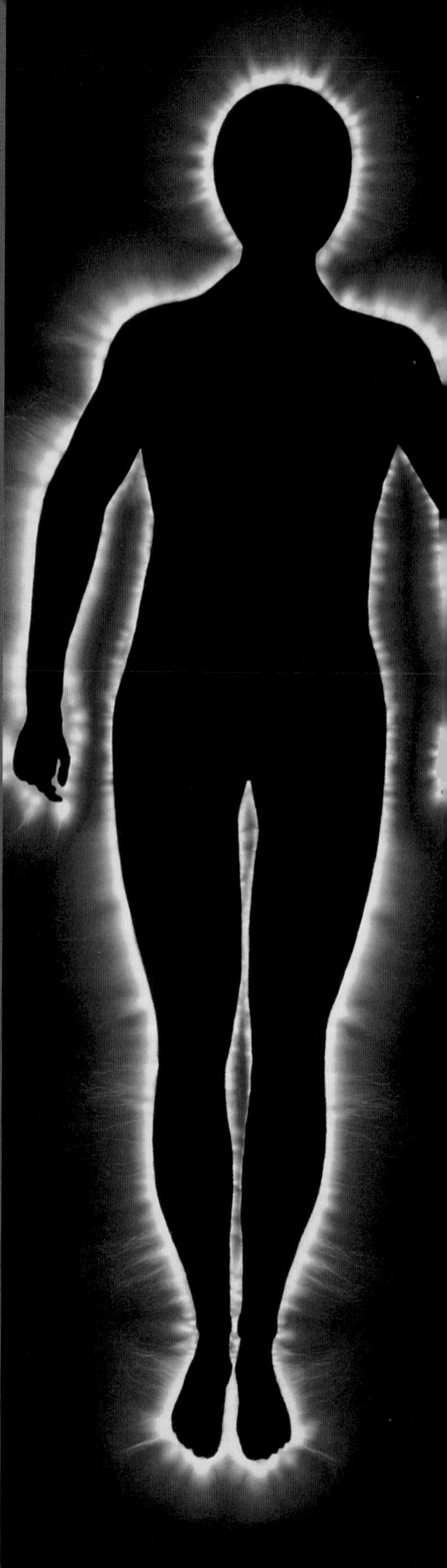

Chapter 1

Mental Powers – the Basics

SOME PEOPLE WANT PROOF that mental powers exist. They want to know what enables certain individuals to read minds, bend spoons, and predict the future. The answer, according to some scientists, is psi – a type of energy that gives the human mind control over matter, space, and even time. The term "psi" comes from the 23rd letter of the Greek alphabet; Greek letters are frequently used to name forces or types of energy, so scientists investigating paranormal phonomena decided it would be a good idea to use a Greek letter for the force they were studying. Psi is sometimes also said to be an acronym for Paranormal Sensory Information.

Don't worry if the exact meaning of the word is sometimes unclear, or if I seem to use it in several different ways throughout this section. Psi is an umbrella term, a single word that stands for everything that's mysterious and inexplicable. It is the strange quality that links feats such as mind reading, spoon-bending, and the ability to see through walls. In this chapter, I look at the theory, history, and future of psi research and ask the crucial question ... does it even exist?

Does psi exist?

PSI HAS A UNIQUE STATUS in the world of science – it is a scientific term for something that no-one is sure exists, may well be impossible to measure, and could have the power to change the world as we know it.

Does it really exist as an actual force? What form does it take and how does it work? Do any or all humans possess it? These are the central mysteries of ***parapsychology***, the branch of science that searches for proof of psi. The story of mental powers is essentially the story of parapsychology and psi.

DEFINITION

Psychology is the study of the mind. The researchers who first started to scientifically investigate the paranormal were mostly psychologists. They decided to call the new field **parapsychology**, *adding* para, *from the Greek for "beside", to the existing word.*

Reality check

Of all the things in this book, psi is perhaps the most likely to exist in reality. It is the only one to be tested under laboratory conditions, and the only one with any solid scientific proof to its name. Scientists have performed the most rigorous experiments possible, finding evidence that clearly says, yes, psi does exist.

Being able to predict *the outcome of a roll of the dice may help prove that psi does exist.*

So why haven't we heard more about psi, and why did I say it's only "the most likely to exist"? The answer is that some types of proof are more convincing than others. Unfortunately, what scientists have found is not very impressive to 0the non-scientist – it's all to do with statistics.

The best proof of psi involves comparatively mundane feats, like guessing 12 correct cards out of 100, instead of 10, or imperceptibly nudging dice as they roll.

This is hardly headline-grabbing stuff, and yet if psi could be proven to exist we might be looking at the greatest scientific discovery of all time.

The real deal

Maybe we don't need psychics and parapsychologists to find real mental powers. There are many documented cases where human beings have been able to produce amazing effects, such as stopping their own hearts, walking on hot coals, or hammering nails through their bodies. These incredible feats are produced through hypnosis and other altered mental states. In the past, scientists said they were impossible, and must be fake – now everyone accepts that they really exist.

A brief history of psi

Only in the last 100 years or so has a clear division opened up between psi phenomena and what we call magic and the supernatural. Right up until the 1920s, few people would have drawn a distinction between ghosts, astrology, and mind reading. Many of the historical figures we will meet in later chapters, from witch doctors to saints, exhibited what, today, we might call psionic, or psi-based, powers.

The real history of psi and parapsychology started in the 19th century, with the birth of spiritualism – a new form of religion based on the belief that it was possible to communicate with the dead. Spiritualism was mysterious and dramatic – objects appeared out of nowhere, musical instruments played themselves, and people floated in mid-air. It captured the imagination of both the public and the scientific establishment.

In 1882, the Society for Psychical Research (SPR) was founded in London. Its aim was to "examine ... in a scientific spirit those faculties of man, real or supposed, which appear to be inexplicable on any generally recognized hypothesis". Although it mainly focused on issues like hauntings and life after death, the SPR also investigated "thought-transference", or telepathy. Within 3 years the SPR was joined by a sister organization in the US, the American Society for Psychical Research (ASPR), which boasted the distinguished psychologist William James among its early members.

Early experiments

The earliest parapsychology experiments were carried out in the 1880s. One person would try to "send" a picture, using only the power of his mind, while another person tried to "receive" it.

But these tests were hard to score – how accurate did the receiver have to be for the test to be a success? – and it was even harder to make sure no-one cheated. Parapsychology researchers decided that if they wanted to investigate psi properly, they would have to do it under controlled conditions in the laboratory.

■ **Can you see what I see?** *Sending and receiving telepathic messages was one of the first psychic phenomena to be studied by the Society for Psychical Research in the 1880s.*

Dupes and dupers

Two of the biggest problems facing parapsychology are cheating and fraud. Pretty much all of the psi effects discussed in this section can be produced by stage magicians, usually much more impressively. In fact, mind-reading tricks are stock elements of high profile acts like the magician David Copperfield, and psychics like Uri Geller (never proved to be a fake) who have made psi phenomena like mind-reading and spoon-bending familiar the world over.

All over the world, *stage magicians follow in the footsteps of Uri Geller wowing audiences with their spoon-bending skills.*

The biggest problem of all for parapsychology is that extraordinary claims require extraordinary evidence. If scientists accept that psi really does exist, they will have to rewrite the laws of physics, and it's going to take more than a bunch of statistics to make them do that.

The usual explanations

Mental powers and the strange happenings associated with them have attracted a host of hypotheses. Explanations of all sorts abound, from the sceptical to the scientific. Fraud is the most common explanation offered by sceptics, whether it's by the experimenter or the person being tested. Even the most eagle-eyed experimenter can be duped, especially when he wants to believe, and since most parapsychologists are extremely keen to find proof of psi, it might be argued that they are easy targets. There's no doubt that cases of cheating and trickery discredit results that seem to be genuine.

Developments in psi experiments were designed especially to make cheating difficult, but some critics say that a determined hoaxer can overcome almost any obstacle to produce convincing results.

The scientific explanation?

Let's assume for the moment that some of the evidence for mental powers is on the level, and that they really do exist – in other words put aside the question of "whether?" This still leaves the question of "how?" Psi phenomena are unusual in the world of unexplained events because although they cannot be explained by current scientific theories they are not necessarily supernatural.

Parapsychologists work on the assumption that if psi does exist, there must be a scientific explanation for it. Usually this is said to be some sort of new form of energy, one that's perfectly natural – we just haven't found it yet.

Unfortunately most theories about how psi works are vague and unsatisfactory. They often involve quantum theory, probably because this is still a poorly understood area of science with lots of room for new discoveries. Most parapsychologists prefer to steer clear of the whole issue.

The research continues ...

In many cases, the institutions that were initially set up to investigate psi are still around today. The SPR and ASPR both still investigate cases and publish a journal, and have now been joined by the Australasian SPR.

The original home of parapsychology – the Foundation for Research on the Nature of Man (FRNM), set up by Joseph and Louisa Rhine at Duke University in the 1930s – is still going strong today and has been joined by a number of research units around the world.

At Princeton University, for instance, the Physical Engineering Anomalies Research lab (PEAR) has performed many experiments on the physical effects of psi. In the UK some universities, such as the Koestler Unit at Edinburgh, have their own parapsychology departments. The professional Parapsychological Association acts as a sort of umbrella organization for academics.

Sceptical inquirers

Keeping a critical watch on these academics, and on the whole field, are ***sceptical*** organizations led by the influential Committee for the Scientific Investigation of Claims of the Paranormal (CSICOP), publishers of the US *Skeptical Inquirer* magazine. For some observers they provide a welcome injection of common sense, but others criticize them for being too dogmatic in their opposition to all things paranormal. The most high profile member of CSICOP is probably former stage magician turned professional debunker, James "The Amazing" Randi.

DEFINITION

Although being **sceptical** *has come to mean opposing any form of belief in the paranormal, true sceptics are open minded – they neither believe nor disbelieve – and are suspicious of dogmatic thinking in either direction.*

In the following chapters you'll read all about the various psi phenomena and hopefully come to your own conclusions as to whether you think psi really does exist.

Chapter 2

Mind Over Matter

IN THIS CHAPTER we'll explore the limits of human capability and look at some incredible phenomena that seem to exceed it. I'll introduce the mysterious (and not so mysterious) abilities of Indian fakirs, the wonders of fire-walking, and the strange world of hypnosis. In the pages that follow I'll try to separate the fiction from the facts, and look at the theories that try to explain them.

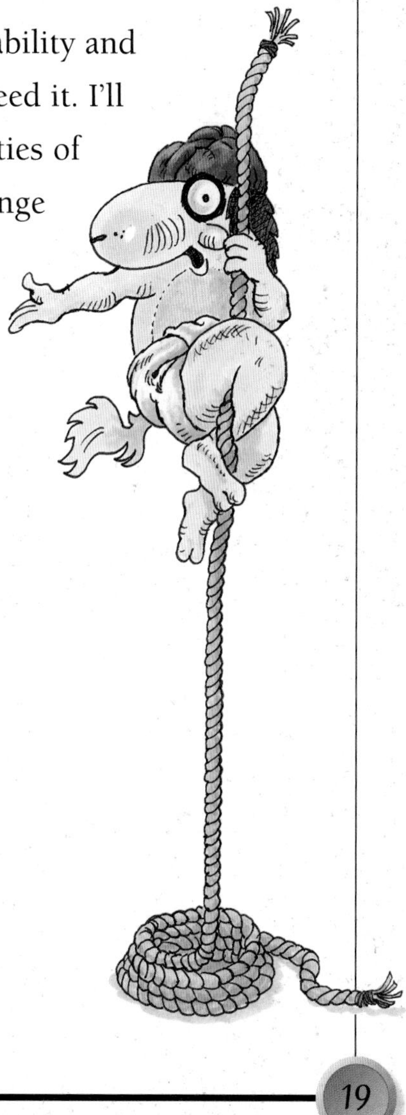

AN EXAMPLE OF MIND OVER MATTER, OR SIMPLY APPLIED PHYSICS?

In this chapter...

- ✓ The unexplored mind
- ✓ Beds of nails
- ✓ The Indian Rope Trick
- ✓ True feats of the holy men
- ✓ Fire, walk on me
- ✓ Hypnosis

The unexplored mind

OUR MINDS CONTROL and direct our bodies, but there are many aspects of the body that do not appear to be under our conscious control. If you get cold, you have to put on more clothes or turn up the heating to get warm. If you have an injury, you have to take a painkiller if you want to relieve the pain. You cannot consciously influence such processes – or can you?

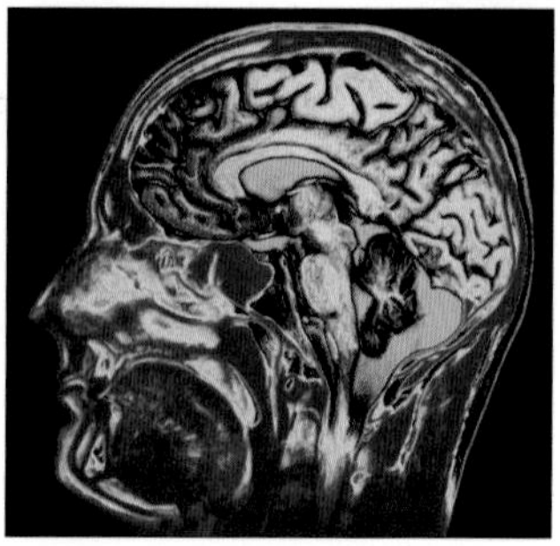

The human mind *may be far more powerful than anyone can imagine.*

Healing powers

Doctors have known for many years that real physical disorders can be produced by the power of the mind – these are called ***psychosomatic*** diseases. Exactly how this process works is still not properly understood, but that hasn't stopped people from trying to reverse the effect and harness the healing power of the mind. Cancer patients, for instance, are sometimes trained to visualize their immune systems destroying cancerous cells, and there is some evidence that this helps to boost their health. People suffering from high blood pressure can be trained through a technique called "biofeedback therapy" to consciously lower their blood pressures.

DEFINITION

The word **psychosomatic** *comes from the Greek:* psycho, *meaning mind, and* soma, *meaning body. Psychosomatic therefore means "of mind and body".*

There are some special cases where people display apparently superhuman abilities, such as fire-walking, body piercing, and hypnosis, which suggest that the mind has enormous untapped potential.

Your unconscious mind and your body

Your brain is connected to your body by two types of nervous system – the somatic and the autonomic. The somatic nervous system carries signals to your muscles that allow you to consciously control them. The autonomic nervous system carries signals from unconscious parts of your brain to parts of your body over which you have no conscious control – the muscles of your intestines, for instance, or the muscles that control the tiny blood vessels in your skin. If you could somehow learn to operate your autonomic nervous system at will, you could stop wounds bleeding, raise your body temperature, and slow down your heart beat.

Beds of nails

HOLY MEN from cultures around the globe can demonstrate the sort of mind-over-matter abilities I've just described. The most famous of these are the **fakirs** *of India, best known for sitting on beds of nails and performing the Indian rope trick.*

DEFINITION

In the West, Indian holy men trained in the mystic arts are commonly called **fakirs**, *from the Arab meaning "poor man".*

How to sit comfortably

The Indian fakir sitting in a lotus position on a bed of nails is a familiar image of exotic Eastern powers, but in reality this is one of the least impressive feats of which holy men are capable.

Sitting or lying on a bed of nails does not require any special powers – simply enough nails. The weight of the person sitting on the nails is spread out so that the weight pressing down on each nail is small – small enough so that the nail does not even pierce the skin. Anyone can perform this trick if they have a bed with a minimum number of nails (the number depends on the weight of the sitter).

Never try sitting on a bed of nails at home, as it is very easy to make mistakes. For instance, if the nails are uneven in length your weight may not be distributed evenly, with painful consequences.

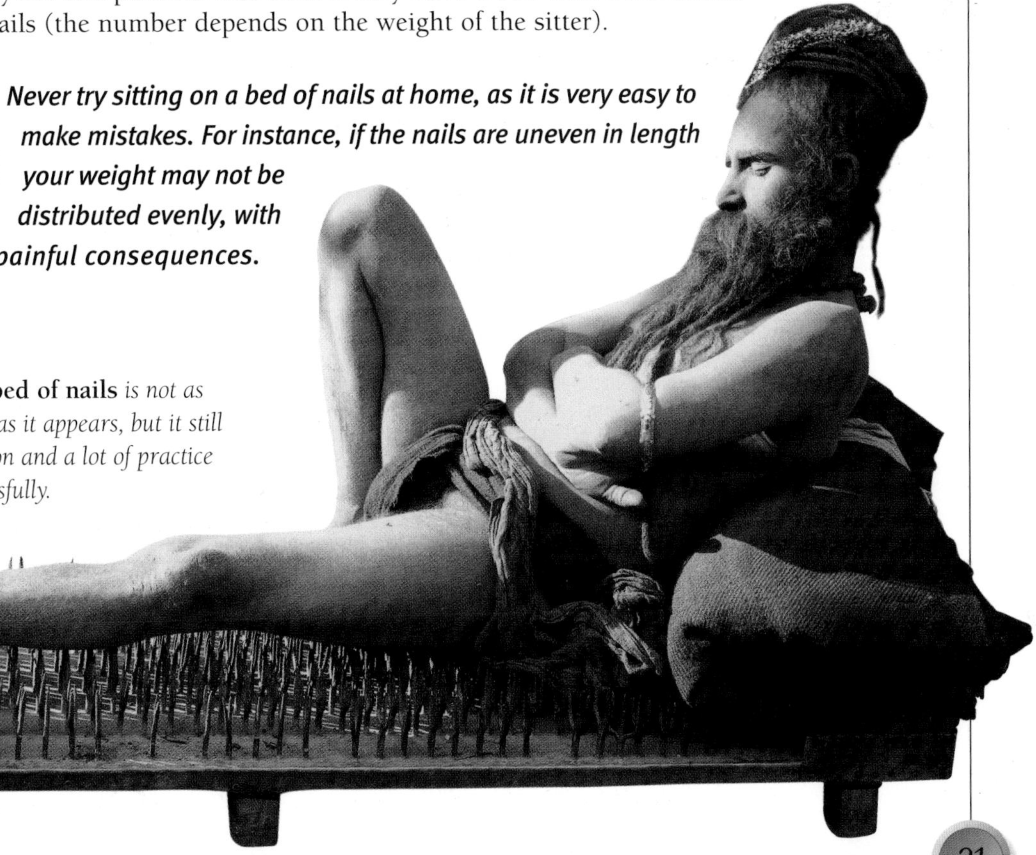

Sitting on a bed of nails *is not as impressive a feat as it appears, but it still takes concentration and a lot of practice to perform successfully.*

The Indian rope trick

ALMOST AS WELL known as the bed of nails is the Indian rope trick. In its classical form, the trick goes as follows. The fakir makes a rope stand on end and his young assistant climbs up it, vanishing at the top. The fakir, brandishing a knife, follows him up and also disappears from view. Bloody chunks of dismembered boy then rain down and the fakir reappears with a suitably gore-stained blade. He puts the chunks into a basket (or covers them with his cloak), from which the whole boy then emerges. Versions of the trick were reported by many British visitors to India in the 19th century, and a variety of theories have been offered to explain it.

Mass hypnosis of the audience

The fakir typically talks throughout the performance, often in a monotonous voice – could he be casting a sort of spell with his voice? In his 1962 book, *Beyond Telepathy*, the scientist Andrija Puharich describes a case in which two psychologists investigated the trick. The performance they saw corresponded to the description above, but when they developed their film of the event, the fakir and his assistant were seen simply standing by the coiled rope for the whole time. In other words the fakir had simply hypnotized the audience into hallucinating the whole experience (using mass telepathy, according to Puharich). Mass hypnosis of this kind is not generally believed to be possible, and such reports have not been verified.

A conjuring trick

Stage magicians regularly recreate the Indian rope trick, and there are a number of suggestions as to how it might be done. These include the use of a bamboo-jointed rope, where the rope is a cleverly constructed prop with a series of bamboo joints that can be locked into place with the flick of a wrist. Alternatively, the top of the rope is attached to an invisible wire slung between two nearby hills.

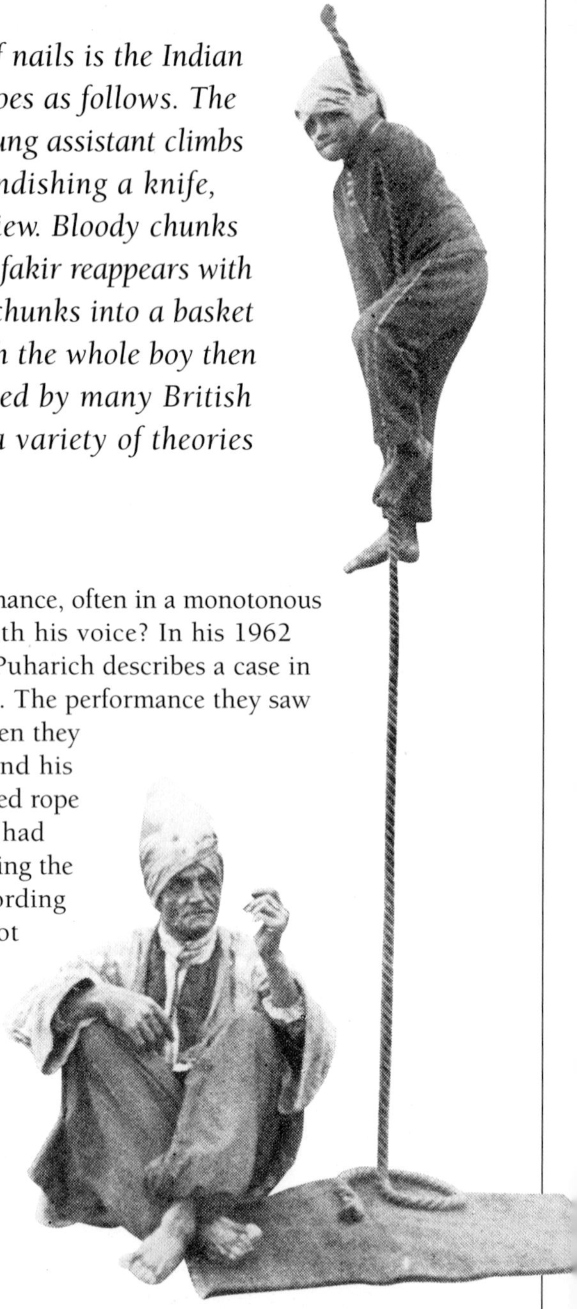

■ **One of the most famous** *photographs of the Indian rope trick shows "Karachi" (English eccentric Arthur Darby) and his son "Kyder".*

A traveller's tale

Disappointingly, it now seems that the most likely explanation is that the rope trick in its most impressive form never actually happened, and was simply a form of traveller's tall tale.

A 1996 survey of original reports of the Indian rope trick showed that the longer the gap between seeing the trick and telling the story, the more impressive the eventual report.

Stories told soon after seeing the trick describe fairly simple performances – ones that could easily be explained. This suggests that the more colourful versions were the result of the tellers embroidering their tales over time, perhaps following the popular and well-known story of how the trick was supposed to look.

True feats of the holy men

BEDS OF NAILS and the Indian rope trick may not amount to much, but fakirs and holy men from other cultures are capable of genuine feats of physical prowess produced by the power of their minds over their bodies.

Not faking it

Fakirs can alter the electrical rhythms of their brains and reduce their blood pressure, heartbeat, and breathing rates to a fraction of the normal levels, by will power alone. Not only does this allow them to adopt difficult yoga positions and then remain motionless for long periods of time, it also allows some adepts to stay under water for more than 6 minutes at a time, or to bury their heads in sand.

Such powers are known as *siddhis* ("accomplishments"), and are acquired through rigorous yoga training. It is claimed that other *siddhis* include the power to levitate, read minds, and see the future.

■ **With his head buried in the sand,** *this yogi in Agra, India, has reduced his heart rate to just two beats a minute and has stopped breathing altogether.*

Tibetan *tumo*

Buddhist monks of Tibet are also able to exert incredible control over their bodies. They can develop a power known as *tumo* – the ability to raise their body temperature through an effort of will. After years of yoga training, adepts can use their mastery of *tumo* to survive naked for an entire winter, living in a cave on a Himalayan mountainside. In 1981, Dr Herbert Benson of Harvard Medical School tested Tibetan monks and showed that they could raise the temperature of their fingers and toes by up to 8 °C (15 °F), simply by an effort of will.

Trivia...

Another power attributed to Tibetan monks is lung-gom *– the ability to run at incredible speeds over deep snow without sinking in.*

Stabbing pains

Deliberate piercing of the body with needles and skewers is a feature of several religions. It is practised by Hindus and Dervishes (members of special Islamic sects), among others. Devotees pierce themselves through the skin, fleshy parts of the arms, legs, and torso, and even through the cheeks. Usually the devotee feels no pain, or is able to shut it out, and often there is little or no bleeding and rapid healing of the wound after the skewer is removed. How is this possible?

People who pierce themselves seem to be able to consciously control their autonomic processes.

Pierced devotees can exert their will power over normally unconscious body processes, such as the opening and closing of capillaries and the release of endorphins (the body's painkillers).

Religious ecstasy

People who pierce themselves are often in a special state known as an ecstatic trance. Through dancing, chanting, and meditation, religious devotees can enter a different state of consciousness – a bit like being self-hypnotized. It is believed that people in an ecstatic trance state can shut out pain and fatigue, and also that this is what gives them the ability to control unconscious body functions such as pain perception.

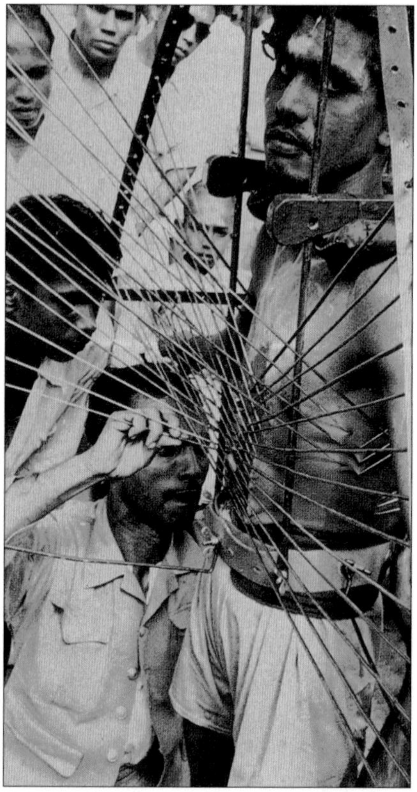

During the Hindu festival *of Thaipusam, religious devotees claim to feel no pain when they are pierced.*

Fire, walk on me

FIRE-WALKING is a feature of many cultures. It is found in religious and magical rituals in such countries as Bali, Mexico, India, South Africa, China, and Fiji. The practice was recorded by ancient Greek and Roman writers including Plato and Virgil, and is even found in some Christian rituals. The villagers of Langadas in Greece, for instance, dance on hot coals to celebrate the Feast of St Constantine.

■ **Fire-walking** *is usually performed in a religious or spiritual context, which might help walkers go into a semi-trance state.*

Hot stuff

Fire-walkers have been observed traversing beds of wood embers, hot coals, white hot stones, and glowing ploughshares, exposing the soles of their feet to temperatures as high as 800 °C (1,472 °F). Despite these extreme temperatures, the feet of fire-walkers remain unscathed. How is this possible?

Quick, march

In 1935 researchers from the University of London watched a young man named Kuda Bux cross a 6 m (20 ft) trench filled with glowing embers at a temperature of about 426 °C (800 °F). Also watching the demonstration was the veteran psychical researcher Harry Price, who proposed a theory that is still cited today. He suggested that although fire-walking looked impressive, in reality the walker's feet were never in much danger of scorching.

Embers, said Price, have a low thermal conductivity – they may be extremely hot, but they will only pass on that heat to surrounding substances relatively slowly. The soles of the walker, which may be quite thick and tough, are in contact with the embers for only a fraction of a second at a time, so they do not have time to burn. Price's theory has some merits – most fire-walks are indeed fairly quick, and the soles of many native fire-walkers are very thick. But it does not explain everything. Some fire-walks are done at a leisurely pace, and some are over material with a high thermal conductivity.

THE LEIDENFROST EFFECT

The Leidenfrost effect is a phenomenon in which an insulating, protective boundary sheet of vapour forms over a liquid exposed to extreme heat (the same effect that allows you to pinch out candles with wet fingers, without getting burnt).

In 1977 Professor Jearl Walker of Cleveland State University, Ohio, had an article published in *Scientific American* that cited the Leidenfrost Effect as a possible explanation for fire-walking. Walker concluded that during a fire-walk, water or sweat on the soles can form a protective layer when the feet come into contact with hot substances. Wetting the feet before the walk is an important part of many fire-walking ceremonies.

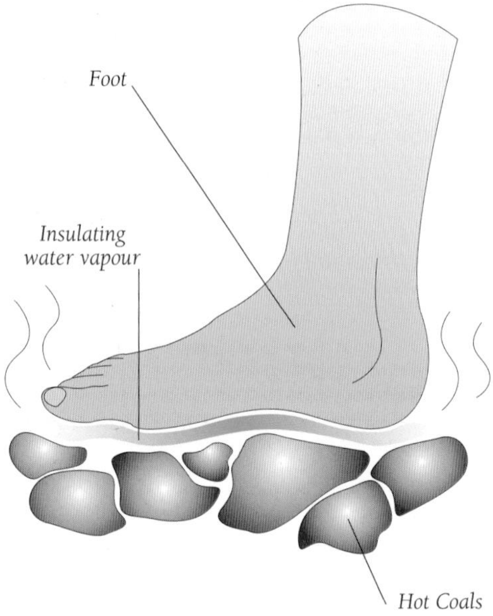

LEIDENFROST EFFECT

The agony and the ecstasy

Like the feats of piercing described earlier, fire-walking often occurs as part of a ritual, in which the walkers may attain a state of religious ecstasy, often with the help of a presiding priest or ***shaman*** who chants or dances. Even in the West, people often work themselves up into a semi-trance state before fire-walking, and completion of the walk is accompanied by a profound sense of euphoria. These facts suggest that mechanisms of endorphin release may help fire-walkers overcome the pain of hot coals, but this theory also has problems.

Not all fire-walkers are in a state of altered consciousness, and endorphins can only block pain, not prevent scorching. Even more tellingly, tests of the soles of walkers immediately before and after a fire-walk show that they are normally sensitive to being touched or pricked with a pin. It seems that religious ecstasy cannot be the whole story either.

DEFINITION

In many cultures throughout history and around the world, the roles of priest, healer, wise man, and magician are combined. Westerners have used various terms to describe the people who perform these complex jobs, including witch-doctor, medicine man, and **shaman**. *The latter term comes from the name given to the holy men of Eastern Siberian tribes such as the Tungus.*

Hypnosis

HYPNOSIS, from the Greek hypnos *meaning "sleep", is a state of consciousness somewhere between sleep and full alertness. Exactly what sort of state is a matter of controversy, and despite extensive research, hypnosis remains something of a mystery. People in a state of hypnosis display remarkable abilities that seem to be beyond the normal range of human faculties.*

It has been claimed that hypnotic subjects have improved memory, superhuman strength, access to past lives, invulnerability to pain, and even telepathic powers.

Can hypnosis tap into paranormal powers, or has hype obscured the less dramatic truth?

Hypnotism may still *be viewed as somewhat macabre, but, in controlled conditions, it can be a useful tool in therapies that treat both mind and body.*

A brief history of hypnosis

Mystics and holy men have been hypnotizing themselves and others for centuries. Greek and Egyptian healers, for instance, sometimes used methods very similar to those of modern hypnotists to put their patients into a trance, so that they could be questioned and advised about their illnesses. Shamans and priests sometimes put themselves into trance states, which may be similar to hypnosis, to help them work magic or communicate with supernatural powers.

The concept of hypnosis as we know it is a relatively recent invention, growing out of the 18th-century movement known as mesmerism, named after the Viennese physician Franz Anton Mesmer. Mesmer discovered that he could heal some of his patients simply by passing his hands over them. Often they would fall into a ***trance*** and become strangely compliant with Mesmer's instructions, a phenomenon known as suggestibility. Today we would say that Mesmer's patients had been hypnotized, but Mesmer and his followers had a different theory.

DEFINITION

A **trance** *is a state of consciousness in which someone does not respond normally to the outside world, acting as if they are not fully awake or aware.*

Mesmer and his trance

Mesmer believed in an invisible force called animal magnetism, similar to electricity, which he could direct through a patient's body to produce a cure. His followers, known as "magnetizers", included the Marquis de Puységur, who first described a mesmeric trance. Puységur called this state "artificial somnambulism", and described how the somnambulist could speak, move around, and follow instructions.

This engraving *shows a hypnotist putting a woman into a trance using the invisible forces of animal magnetism.*

Scottish physician James Braid (1795–1860) developed his own theory about mesmerism. He did not believe that animal magnetism was involved, and came up with a theory that he called neurohypnotism, later shortened to hypnotism. From the 1880s onwards, hypnosis was used as a form of psychotherapy, and stories grew up about the strange effects of the hypnotic trance. People were said to develop hyper-acute senses, and be able to recall long-forgotten incidents in minute detail.

Hypnosis and suggestibility

Today it is clear that while hypnosis is not a paranormal phenomenon, it can produce some incredible, and inexplicable, results. One of the central features of hypnosis is that people will follow suggestions to a remarkable extent, including some instructions that should be impossible to obey – not feeling pain, for instance. People will even follow suggestions made to them during hypnosis after they have come out of the trance – this is known as post-hypnotic suggestion.

People under hypnosis cannot be made to act against strongly held moral values (in other words, do things they really don't want to do).

Suggestibility is probably responsible for some of the more bizarre behaviour that hypnosis can produce. A common trick performed by stage hypnotists is regression, in which a hypnotized person is told that he or she is a child. The person behaves accordingly, speaking like a child and often pretending to be at nursery school or in a similar situation.

Has the hypnotic subject really regressed to childhood, somehow resetting his or her mental clock and reactivating childish mental structures, or is he or she simply pretending (albeit unconsciously)? It seems likely that the latter is true, and that the hypnotized person is acting – unconsciously playing along with the hypnotist.

Hypnosis and pain

One of the first and most dramatic uses of hypnosis was in surgery, where it was used as an anaesthetic. As early as 1842, an English surgeon named Ward amputated a man's leg while he was in a mesmeric trance. This was before the development of chemical anaesthetics, such as chloroform, yet the man felt no pain. Up until 1859 James Esdaile, a surgeon in India, performed over 300 operations using hypnosis as the only form of pain control. Today we have sophisticated anaesthetic drugs, but very occasionally hypnosis is still used to block out all pain. How it works is not clear.

Experiments show that the hypnotized brain registers pain signals as normal, but that the conscious mind seems to shut these signals out.

In a remarkable test by Stanford University psychologist E.R. Hilgard, a hypnotized man was told that he would feel no pain and was then pricked with a pin and questioned about his sensations. Although he verbally denied experiencing any pain, a written answer gave the opposite response – at least one part of his consciousness did feel the pin. This psychological phenomenon is known as dissociation.

INTERNET

www.hypnos.co.uk

This site lets you download recorded hypnosis sessions to help treat a range of problems, including stopping smoking, asthma, and weight control.

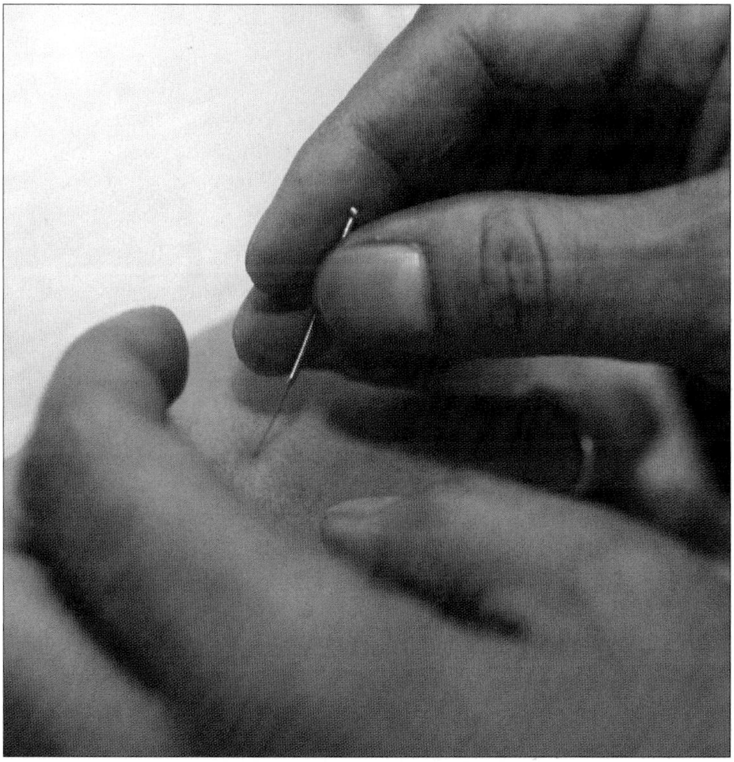

The prick of a pin *will naturally result in pain signals being sent to the brain. However, the hypnotized mind may not register the pain on a conscious level.*

Hypnosis and memory

Many people under hypnosis seem to be able to remember things that they cannot recall when fully conscious – such as childhood memories or precise descriptions of things seen only fleetingly. Some hypnotists even claim that hypnosis can reveal memories of past lives.

Controlled experiments, however, show that hypnosis does not boost a person's ability to perform memory tests – for example, remembering lists of words and numbers. Some psychologists suggest that what seem to be vivid childhood memories might actually be unconsciously invented in response to the hypnotist's suggestion. One memory effect that hypnosis can reliably produce is known as ***post-hypnotic amnesia***. Despite not remembering what happened during hypnosis, the person does retain the memories in some part of his or her consciousness, because he or she can be made to reveal them later.

DEFINITION

In **post-hypnotic amnesia**, *a hypnotized person has no conscious recollection of what happened during hypnosis.*

THE FALSE MEMORY SCANDAL

The relationship between hypnosis and memory has become a serious issue in recent years with the development of the "false memory" controversy. During the 1980s and 90s widespread allegations of child abuse and satanic rituals tore apart families and whole communities. Many of the allegations were based on "recovered memories" – memories that had apparently been suppressed because of their traumatic nature, but were recovered through hypnosis. Subsequent investigations suggested that in most cases the hypnotists had unwittingly "implanted" memories in the minds of their subjects, through being too eager to find evidence of abuse. Despite thousands of hours of police work, not one successful prosecution for satanic abuse has been brought.

Hypnosis and the body

In the late 19th century it was often claimed that hypnosis could increase the range and power of a person's senses. Although laboratory findings have not backed up these claims, it is true that under hypnosis a person's attention can be focused on specific sounds, sights, or other sensations, while distractions are excluded. It may also be possible, through suggestion, to make a hypnotized person hallucinate – see or hear things that aren't there.

Trivia...

Sigmund Freud first encountered hypnosis as a young medical student studying in France. He later used it extensively in the work that led to the development of his theories of the subconscious.

Whether through meditation or hypnosis, *the mind can exert a powerful influence on the body – an influence that science still cannot explain.*

Hypnosis may also be able to tap into psychosomatic powers similar to those of fakirs and yoga adepts. A hypnotic suggestion that a burning cigarette has been applied to the skin can cause a hypnotized person to produce a blister at that spot. This should be impossible, since the processes that form a blister are not under conscious, or even nervous, control.

This power can be used for beneficial purposes. Since the days of Mesmer, hypnosis has helped to treat and even cure a variety of medical conditions. Many of these have been physical problems, and yet doctors argue that hypnosis is a purely psychological phenomenon.

A simple summary

- ✓ Your mind may have untapped potential to boost the functioning and health of your body.
- ✓ Although the feats for which fakirs are best known – the bed of nails and the Indian rope trick – can be explained as tricks, fakirs also have impressive psychosomatic powers.
- ✓ Fire-walking is possible thanks to a combination of physics and self-belief, and provides a dramatic illustration of the power of the mind.
- ✓ Hypnosis is a poorly understood but potent method for changing the normal relationship between the conscious and unconscious mind, and between the mind and the body.

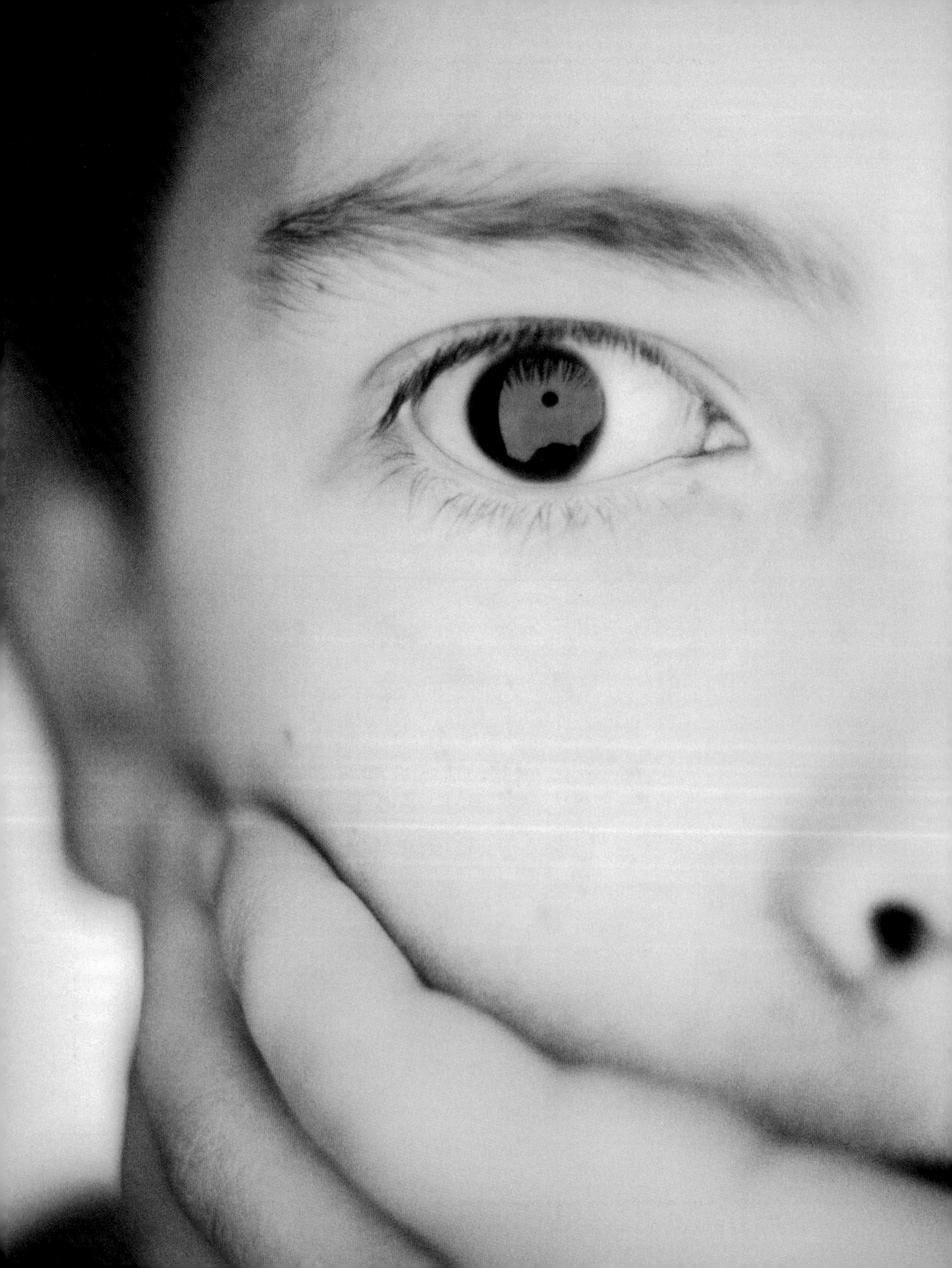

Chapter 3

ESP and Psychokinesis

ESP AND PSYCHOKINESIS are the best known types of psi power. Between them they include a wide range of incredible powers and phenomena, from psychic spies to telepathic pets. I'll start off by introducing the hard evidence that these powers really exist, before moving on to the more fantastic stuff about mind-reading pigs and spoon-bending humans.

In this chapter...

What are ESP and psychokinesis?

ESP STANDS FOR Extra-Sensory Perception, meaning the ability to perceive information without the use of the senses known to science. J.B. Rhine coined the phrase in 1934 as an umbrella term to cover three types of paranormal ability.

Categories of ESP

The three types of ESP are telepathy, clairvoyance, and precognition.

1. **Telepathy** is the ability to receive and sometimes communicate information between two minds, without the use of normal senses. Other names for telepathy include mind-reading, mental radio, and thought transference

2. **Clairvoyance** is the ability to perceive information about objects, places, and events without the use of normal senses. Other names for it include remote viewing and far sight, known in Celtic lore as "second sight"

3. **Precognition** is the ability to perceive information about the future (see Chapter 4)

Trivia...

There are actually more than five senses. In addition to vision, hearing, touch, taste, and smell, you can also sense temperature variations, the position of your muscles (known as proprioception), and the force of gravity (which is how you know what angle your head is at when your eyes are closed).

■ **Have you ever** *been thinking about a friend when that very person happens to call you? Coincidence or ESP?*

If these powers truly exist, it could be surprisingly difficult to tell the difference between them.

Suppose, for instance, that a psychic perceives the location of a hidden item. Is he or she using clairvoyance to determine the object's location, or telepathy to read the mind of the person who hid it? Or suppose that a psychic predicts what someone is going to say, and is then proved right. Did he or she use precognition to see the future, or implant the thought in the speaker's mind by telepathy?

Some of the experiments used to test ESP powers are carefully designed to rule out such uncertainty, but in many cases there is no way of telling which power is operating. This sort of confusion is one reason why many parapsychologists prefer to use the blanket term "psi".

Psychokinesis

Psychokinesis, PK for short, is the ability to exert physical force using only the power of the mind. It is also known as telekinesis. Normally PK involves the movement of objects, such as bending spoons or levitating bodies, but it is sometimes used to mean the mental generation of any form of energy, including heat and electricity.

Levitation is one example *of macro-PK, in which people or large objects are moved through space or into mid-air purely by the power of the mind.*

Feats like spoon-bending and levitation are examples of what parapsychologists call macro-PK, because they involve PK operating on relatively large scale objects or systems.

However, the most significant results in experiments come from attempts to use PK on a minute scale – on an atomic or sub-atomic level – when it is known as micro-PK. Examples include attempting to influence a computer read-out.

Teleportation – the movement of people or objects between two points without crossing the distance between them – may be a special case of psychokinesis, if it is achieved using the power of the mind.

In the laboratory

THE MOST STRIKING EVIDENCE for ESP, psychokinesis, and other paranormal forces comes from reports of personal experiences. Millions of people have stories to tell of strange coincidences, dreams, visions, and encounters. Surveys show that at least 50 per cent of people believe in ESP, for instance, and this is probably largely due to personal experiences. Scientists call this sort of information anecdotal evidence.

Anecdotal evidence is very unreliable. Hundreds of experiments have shown that humans in general are surprisingly bad at perceiving and recalling events accurately. This means that anecdotal evidence is of limited use in scientific investigations, and particularly in parapsychology, a field rife with fraud, mistakes, and misinterpretation.

In order to find convincing evidence for the existence of ESP and psychokinesis, one must turn to the laboratory, and experimental evidence.

Auto-Ganzfeld experiments

Biologist J. B. Rhine, together with his wife, carried out the first laboratory investigations of psi in the 1930s. These experiments laid the foundations for parasychology experiments to come, culminating in the development of the auto-Ganzfeld experiment.

The auto-Ganzfeld experiment now provides the best evidence for ESP.

In a Ganzfeld experiment, the subject sits in a comfortable reclining chair with half ping-pong balls over his eyes and white noise playing through headphones. The effect is to provide a uniform field (or *ganzfeld*, in German) of light and sound, minimizing distractions from the outside world and helping the subjects to focus their attention inwards. Both anecdotal and experimental evidence show that ESP appears to function most strongly under such conditions.

While in the Ganzfeld experiment set-up, the subject attempts to "receive" a picture being "sent" by someone in another room. He or she is then presented with four pictures and chooses the one he or she thinks was being sent.

Psychologist Charles Honorton originally developed this technique in the early 1970s. After initial criticism, the experiment was automated to minimize the possibility of intentional or unintentional fraud – hence auto-Ganzfeld.

■ **To conduct the auto-Ganzfeld experiment** *a controlled environment must be created in which a subject attempts to "receive" a telepathic message from a sender. The message is usually a picture.*

Results obtained with the auto-Ganzfeld experiment consistently show that people get the right answer about 35 per cent of the time, significantly higher than the 25 per cent success rate predicted by chance.

The only way to account for this remarkable result is through some form of telepathy, unless there are devastating flaws in the experiment that no one has spotted yet.

Drawing conclusions

In practically any other field of science, this would be regarded as convincing proof. Critics and sceptics, however, argue that there are problems with both the methods and the statistics. Are they simply scared to admit that ESP and psychokinesis might exist – that there are powers that we cannot explain? After all, science is notoriously bad at accepting new theories that challenge the existing order.

All we can really say is that these results are exciting and intriguing, and worth investigating further.

Zener cards

In his mind-reading experiments during the 1930s, J.B. Rhine used a set of cards, named after their designer, Dr Karl Zener, to test the ESP of his subjects. A pack of Zener cards consists of 25 cards printed with a set of five symbols – a star, a circle, a square, three wavy lines, and a cross. Zener cards have been heavily criticized (in early versions, the symbols on the front of the cards could be seen through the back), but have nonetheless become one of the most recognizable icons of the paranormal world.

Are you psychic?

To carry out your own Rhine test, you will need: a friend; pen and paper; a pack of Zener cards. You can buy Zener cards, or you can make your own – just be sure to use thick card so that your partner can't see through them.

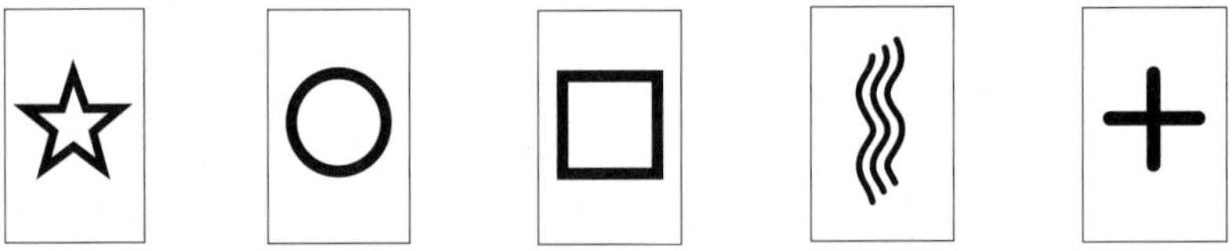

ZENER CARDS

1. Sit across a table from your friend. You are the "sender", and he or she is the "receiver". Shuffle the pack, put it face down on the table, and lift off the top cards one by one.

2. Look at each card in turn (make sure your friend can't see the front) and try to send the image to your friend's mind.

3. After a second, he or she should guess which symbol you are trying to send. If the receiver gets it right, it's a "hit". Record how many hits he or she gets as you go through the pack.

4. Shuffle the pack carefully and go through it again – the more times the better.

According to chance, the receiver should only be right about 20 per cent of the time – 1 in 5. If you score higher than this – for example, if your friend scored 8 or more out of 25 – congratulate yourselves – one or other, or possibly both of you, could be psychic.

Psychic spies

IN THE EARLY 1970s rumours that the Soviets were researching ESP for espionage purposes led the US government to invest in some research of its own. The result was one of the most extraordinary chapters in the history of the paranormal – a two-decade-long programme of psychic spying funded by the most shadowy security agencies in the US.

DEFINITION

Remote viewing *is a specific type of clairvoyance, in which a psychic is apparently able to mentally travel to a distant and/or unknown location and observe what is going on there. It is linked to phenomena such as astral travel.*

Remote viewing

DEFINITION

Some spiritualists believe that, in addition to our physical bodies, we each have an **astral body** *– similar to a soul or spirit – that can leave our real bodies and visit other locations through astral travel.*

The CIA funded Harold Puthoff and Russell Targ of the Stanford Research Institute to investigate a form of ESP: ***remote viewing***.

Puthoff and Targ had initial successes, especially with a test subject named Ingo Swann, an artist from New York. Given nothing more than map co-ordinates, Swann could apparently use his ***astral body*** to view and describe a distant location that he had never seen before. In one test he was given co-ordinates for the middle of Africa's Lake Victoria and correctly identified a small island that even the experimenters did not know existed.

Operation Stargate

These results encouraged the Defence Department to take over the programme, which was now called Operation Stargate. Based at Fort Meade, Maryland, headquarters of the National Security Agency (NSA), Operation Stargate was to run under the auspices of the NSA and Defence Intelligence Agency (DIA) for two decades at a cost of more than $20 million, and involved both research and attempts at actual psychic spying.

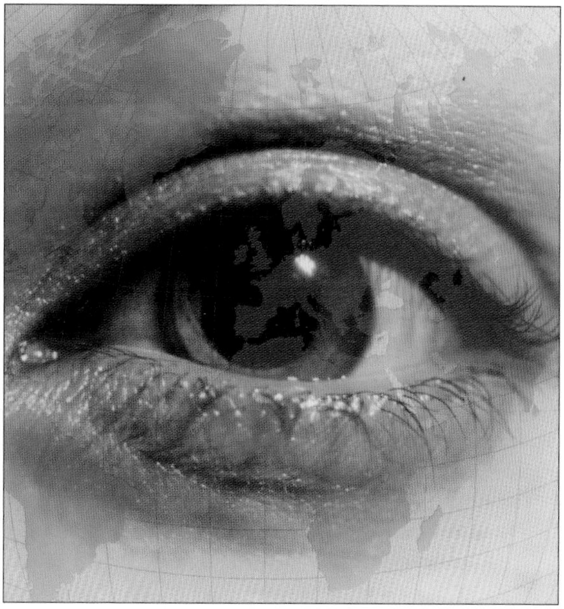

■ **Remote viewers** *believe that it is possible for the mind's eye to leave the body and travel to a distant location.*

Trivia...

US Army officer David Morehouse, one of Operation Stargate's "Naturals", was discharged in 1994 after being charged with theft, sodomy, adultery, and conduct unbecoming of an officer, not to mention being hospitalized for seeing angels and having suicidal urges.

The Naturals

During its heyday in the late 1970s and early 80s, Operation Stargate employed a core of six remote viewers who appeared to be naturally gifted with psychic powers – the Naturals – some of whom are now well-known names in the paranormal community. Men like Courtney Brown, Ed Dames, and David Morehouse (who described himself as a "psychic warrior") apparently scored some remarkable successes, claiming to have located PLO training camps, secret Soviet submarine bases, kidnapped generals, and crashed aircraft for their NSA and DIA paymasters.

The validity of these claims is hard to judge because the psychic spying was not done under controlled conditions.

The Naturals were given as much background information as possible, and even then the remote viewing "intelligence" that they obtained was effectively useless, since it had to be checked by conventional means.

The Witches

By the late 1980s Operation Stargate was running into trouble. New recruits from New Age and occult backgrounds, derisively nicknamed "The Witches" by the Naturals, had a negative impact, while efforts to improve remote viewing capability had serious mental health repercussions.

As in the auto-Ganzfeld experiments, the best conditions for remote viewing are thought to be those that enhance internal imagery. The Naturals underwent constant intensive training in imaginative techniques. Perhaps inevitably their grasp on reality began to weaken. Their reports got weirder, with claims of alien encounters, UFO bases, genetic engineering conspiracies, and machines on Mars. Brown claimed to have uncovered a subterranean tunnel network beneath New Mexico, filled with aliens in cahoots with the government.

According to CIA-trained *psychic spies, UFOs commute daily from bases in the American Midwest.*

The end of the line

In 1995 the CIA commissioned a review of the programme by outside experts.

Although there was some disagreement about the validity of Operation Stargate's remote viewing tests, the overall recommendation was that the programme had no espionage value and was a waste of public money.

The programme was duly shut down leaving the mentally scarred psychic spies to fend for themselves. Courtney Brown, for instance, still practises remote viewing and now has a flourishing career as a paranormal pundit and author. In 1997 he claimed to have identified an invisible UFO filled with reptilian aliens travelling behind comet Hale-Bopp. Similar beliefs led to the mass suicide of more than 40 members of the "Heaven's Gate" cult that same year.

■ **Comet Hale-Bopp,** *seen here on the left, is believed by some remote viewers to be accompanied by a spaceship full of aliens.*

Telepathic pets

ESP ABILITIES AMONG animals are referred to as animal psi, or anpsi for short. The existence of anpsi is suggested by a number of remarkable phenomena in the animal world.

Animal magic

Biologists have long been fascinated by the incredible homing abilities of some animals, including pigeons, bees, and butterflies. New sensory abilities that help to explain homing have been discovered, including sensitivity to magnetic fields and polarized light, but according to some researchers only a form of anpsi can explain the remarkable feats of some household pets that become separated from their owners.

■ **When the Earl of Southampton** *was imprisoned in The Tower of London in 1600, his cat sought him out and came down the chimney to find him.*

Famous cases of "incredible journeys" include: a collie that found its way home from India to Scotland by stowing away on a ship; an Australian cat, named Puss, who in 1977 crossed over a thousand miles of outback to find its owner; an Irish terrier/collie cross named Prince, who in 1914 crossed the English Channel to find its master who was in the army; and Sugar the cat, from Oregon, who walked from Oklahoma to California – a journey of 14 months and 2,415 km (1,500 miles). In some cases pets find their owners at their new homes – places that the pet has never visited in its life.

Toby the Sapient Pig

Research into anpsi started in earnest in the early 1920s, when Dr W. Bechterer claimed to have shown that a fox terrier called Pikki could recover selected objects following telepathic directions from humans.

However, Pikki may well have been responding to minute non-verbal clues inadvertently given by his handlers, in a similar fashion to Clever Hans, the intelligent horse of turn of the 20th-century Germany. This explanation could possibly also apply to another animal prodigy, this time of the 19th century – Toby the Sapient Pig. Toby the pig, it was claimed, could not only spell, read, and play cards, but could also "discover a person's thoughts".

INTERNET

www.globalpsychics.com

Visit this web site and link to "Animals Talk" to meet Laura Simpson, a real life Dr Doolittle (or Animal Communicator), who telepathically communes with the animal world.

CURSE OF THE PHARAOH

Some pets appear to know when their master has died. One of the most famous cases is that of Lord Carnarvon, victim of the Curse of Tutankhamen. When the peer died in Egypt, on 6 April, 1923, shortly after entering the pharaoh's tomb, his dog in faraway England was supposed to have set up a mournful howling. (Like much else concerning the story of the Pharaoh's Curse, this detail may have been a colourful later addition.)

■ **Could the curse of Tutankhamen** *have caused Lord Carnarvon's death? And how could his dog, in another continent, know that his master was dead?*

Dogs that know when their owner is coming home

This is the title of a book by maverick scientist Rupert Sheldrake, whose own research has convinced him that some pets do indeed have a telepathic link with their owners.

Anecdotal stories of pets who become excited long before they can hear or smell their masters encouraged him to investigate one such case in detail. Between 1994 and 1995 he collected observations of a dog called Jaytee, from Lancashire, England, who would get very excited shortly before his owner got home. Jaytee seemed to know when his owner would be arriving, regardless of the time of day or mode of transport that she used. Sheldrake argues that some form of anpsi must be responsible.

The beauty of this experiment is that it can be repeated by anyone with a pet and someone to record its antics.

The most impressive evidence for anspi comes from instances when an owner arrives home unexpectedly, without previously informing anyone.

These conditions minimize the chance that the pet is reacting to the time of day or the expectation of others in the house.

Spoon benders

SINCE THE BEGINNING of psychic research the most impressive cases of psychokinetic (PK) ability have been those involving macro-PK. In the days of spiritualism these abilities were known as physical mediumship. PK powers were regularly demonstrated by famous mediums such as Eusapia Palladino (see p. 47) and Daniel Dunglas Home, who frequently levitated himself and other objects, including musical instruments that then played themselves.

The most famous practitioner of macro-PK – probably the most famous psychic, period – is Israeli-born spoon bender Uri Geller.

Geller is one of the few macro-PK practitioners never to have been convincingly unmasked as a fraud.

All done with wires

Almost all the major mediums were debunked in the 19th and early 20th centuries. Only Home was never caught cheating, but today his feats and powers are generally suspected of being fraudulent – they can all be recreated by stage magicians.

In the early 1900s a Polish medium named Stanislawa Tomczyk came to prominence, partly thanks to her PK abilities. She was apparently able to stop clocks and move small objects such as matchboxes. The eminent psychologist Dr Julien Ochorowicz investigated Tomczyk and concluded that she was genuine, despite making some intensely suspect observations. He attributed her PK powers to ultra-fine threads that shot out from her fingers, connecting them to the target objects. These threads could even be photographed.

Who's pulling the strings? *Fraudulent medium Stanislawa Tomczyk "performed" psychokinesis with the aid of thin thread.*

Ochorowicz somehow managed to avoid the obvious interpretation, which was that Tomczyk was using perfectly ordinary thread to move the objects. Similar tricks were employed by Russian housewife and pyschic Ninel Kulagina, who was caught using invisible thread to lift tennis balls and hidden magnets to move salt cellars.

Project Alpha

Sceptics argue that all claims of PK abilities can be explained as similar trickery. James Randi decided to prove how easily a parapsychology laboratory, with all its supposed controls against cheating, could be deceived. In the early 1980s he recruited two young stage conjurers for something he called Project Alpha.

Sceptic James Randi *(left) cast doubts on the validity of controlled PK experiments. He fooled laboratory psychologists into believing the tricks of a conjurer (right) were due to psychic ability.*

The pair went for testing at the McDonnell Laboratory for Psychical Research, at Washington University in St Louis, where they bent spoons and stopped clocks to order.

Despite leaving a trail of clues the fake psychics employed by Randi's Project Alpha were declared genuine by parapsychologists.

Uri Geller

Israeli-born psychic Uri Geller claims to have received his powers at the age of three. A mysterious silvery light knocked him out as he played in the garden, and soon afterwards he began to realize that he had psychic abilities.

> ***Trivia...***
>
> *A Swedish woman who had watched Geller on TV blamed him when she became pregnant – the coil that she used as birth control had mysteriously straightened.*

He came to prominence in 1973 after a British television appearance during which he restarted stopped watches and bent a fork. In the years that followed Geller became an international celebrity, appearing on dozens of TV programmes and claiming a huge range of paranormal powers. He bent spoons by the hundred, stopped the clocks of people watching him on TV, found precious metals for mining companies, stopped an ocean liner in its tracks, and claimed partial credit for ending the Cold War by beaming peace messages into the brain of Soviet leader Mikhail Gorbachev.

Despite repeated laboratory tests, Geller has never been caught cheating or been proved to be a fake, and is renowned for suing anyone that says otherwise.

Testing Uri

The results of laboratory testing have been ambiguous and sceptics point to a number of suspicious facts that cast doubts on Geller's claims.

1. Geller's scores in lab tests are far from perfect, but as he points out himself this may be evidence in his favour – "If I were a professional magician, I would practise to the point where I would never fail …" he says in his 1975 autobiography

2. Controls in some of the labs where Geller has been tested have been criticized as too lax

3. Scientists who have worked with Geller have admitted that he creates an atmosphere that makes controlled investigation difficult – "Geller works in a high state of excitement which communicates to experimenters, making it difficult to keep your mind on what's happening", says Professor David Bohm. "He exudes sincerity, which makes people really want to believe him", was the verdict of Dr Joseph Hanlon, who investigated Geller for *New Scientist* in the 1970s

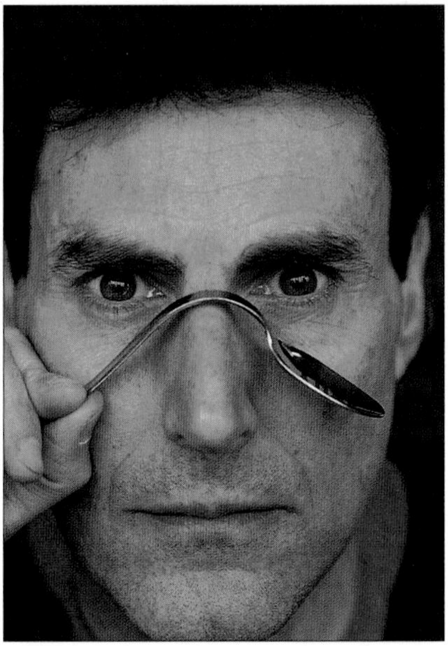

Has Uri Geller *been pulling the wool over our eyes for almost 30 years or does he really possess paranormal powers?*

4. Sceptics claim that Geller cannot perform when trained magicians provide the controls. Geller argues that he does not respond well when he has a hostile audience

5. Randi claims that hidden camera footage of Geller shows that the spoon bending is achieved by simple sleight of hand. Geller allegedly bends the spoon manually, and then moves his hand to make it look as if the already-bent spoon is slowly changing

6. Randi claims that all of Geller's "stunts" can be reproduced using stage magic

7. Geller himself has a habit of adding to the controversy with ambiguous statements such as, "No one knows if I am real or not"

The Geller controversy illustrates the problems and pitfalls of investigating psi phenomena by looking at "gifted" individuals.

Whether or not Geller's powers are genuine, they are shrouded in so much doubt that they can never be taken as serious proof of the existence of psi. Once again, parapsychologists are forced to turn to the laboratory in the search for proof.

Thoughtography

THOUGHTOGRAPHY, ALSO CALLED thought or mental photography, is the ability to project images onto surfaces, usually photographic film, using only the power of the mind. It may be a special case of PK. Professor Tomokichi Fukurai, of Tokyo University, coined the term thoughtography in 1910.

Thoughtography through the ages

The earliest examples are probably images produced on photographic plates by psychics in the late 19th century, known as dorchagraphs, although in 1990 the *Journal of the Society for Psychical Research* suggested that the Turin Shroud might have been produced by medieval thoughtography.

Fukurai discovered that a woman named Ikuko Nagao could apparently make Japanese characters and other shapes appear on plates of film (no camera was involved). The professor published the plates in a book called *Clairvoyance and Thoughtography*, and was promptly hounded from his post.

Images are not only projected onto film. In the 1890s the great Italian medium Eusapia Palladino could apparently impress her features into putty that was sealed in a jar, using only her will. In 1935 a Pennsylvanian woman, Mrs Gertrude Smith, claimed to be able to produce images on the shells of eggs laid by her hens, simply by thinking about it. She could even make the shells change shape.

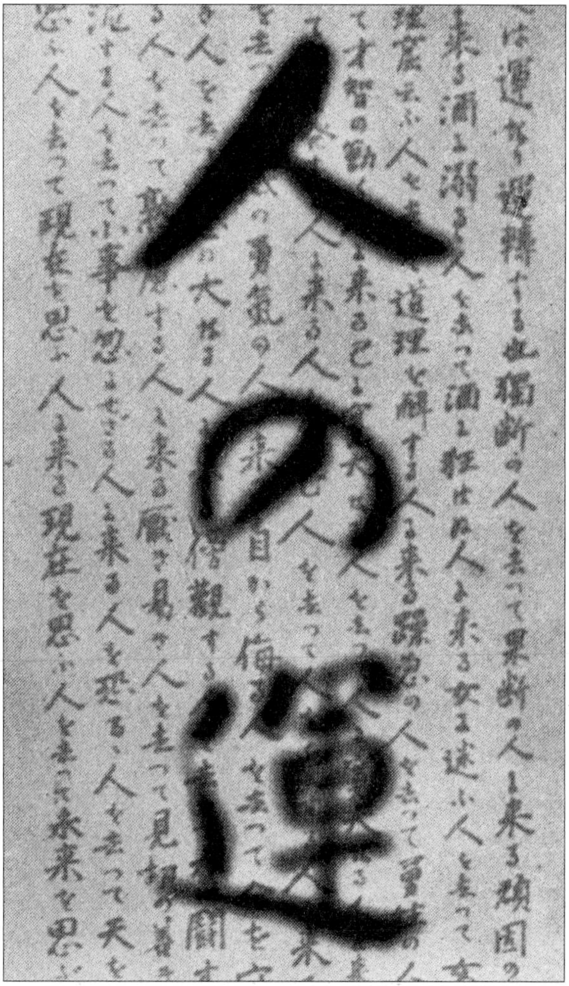

■ **Could it be** *that this photographic image was produced by the power of thoughtography alone? The artist's claims that it was were met with scepticism.*

Firestarter

A SPECIAL CASE OF PSYCHOKINESIS seems to be the ability to start fires without using any apparent means of ignition. People afflicted with this strange power are known as firestarters (Charles Fort called them fire genii).

Firestarting is not normally under the conscious control of the firestarter, which makes it dangerous and unwanted.

A rare exception is the early example of A.W. Underwood of Paw Paw, Michigan. In 1882 he was reported to be able to set things alight simply by breathing on them. He claimed the talent was useful for lighting his camp-fire when he was out hunting.

More typical is the 1929 case of Lily White from Antigua, who had to borrow clothes from her neighbours because hers kept catching fire.

Kid's stuff

Children and young adults seem particularly prone to the phenomenon of firestarting. In 1982 a comic book belonging to nine-year-old Italian Benedetto Supino caught fire while he was reading it. Subsequently his sheets (a favourite target for PK induced flames), furniture, and other household goods mysteriously ignited, and he was even able to make a plastic box combust just by staring at it. Similarly, in 1986, 13-year-old Russian "fire boy" Sascha K was plagued by hundreds of small domestic fires, which had no apparent cause.

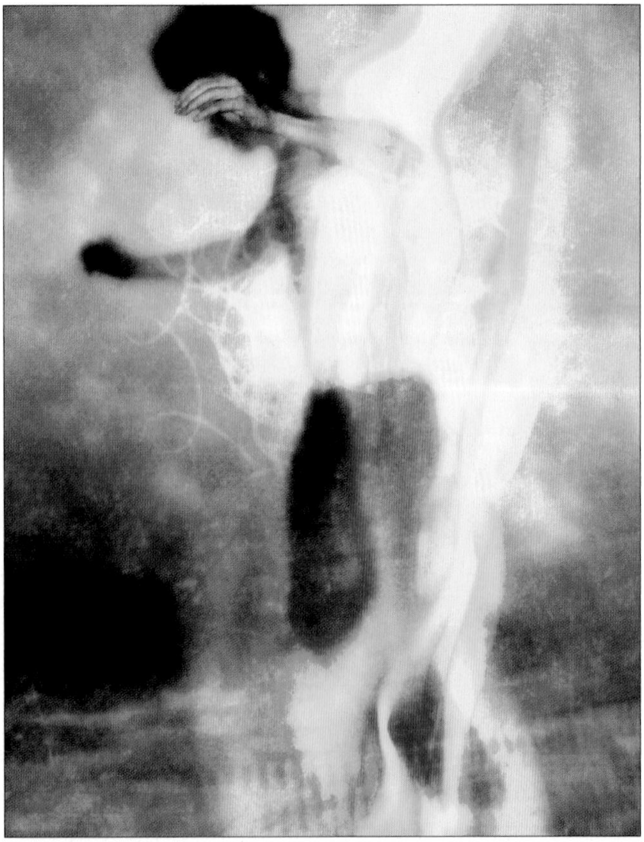

■ **The mysterious** *ability to start fires without ignition tends to be the reserve of children and teenagers.*

The usual explanation given by the authorities is that firestarters are mini-pyromaniacs, responsible for starting the fires themselves through normal means, for whatever reason (attention seeking? mental illness?). However, in some cases witnesses attest that the firestarters could not have set the fires themselves.

Burning guilt

One such case was that of Scottish au pair Charlotte Compton. In 1983 she was tried for arson and attempted murder in Leghorn, Italy, on the basis that a fire had broken out near the little girls in her charge. She was found guilty despite the fact that she had been downstairs with the family at the time. The grandmother of the family accused her of having the evil eye (the power to cause misfortune with a glance), which was evidently good enough for the jury.

A simple summary

✓ There are many different sub-categories and special types of ESP and psychokinesis (PK), including telepathy, clairvoyance, remote viewing, precognition, macro and micro-PK, firestarting, and thoughtography.

✓ Laboratory studies provide convincing evidence for the existence of psychokinesis and ESP. However, controversy still rages over the validity of these studies, and the effects they show are relatively small.

✓ Evidence from outside the laboratory, known as anecdotal evidence, is often more striking, but much less reliable.

✓ There are numerous reports of ESP phenomena in the real world, including psychic spies, and hundreds of cases of supposedly telepathic animals. Many of these reports turn out to have mundane explanations such as cheating; others are confused or suspect. But there is a hard core of reports that seem inexplicable.

✓ PK phenomena such as spoon-bending, thoughtography, and firestarting seem to be equally unreliable in their evidence as ESP phenomena, but again, there are some strange cases that seem to be genuine yet defy explanation.

Chapter 4

Precognition

MANKIND HAS ALWAYS BEEN EAGER for knowledge of the future, and has celebrated those who seem to have the gift of prophecy. But is it really possible to see into the future and if so, could it be a gift that we all possess? In this chapter I'll explain what precognition is, look at some of the famous cases and experiments that may prove its existence, and then discuss how it might be possible.

In this chapter...

- ✓ **What is precognition?**
- ✓ **Famous cases of precognition**
- ✓ **Nostradamus**
- ✓ **Is precognition possible?**
- ✓ **Just a coincidence?**

PREDICT THE FUTURE SUCCESSFULLY AND YOU COULD MAKE A MINT

What is precognition?

ALSO KNOWN AS prophecy, foretelling, or having a premonition, **precognition** *can take the form of a simple hunch or a full-blown vision of the future. Another form of foretelling, known as divination, is slightly different, because it involves the use of objects, such as cards, tea leaves, or chicken's entrails, as a guide to the future.*

DEFINITION

Precognition *is the ability to perceive information about the future, without using any known senses.*

An everyday wonder?

Precognition seems to be common but the majority of premonitions are never recorded, and are quickly forgotten when they fail to come true. Full-blown precognitive visions occur most commonly during dreams, or just before or after sleep. Even the premonitions that are confirmed are not usually recorded until after the event, making them more or less useless as hard evidence for the reality of precognition.

The paranormal researcher is interested in the relatively few instances when a premonition is recorded (either by being written down or by being reliably witnessed) before the event it refers to.

Precognition may have survival value. According to American researcher William Cox, statistics show that trains involved in accidents carry fewer passengers than the same trains travelling at the same time on previous or succeeding days.

Trivia...

Most people's premonitions refer to their own lives or the lives of those close to them.

■ **The oracle of Delphi** *is one of the most famous historical cases of precognition. In Ancient Greece, the Priestess of Delphi read prophetic oracles to the town's people, which were believed to be the word of God.*

Famous cases of precognition

THERE ARE MANY STORIES of predictions, prophecies, and premonitions that came true in real-life events. In fact, some of the world's most famous disasters were foreseen by several individuals before they happened. Here are some of the best known ones.

The fate of the Titanic

The sinking of the Titanic is probably the most famous peacetime disaster of the 20th century. It was also one of the most predicted.

Before the Titanic sank, there were over a hundred premonitions forewarning of the event.

George Behe, author of *Titanic: Psychic Forewarnings of a Tragedy*, recorded these premonitions associated with the sinking, including several stories written many years earlier that seemed to foretell the exact same circumstances.

When the Titanic *collided with an iceberg in 1912, the damage done to the luxury liner sealed her fate. There were many similarities between the tragedy and prophetic warnings issued before the event.*

The book *Futility: The Wreck of the Titan*, written by Morgan Robertson in 1898, details the fate of a huge, supposedly unsinkable ocean liner named the *Titan*, which collides with an iceberg in the mid-Atlantic during her maiden voyage. In the story, most of the passengers drown because there aren't enough lifeboats – a well-documented problem with the Titanic.

INTERNET

www.encyclopedia-titanica.org/

This site offers unique information about the Titanic, including passenger biographies and cargo lists.

Even the obscure details of Robertson's novel, written before the Titanic was on the drawing board, are chillingly accurate. His Titan has a massive displacement (a measure of the size of the ship) of 70,000 tons, far larger than any ship built at the time of writing, but similar to the 66,000 ton displacement of the real Titanic. The fictional Titan even has a similar number of passengers and lifeboats.

The English journalist W.T. Stead wrote some similar tales during the 1880s, and became an expert on the inadequate safety precautions of liners. In 1910 he visited several psychics who gave dire warnings about his involvement in a maritime catastrophe in April of 1912. Mystifyingly, Stead nonetheless booked passage on the Titanic, which duly took him to the bottom on 10 April 1912.

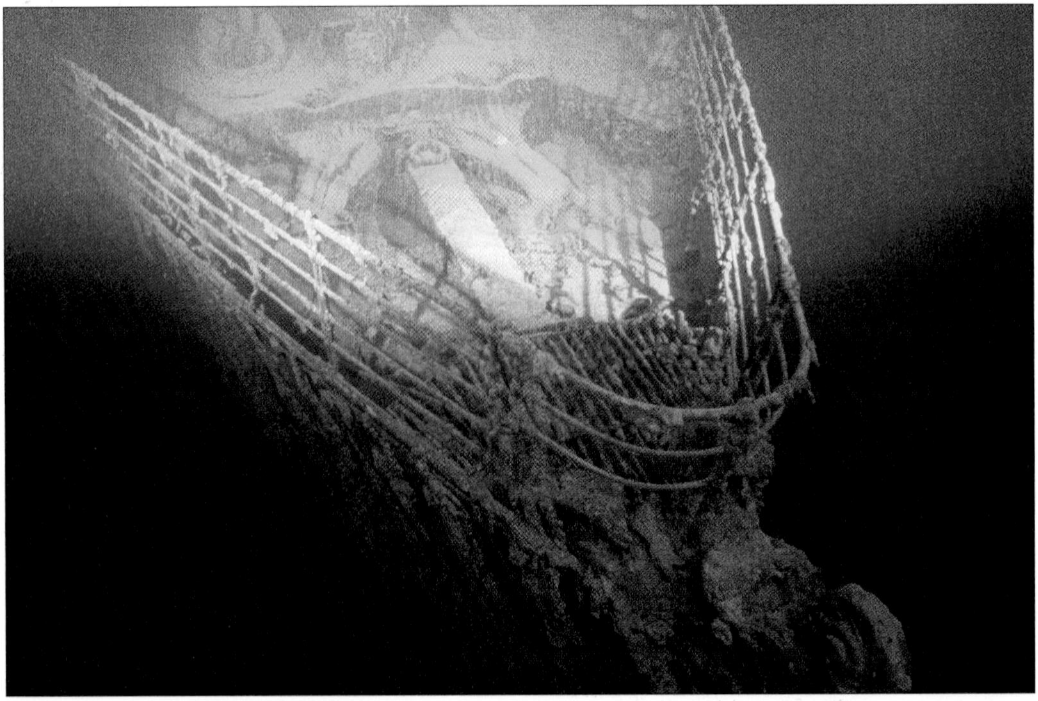

■ **Since the Titanic** *came to rest in its watery grave at the bottom of the Atlantic Ocean, its sinking has been the subject of much speculation. Was the fate of the oceanliner on its maiden voyage really foreseen?*

Profitable premonitions

In 1946 a young Oxford student and racing enthusiast named John Godley (later Lord Kilbracken) dreamt the names of two horses that would win a race the day before the event. Over the next 3 months, he had two more such dreams, and made a considerable amount of money. This is a rare case of precognition paying off in the world of gambling. Unfortunately Kilbracken's "gift" was unreliable, and his subsequent successes were few and far between. A possible non-paranormal explanation is that Kilbracken was making accurate guesses on the basis of his extensive racing knowledge.

■ **A win at the races** – *perhaps that "lucky streak" is down to precognition rather than just chance?*

Playing the stock market is another form of gambling, and many top financiers admit to following hunches. In 1906, for no apparent reason, Wall Street wizard Jesse Livermore had a strong urge to sell stocks in the Union Pacific Railroad. A few days later, the San Francisco earthquake sent the company's stock price plunging and Livermore made a fortune.

More recently, a group called Delphi Associates used precognition to try to predict the price fluctuations of silver futures. To begin with they were highly successful, guessing correctly nine times in a row. Like Kilbracken, however, their success was short-lived.

Even if precognition really exists, it seems to be too unreliable to predict fluctuations in stock prices.

Dead presidents

US President Abraham Lincoln famously foresaw his own death in a dream. In the dream he followed the sound of sobbing through the White House to the East Room, where he saw people filing past an open coffin, with soldiers standing guard. "Who is dead in the White House?" he asked one of the soldiers. "The President. He was killed by an assassin", came the answer. Just a few days later the dream was fulfilled. Shot dead by John Wilkes Booth, Lincoln's body lay in state in the East Room.

US President *Abraham Lincoln, who was assassinated while at the theatre in 1865, foresaw his death in a dream. Typically of precognition, the exact circumstances were not revealed.*

The assassination of John F. Kennedy, on 22 November 1963, was also foreseen. In the summer of 1963, comedian Red Skelton claims to have woken up to find himself writing "President Kennedy will be killed in November" on a piece of paper.

American psychic Jeane Dixon claims that she was warned of Kennedy's assassination as early as 1952, when a mysterious voice told her that a Democrat elected in 1960 would be killed in office. Dixon also predicted the death of Robert Kennedy, telling an audience at the Ambassador Hotel, Los Angeles, that he would never become president because of "a tragedy right here". Indeed, just one week later, Kennedy was shot in the very same hotel.

Lincoln and Kennedy were connected by a whole series of strange links. Lincoln was assassinated in the Ford Theatre; Kennedy while travelling in a Ford Lincoln. Kennedy's secretary, who told him not to go to Dallas, was called Evelyn Lincoln. Both presidents were killed while sitting next to their wives, and both were shot in the back of the head. Lincoln's assassin ran from the theatre to a warehouse; Kennedy's from a warehouse to a theatre. Both men were succeeded by presidents called Johnson. Perhaps most spookily, both men spoke about being assassinated less than a day before it happened.

Collecting prophecies

Following the Aberfan tragedy of 1966, when part of a Welsh mining town was covered by a landslide killing 128 children and 16 adults, English psychiatrist J.C. Barker collected dozens of reports of premonitions of the disaster. His research led him to suggest that a bureau should be set up to collect precognitions, which could then be used for research, and perhaps to avert future disasters. The British Premonitions Bureau was duly set up in 1967 and collected many reports, none of which turned out to be much use. It was subsequently shut down.

■ **The Aberfan slurry** *catastophe in Wales was supposedly predicted many times before it happened. Perhaps heavy rain weakening the collapsing coal tip made the threat of impending disaster clear for all to see?*

Many major disasters seem to come attached with claims that they were foreseen. This has led some people to ask the obvious question: "Couldn't they have been prevented?"

Nostradamus

THERE HAVE BEEN many famous seers throughout history dating right back to the prophets of the Old Testament and the ancient Greek oracle at Delphi. The most famous of all is probably Nostradamus – real name Michel de Nostredame – born in Provence, France, in 1503.

MURAL OF NOSTRADAMUS, FRANCE

Originally a physician specializing in treatment of the plague, Nostradamus gained widespread notoriety with the publication of his *Centuries*, an **almanac** of four-line verses, or quatrains, arranged in groups of a hundred. The quatrains are prophecies of the near and distant future that came to Nostradamus in vivid visions. He believed them to be divinely inspired.

DEFINITION

An **almanac** *is a calendar giving astronomical and other information.*

Nostradamus has been credited with dozens of successful predictions, including the deaths of Henry II and Louis XVI of France, the Great Fire of London, the rise of Napoleon, World War II, the atomic bomb, the end of the Cold War, and the fall of the Berlin Wall.

■ **According to Nostradamus's followers,** *he predicted the fall of the Berlin Wall, which divided Eastern from Western Germany. But the parallel was drawn after, not before the wall was taken down.*

Trivia...

Nostradamus's prophecies were first published in 1555, and have been continuously in print ever since. Only the Bible has been in print for longer.

Sceptics argue that all of Nostradamus's successes have been determined after the event, and are entirely due to interpretations being made to fit. There is a lot of truth to these criticisms. The quatrains are not straightforward predictions – they are extremely cryptic and have to be interpreted. They were written in a complex mix of Greek, Latin, French, Italian, and Nostradamus's native Provençal, and different translations can vary widely. Some interpreters even argue that Nostradamus was using a code, or that the quatrains need to be rearranged in order to be understood. The most likely explanation of his apparent success seems to be that it is due to "the ingenuity of his interpreters", in the words of Nostradamus researcher David Pitt Francis.

Different interpreters of Nostradamus's prophesies sometimes use the same quatrain to refer to completely different events.

One way to test the success rate would be to use the prophecies to actually predict something, rather than simply fit them to past events. For instance, several books on Nostradamus written in the 1980s refer to his glum view of the end of the 20th century, which he predicted would descend into apocalyptic war after the coming of an Antichrist, with Armageddon scheduled for 1999. It would seem that Nostradamus fails this test.

NOSTRADAMUS AND HITLER

One of the most celebrated quatrains, number 2:24, illustrates some of the problems with interpreting Nostradamus. In Erika Cheetham's 1973 translation it is given as:

Beast wild with hunger will cross the rivers,

the greater part of the battle will be against Hitler.

He will cause great men to be dragged in a cage of iron,

when the son of Germany obeys no law.

INTERNET

www.nostradamususa.com

This is the web site of the Nostradamus Society of America.

Obviously this sounds like an extraordinarily accurate prophecy. It turns out, however, that the original version says "Hister", an old name for the River Danube. Given that Germany was a regular battleground in the 16th century, Nostradamus's prediction becomes much less impressive.

Is precognition possible?

PRECOGNITION SEEMS to break even more laws of nature than extra-sensory perception. Not only are people receiving information without using any known senses, but the information appears to be travelling backwards in time.

Serious physicists have suggested that according to the mysterious and poorly understood laws of* quantum physics, *precognition may actually be possible.

In the laboratory

As with many types of paranormal phenomena, the anecdotal evidence for the existence of precognitive powers is not convincing. What about experimental evidence?

Laboratory studies of precognition are similar to ESP studies but involve the subject guessing the order of a sequence of events before that order is determined.

DEFINITION

Quantum physics *is a branch of science that deals with the world of subatomic particles and events.*

The combined results of 50 years of these experiments suggest that a small but significant precognition effect does exist. The same criticisms apply to these experiments as they do to ESP and PK experiments.

Tiny time travellers

Some theories of quantum physics predict the existence of a particle called a tachyon, which travels faster than the speed of light and could travel back in time. This particle has never been detected, and may be purely imaginary. If it did exist, however, perhaps the tachyon might be involved in precognition.

The trouble with theories involving psi and quantum physics is that they are always a bit woolly on the details. No one has explained exactly how tachyons might interact with the human mind to produce precognition. The real explanation behind amazing stories of prophecy may be a lot more mundane.

■ **The cult British television series,** Doctor Who, *was fiction based on the theory of time travel. The Doctor used the tardis to travel back through time. Can tachyons do the same?*

Just a coincidence?

THE MAIN NON-PARANORMAL explanation for precognition is that it is all down to coincidence. What looks like an amazing prophecy is really just a lucky guess. This is not as farfetched as it sounds, for two reasons: the premonitions that come true make up only a tiny fraction of all the premonitions that people have; and coincidences are often not as unlikely as they seem.

Dream of doom

In May 1979, Cincinnati office manager David Booth had recurrent dreams in which he saw an American Airlines aeroplane roll over in mid-air and crash with a terrible explosion. Shaken by this terrible premonition he called the airline, the Federal Aviation Authority, and the local airport to warn them, but there was little they could do.

Four days later an American Airlines plane crashed in Chicago, rolling over in mid-air before plunging earthwards in exactly the way Booth had dreamed. Over 270 people were killed.

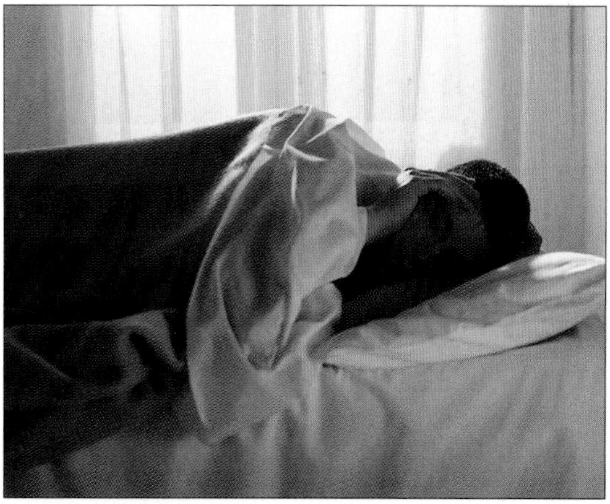

■ **It is common** *for dreams to contain portentous visions and scenarios, but this could be attributed to the subconscious ordering of logical thoughts.*

David Booth's premonition seems to be awful proof that precognition does exist – after all, it couldn't just have been a fluke could it?

Weighing the odds

Here's how a sceptic might look at David Booth's dream: each night in the US there are probably dozens of people who dream about an air disaster. Most of these dreams probably feature the most popular airlines and the most common types of aeorplane, and any of them that feature a crash on take off or landing are more likely to be accurate.

Statistically speaking, there is a good chance that any aviation disaster will have been preceded by a disturbingly accurate dream "premonition".

In this context, it no longer seems so unlikely that Booth's dream was simply part of a dreadful coincidence.

Predicting disaster

Massachusetts teacher Richard Newton made a similar prediction in 1978. He forecast that on 11 March 1979, a plane with a red tail logo would crash outside a city in the northern hemisphere, killing 45 people.

Newton was almost exactly right. On 14 March 1979, a Royal Jordanian Airlines jet (with a red tail logo) crashed at Ad Dawhah, Qatar, killing 47 people. Again, the chilling accuracy of Newton's prediction seems like solid proof that precognition does exist.

Predicting a plane crash *on the strength of calculated probability can be very accurate. Many airlines would have fitted Richard Newton's prediction that a plane with a red logo would crash.*

Except that Newton had made his prediction solely on the basis of statistical probability. He knew that most crashes happen as planes take off from or land at airports, and that most of the world's airports are outside cities in the northern hemisphere. Over half of the world's commercial airlines at the time had red tail logos, and statistics showed that March was the worst month for crashes, and that the average number of people killed in a crash was 45.

Using the logic of probability to predict an event could at times be construed as unexplained precognition.

Explained, or explained away?

Students of strange phenomena learn to be wary of "neat" or "glib" explanations like this one. It may well be true, but then again it doesn't tell the whole story.

Why did Booth dream of such a precise and unusual cause of disaster (rolling over in mid-air)? What about the fact that his dreams were recurrent, and affected him so strongly that he risked ridicule to alert the authorities? The circumstances would suggest that there is more to Booth's dream than many gave him credit for.

There is a difference between explaining something, and explaining it away.

INTERNET

yaron.clever.net/precog

Yaron Mayer, former member of the Israeli Parapsychology Association, has set up his own Central Premonitions Registry, where you can officially log any premonitions or prophetic dreams that you have.

A simple summary

✓ Precognition may be quite common, but its accuracy is hard to gauge.

✓ Most premonitions occur during a dream, or just before falling asleep or waking up.

✓ Significant events, particularly disasters, seem to trigger premonitions.

✓ Premonitions tend not to be reliable enough to be profitable in the world of gambling.

✓ There have been many famous prophets through the ages, but their powers may exist mainly in the minds of their fans.

✓ There is some evidence from the laboratory to suggest that precognition really exists.

✓ Misinterpreted coincidence seems a more probable theory than precognition.

✓ There is no explanation for how precognition can be so accurate.

Chapter 5

Psychic Healing

IN THIS CHAPTER I'll introduce many different types of unconventional healing and health-related topics such, as body auras. They may not all be strictly psychic – some are religious or spiritual in nature, others appear to relate to physical energies of the body rather than the mind – but they all have one thing in common: all of them seem to defy the rules and logic of conventional western medicine.

In this chapter...

- ✓ **What are psychic and spiritual healing?**
- ✓ **Psychic healing in history**
- ✓ **The healing spirit**
- ✓ **The placebo effect**
- ✓ **Auras**
- ✓ **Kirlian photography**

What are psychic and spiritual healing?

PSYCHIC HEALING is physical or mental healing produced by the power of one person's mind on another person's body (sometimes the power is said to come from the sick people themselves). Spiritual healing is closely related, but involves healing produced by a supernatural force – a person's spirit or soul, or a higher power that is brought to bear by the healer through ***channelling****.*

DEFINITION

The ability to allow another spirit or consciousness to act or speak through you is known as **channelling**. *The thing or person being channelled does not have to be alive, or even to have existed in real life. Sometimes it is conscious, and takes over the body of the channeller, speaking in its own voice. Sometimes it is simply a force or power that passes through the channeller.*

Between them these categories include several different types of healing, including faith healing, therapeutic touch, psychic surgery, shamanic healing, and many types of complementary medicine. For the purposes of simplicity, I'm going to use "psychic healing" as an umbrella term when referring to these techniques collectively.

Psychic healing in history

PSYCHIC HEALING HAS BEEN AROUND in various forms much longer than recorded history – probably as long as mankind.

Witch doctors and medicine men

The earliest forms of healing were probably similar to those still practised by shamans in tribal cultures today. These involve a mix of herbal medicines, many of which are now used in slightly different forms by western medicine, and religious or magical practices, such as chanting, spells, talismans, or meditation.

■ **Thenyemba, the great witchdoctor** *of the Hambukushu people of Botswana, conducts a ceremony to appease the spirits of the ancestors of an unwell patient.*

The shaman's psychic gifts were one element of the healing process. Some Australian Aboriginal tribes, for example, practise a form of healing magic where one of the elders chants and touches the sick person with a spear or stick. In much of the world psychic healing methods still play an important role in healthcare.

The royal touch

The major figures of several organized religions have been credited with miraculous powers of healing. Their ability to make the lame walk again, heal lepers, and even raise the dead was evidence of their divine power. Christ and his followers, such as St Paul, could even cure mental illnesses by casting out devils. Effectively they were practising faith healing.

This tradition of divine healing power continued in the West in the form of the royal touch. People believed that kings, queens, and emperors could heal simply by touch. In England the royal touch was believed to be specifically effective against scrofula – tuberculosis of the lymph nodes.

Trivia...

Samuel Johnson (1709–84), the great English man of letters and compiler of the first dictionary, sought treatment for his scrofula from Queen Anne.

Laying on hands

The royal touch and the healing miracles of Jesus are both examples of the practice of laying on hands. By placing his or her hands on the sick person, the healer passes on some mysterious healing force. Laying on hands was practised long before Christ. It is mentioned in Indian texts from 500 BCE and practised by the ancient Greek physician Hippocrates, around 400 BCE.

INTERNET

www.therapeutic-touch.org

This is the official web site of the international organization founded by Dolores Krieger.

The most modern form of laying on hands is the Therapeutic Touch technique developed in the 1980s by Dolores Krieger, a professor of nursing from New York University.

Despite its name, Therapeutic Touch actually involves passing the hands over the body without touching it, and is mainly used to diagnose a person's condition.

Krieger claims that an experienced practitioner can achieve up to 80 per cent accuracy. Sceptics would argue that they are unconsciously using their experience to evaluate clues from the patient's medical history and appearance, and then formulating a diagnosis.

THE HEALING POWER OF DOLPHINS

An increasingly popular healing therapy is swimming with dolphins. Simply being in the water with dolphins is said to help treat or enhance the quality of life of people, particularly children, suffering from diseases such as autism and Down's Syndrome. Both captive and wild dolphins are used – for instance, in Dingle in the southwest of Ireland, sick children regularly swim with a friendly wild dolphin known as Fungi. No one knows for sure if "dolphin treatment" really works, and if so, how.

■ **Dolphin therapy** – *can it treat disease?*

The healing spirit

SEVERAL IMPORTANT TYPES of psychic healing depend on some form of spiritual power, which is channelled through an individual.

Faith healers

Following on from Jesus and the Apostles, many Christian saints were said to be able to cure illness, gaining personal followings as a result of their miraculous powers. As the Church became more established and organized it often felt threatened by these "mini-cults" and tended to discourage faith healing. Today most faith healing is performed outside the established churches by preachers known as charismatics, who often bring about dramatic cures as part of large prayer meetings. Typically they do not claim to be personally gifted, but say that they are channelling divine power.

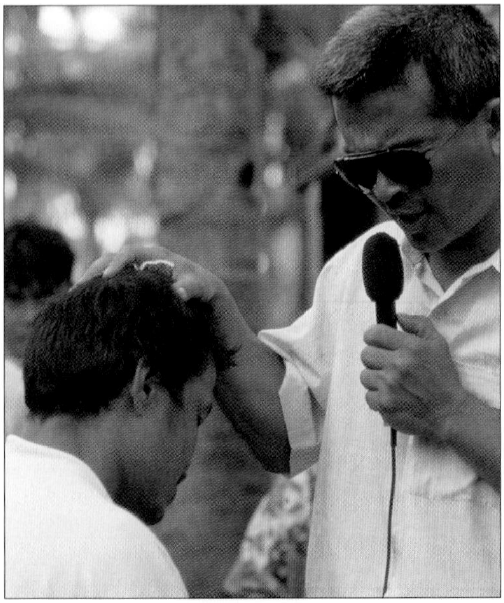

■ **A faith healer** *prays over a patient at a Malatapay market in Negros, the Philippines.*

Official disapproval is less of a problem for less-centralized religions. For instance, in India hundreds of Hindu gurus practise forms of faith healing, often drawing huge crowds of people wanting to be touched or hugged.

Spiritual healers

The growing popularity of the spiritualist movement in the 19th century led to many claims of healing powers. Again, many such healers do not claim to be exerting power themselves, but to be following advice from or channelling the powers of a spirit.

The most famous spiritualist healer was probably the American Edgar Cayce (1877–1945). Cayce discovered his powers after curing himself of dumbness while under hypnosis. He did not heal directly, but would go into a trance and pass on diagnoses and treatments from the spirit world. Cayce attributed his gift to a power he called the Universal Consciousness.

Trivia...

José de Freitas was estimated to have treated more than half a million people between 1950 and 1964. However, Brazilian law held spirit healing to be a crime, and in 1964 de Freitas was convicted and sentenced to 16 months in prison.

Other spiritual healers were more precise about the sources of their powers. Famous Brazilian spiritual healer José de Freitas, known as Arigo (the "simpleton"), claimed to be guided by a fat, bald German named Dr Adolf Fritz, while English spiritualist Harry Edwards was helped by Louis Pasteur and Joseph Lister (fathers of vaccination and antiseptics respectively). Both men operated from around the 1940s.

Psychic surgery

Psychic surgery is a particularly striking form of psychic healing, mainly found in South America and the Philippines. Psychic surgeons perform gory-looking operations with no anaesthetic, using their hands or simple tools (penknives or dirty scalpels for example), sometimes appearing to reach inside the patient's body. They remove diseased tissues, curing the patient, who is usually left with no visible scarring or wounds.

If this sounds too incredible to be true it's because it probably is. In a famous exposé in 1979, a BBC documentary crew investigated psychic surgeons David and Helen Elizalde. Normally the tissue that is supposedly removed from the patient is quickly disposed of, but in this case a sample was recovered and tested. It proved to be pig's blood.

It is now generally assumed that most psychic surgery is actually sleight-of-hand.

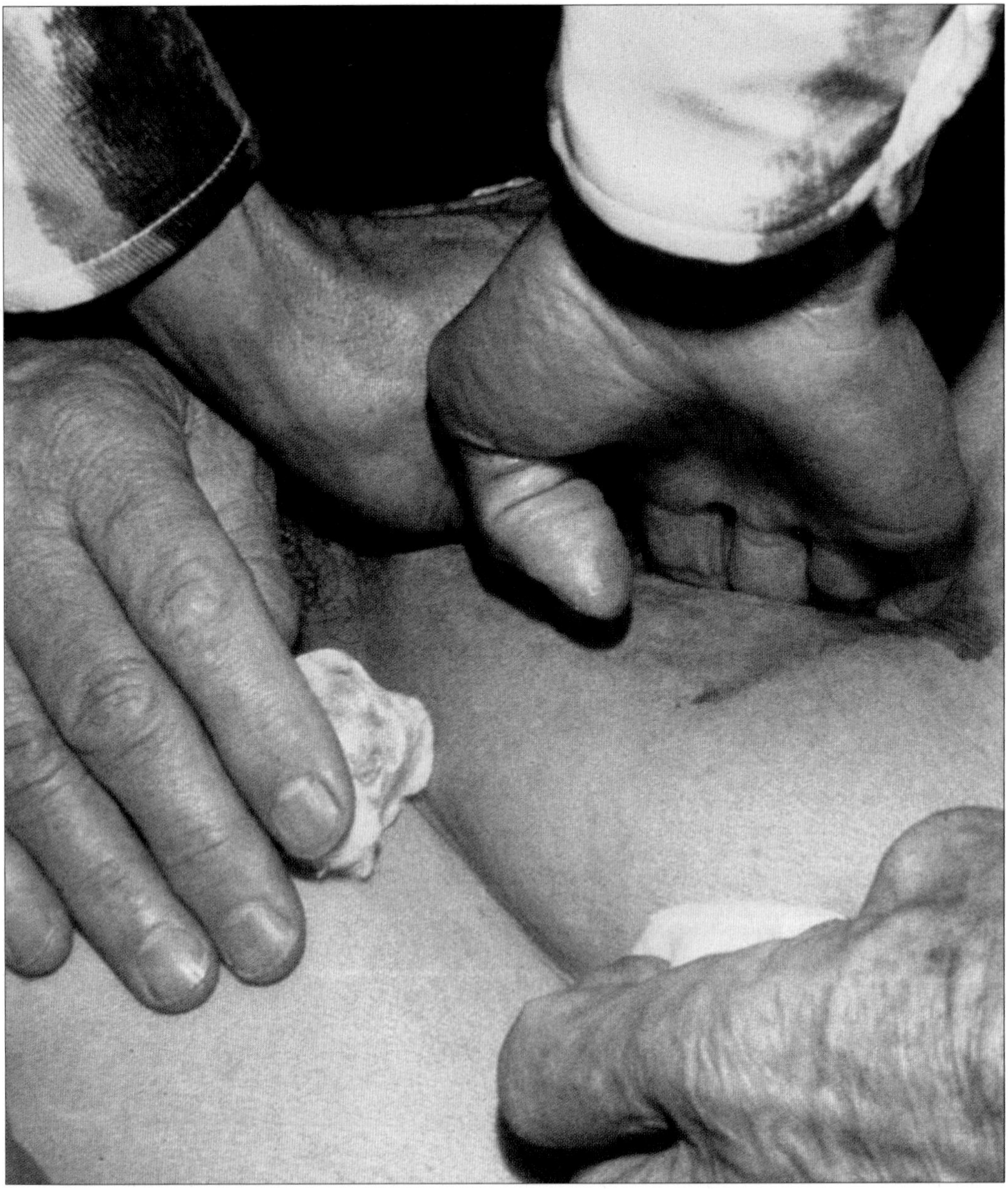

■ **Filipino psychic surgeon Feliciano Omilles,** *shown here working in Mexico in the early 1970s, appears to insert his hand deep into the fleshy tissue of his patient's chest.*

The "surgeon" uses pig's blood to create a gory appearance, and manipulates fleshy parts of the body so that it looks as if his or her hand is inside the patient. The removed tissue is fake. However, not all psychic surgeons have been unmasked in this way, and there are thousands of apparently genuine reports of successful "operations".

The placebo effect

IF PSYCHIC HEALING can produce such remarkable effects, why do conventional doctors ignore it? Sceptics argue that there are no paranormal or supernatural powers at work, and that psychic healing can be explained purely by the ***placebo effect****.*

Sceptics argue that psychic healing works merely because patients believe in it.

DEFINITION

A placebo is a fake medicine, with no active components, which the patient thinks is real. Doctors have discovered that a placebo can treat and even cure an illness – this is known as the **placebo effect**.

Difficult to swallow

The majority of illnesses successfully treated by psychic healing are ones that are believed to have a large psychosomatic element – migraines, allergies, aches, and pains. These are diseases that one would expect to respond to the placebo effect. However, there are also many tales of severe diseases such as cancer being cured. Conventional medicine labels such cures as "spontaneous remissions". Can the placebo effect really account for these?

NATURAL RECOVERY RATES

Another reason why conventional medicine remains unimpressed by psychic healing is because, overall, its claims are not as impressive as they might appear. Psychic, faith, and spiritual healers usually claim a 70 to 75 per cent success rate at treating disease. Conventional doctors point out that up to 80 per cent of patients with diseases get better on their own anyway, if left for long enough. In other words most, if not all, of the patients "cured" by psychic healers would have recovered naturally.

The power of placebo

There is no doubt that the placebo effect can produce some remarkable cures. For instance, in America in the 1950s Dr Philip West used a so-called "wonder drug", called Krebiozen, to treat a man with advanced cancer. The patient responded well and his tumours shrank, until he came across an article debunking the new drug and suffered a relapse. West managed to convince his patient that the drug was effective, and administered an injection of water, pretending that it was an extra-strength dose of Krebiozen. Once again, the man's tumours went into remission, until the American Medical Association announced that tests had proved Krebiozen useless. West's patient relapsed for a final time and died within days.

A slightly different example is that of physicist Dr Lawrence Le Shan, who was researching long-distance psychic healing, which involves a healer focusing on a patient who is not present. Le Shan made a date with a "patient" by post, agreeing that at a certain time they would both concentrate on healing the man's illness. Le Shan, however, completely forgot the appointment and failed to attempt the healing. A few days later he was contacted by the patient's doctor, who told him that the man had recovered from his illness anyway!

The real mystery

Extraordinary stories like these, together with the apparent successes of psychic healing, have led to the birth of a new branch of medical science called psychoneuro-immunology (PNI). This is the study of how the mind can affect the body's natural defence systems.

We've already met some aspects of PNI in Chapter 2, where we saw that the mind can exert amazing control over the body. The incredible claims of psychic healing provide more evidence that conventional medicine does not properly understand the limits of this control.

Perhaps the real mystery of psychic healing is not the existence of psychic powers, but of the untapped healing potential of our own minds and bodies.

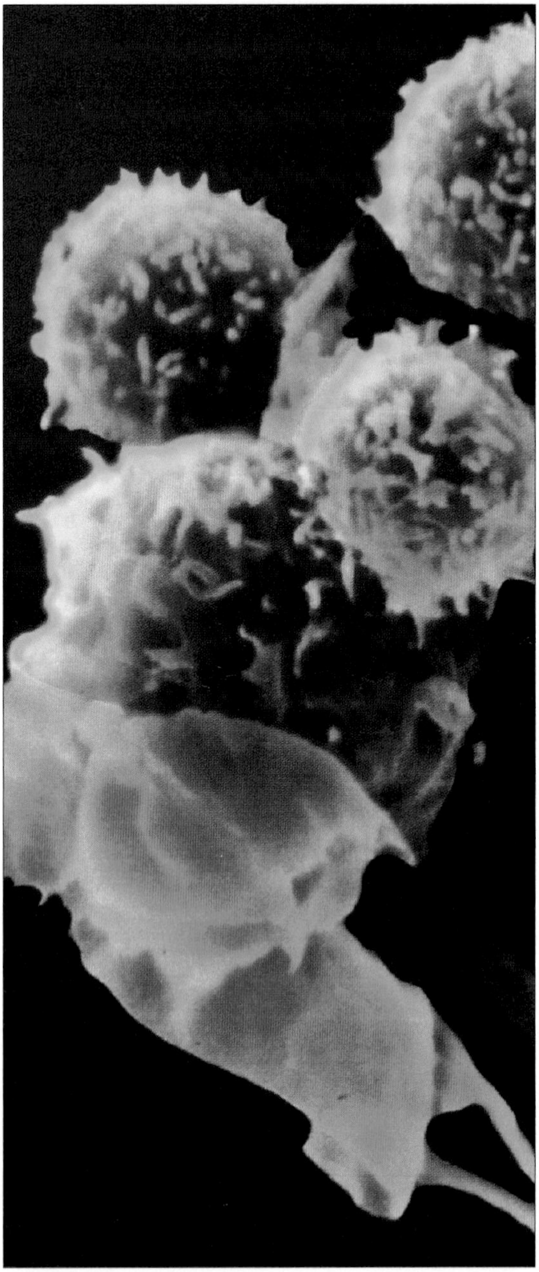

This magnified image *shows naturally-occurring T-lymphocyte cells (blue) attacking a cancer cell (orange). Stories of healing through positive thinking suggest that the mind can somehow affect the function of T-cells.*

Auras

AURAS, ALSO KNOWN AS auric fields or auric hazes, are glowing outlines that surround people or objects, according to psychics. They usually extend only a few centimetres from the body and can vary in colour and brightness.

The halo effect

Belief in the existence of auras is an element of occult, spiritualist, and ***New Age belief***. Auras have been used since the 19th century to make health and character assessments.

It is usually said that you have to be psychic, or develop psychic abilities, in order to see an aura unaided.

DEFINITION

During the Sixties, there was an explosion of interest in mystical and eastern topics, and attempts were made to fuse elements of different belief systems (e.g., Hinduism, medieval western alchemy, and spiritualism). The resulting mixture is collectively termed **New Age belief**, *and covers a wide range of topics, from dolphin healing to sightings of angels.*

Crystal clear

According to New Age theory, auras are a manifestation of the electromagnetic field that surrounds all things. This means that animals, plants, and even rocks may have auras. New Age health practitioners sometimes use auras to help diagnose physical, mental, and spiritual illness.

The strength and colour of a person's aura is said to reflect their state of health and elements of their character and personality.

For instance, an orange/green aura is said to indicate health and vitality, while indigo indicates psychic abilities.

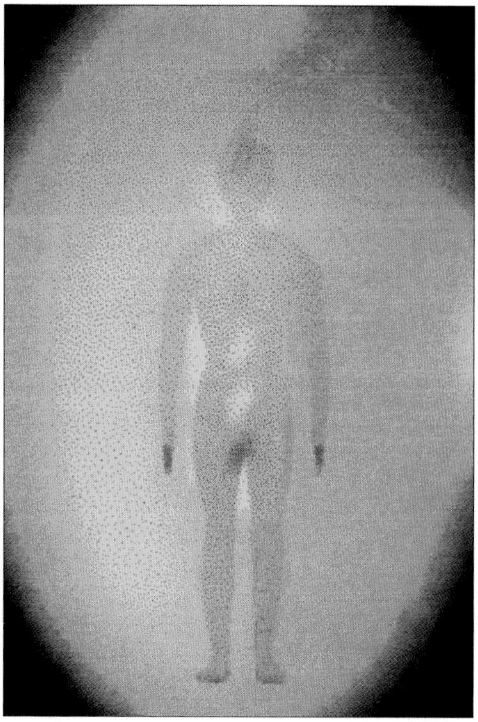

The full body aura *of a healthy woman, produced by computer after the subject's hand was analysed.*

A common New Age belief is that crystals can be used to influence and extend auras – to as much as 7.6 m (25 ft) around the body – improving health and wellbeing. Conventional science argues that auras do not exist, but the human body does produce a very weak ***electrostatic field***. It is not impossible that specific health complaints, for instance, could subtly alter the pattern and strength of this field. However, this is purely speculation. No one knows how this field might relate to health or mental states, and it is invisible to the naked eye.

DEFINITION

The activity of the cells in the human body generates a static charge, which in turn generates a minute field of attraction or repulsion to other charged surfaces. This field is called an **electrostatic field**.

Seeing the aura

Psychics and New Age healers claim to be able to see auras, and they also say that anyone can develop this skill through relaxation, meditation, and visualization. (A good object to practise on is a small magnet – its magnetic field is supposed to produce a clearly defined aura.)

Trivia...

Auras are modern relations of the halos of Christian saints and the bodily radiance attributed to Buddha. They are also found in Australian Aboriginal and Native American beliefs.

In 1909, English doctor Walter Kilner of St Thomas's Hospital, London, developed a device that he claimed would allow anyone to see auras with no training or special powers. He used a special blue dye (dicyanin) sandwiched between two plates of glass to create a screen, and later a pair of goggles, that made auras visible. It is now generally accepted that the auras are an optical effect created by the dye, but you can still buy Kilner goggles.

Dr Kilner believed *that when using the goggles he had invented (right), the wearer could see three distinct layers of an individual's aura, extending about 30 cm (12 in) from the body.*

Kirlian photography

BY FAR THE BEST KNOWN METHOD for visualizing auras is Kirlian photography. A Kirlian photograph is the image produced by passing a high voltage electric current through an object on a photographic plate. Images of hands taken this way seem to reveal a glowing aura (or corona), often with radiating streaks of light.

A shocking discovery

Russian electrician Semyon Kirlian discovered the phenomenon in 1939. After noticing that an electrode placed next to a person's fingers would discharge flashes of light, he decided to try and photograph the discharges. Together with his wife, Valentina, Kirlian developed an apparatus that could produce detailed and beautiful photographs of energy fields radiating from objects and body parts. But what were they actually seeing?

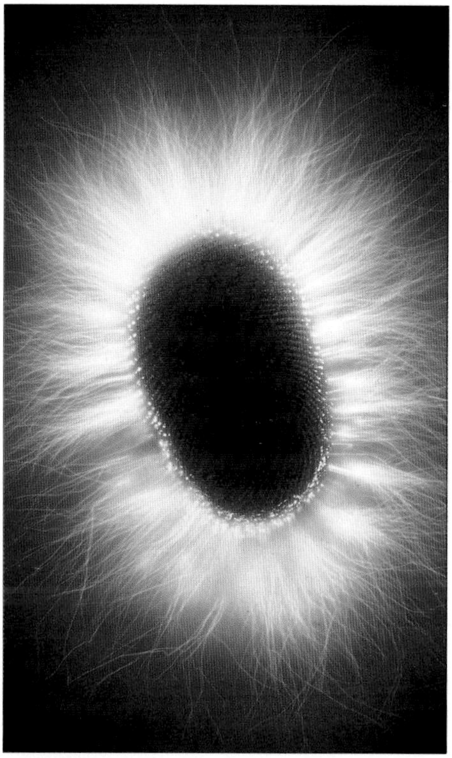

Kirlian photographs, *like this one of a fingertip, illustrate the discharge that results from high-energy interactions between the subject and a strongly-applied electric field.*

Biological plasma

According to the Kirlians and their followers (including the New Age community), the process captures on film the aura that surrounds all living things, an aura composed of some sort of electromagnetic field.

Kirlian called this field biological plasma, also known as bioplasma or bioplasmic energy. After noticing that the corona around Kirlian's hand in a photo taken shortly before he came down with flu was dull and blurred, the Kirlians developed the theory that their photographs could be used to diagnose illnesses. Broken, dull, or vague coronas are held to be indicative of illness, while bright, colourful, unbroken coronas show health and vitality. Some research backs up the Kirlians' claims. Doctors in New York claim that the coronas of schizophrenic patients are broken before treatment and unbroken afterwards. Thelma Moss, of the School of Medicine at UCLA, has found that coronas around a person's fingertips are larger when the person is more relaxed.

Kirlian photography of the hands of psychic healers are said to show strong discharges of healing "energy", as streaks radiating out from the fingers and strong orange glows around the palms. The conventional scientific view is that there is no evidence for the existence of bioplasmic energy, and that Kirlian photographs show a phenomenon called Lichtenburg figures (after their discoverer, Jeri Lichtenburg). These are photographic effects produced by the ionization of air by discharges of static electricity. In other words, Kirlian photographs reveal nothing more than colourful bursts of static electricity.

INTERNET

www.kirlianlab.com

Go to this site to buy your own Kirlian apparatus and other hardware, incorporating all the latest digital technology.

Leaf life

One of the strongest pieces of evidence backing up the claims of the Kirlians was their famous picture of a damaged leaf. The full outline of the leaf's corona continues to show up on a Kirlian photograph, even after the tip of the leaf has been removed. The outline of the missing part grows dull and fades after a few minutes.

It is argued that the living tissue of the leaf somehow maintains a bioplasmic field that "remembers" its original form. Sceptics argue that the damaged leaf corona is simply an effect produced by not properly cleaning the electrified plate on which the leaf sits. However, at least one researcher claims to have produced the same effect with carefully cleaned electrodes.

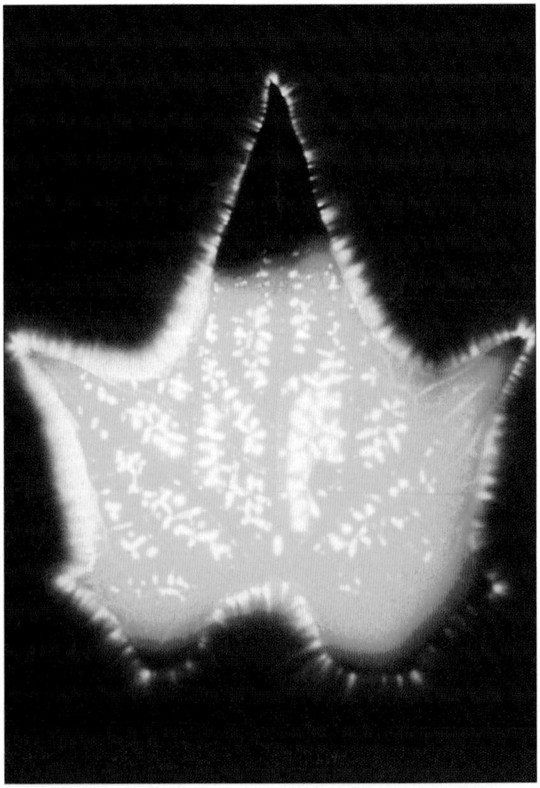

■ **The "phantom leaf effect".** *The bioplasmic field of the entire leaf remains intact in this classic Kirlian photograph, even after the uppermost tip of the leaf has been removed.*

YOU SEE WHAT YOU WANT TO SEE

Kirlian photography is a good example of how the scientific and "alternative" communities can view the same phenomenon in quite different ways. Conventional scientists claim to have explained Kirlian photography long ago, as a meaningless effect produced by static electricity.

This doesn't seem to bother New Age healers and Kirlian photographers, however, who continue to use the technique to diagnose illness and make personality assessments. The bottom line is that it often doesn't matter what the scientists say – people will interpret and use a phenomenon however they want.

A simple summary

✓ Psychic healing methods have been around for a very long time and still hold considerable appeal for many people.

✓ Some forms of psychic healing are fake, based on illusion and trickery.

✓ Conventional medicine attributes the apparent successes of psychic healing to the placebo effect, which can produce powerful results. But not all the claims made by psychic healers can be explained this way.

✓ Psychic healers claim that everyone has an aura that reveals their personality and state of physical and spiritual health, and that Kirlian photography is one way of visualizing that aura.

✓ Conventional science dismisses the claims of Kirlian photography and the existence of auras, but admits that the human body does generate some forms of electromagnetic field.

PART TWO

Spirit

In Part Two you'll encounter some incredible and terrifying phenomena – spirits of the dead, spells and curses, angels and demons – supernatural happenings that challenge the most basic assumptions of the rational world.

Chapter 6

The Spirit World – the Basics

In part one we looked at a variety of psychic phenomena that belong to the realm of the mind. In this section we turn to the realm of the spirit, and look at phenomena that are connected, in one way or another, to the existence of powers beyond the human mind, beyond even the natural world. To help you try to make sense of the reported ghost sightings, levitations, spells, and visions, this chapter introduces some of the basic concepts of the supernatural world: what are the common elements of supernatural phenomena, do they really exist, and if not, what might be causing them?

If these phenomena are real they raise fundamental questions. Are there other dimensions or planes of existence? Is there life after death? Do higher powers watch over us, controlling time and matter in ways we cannot conceive? Is there such a thing as the human soul, and are supernatural forces engaged in a constant struggle for its control? All in all, heavy stuff. Read on and I'll try to help you find your own answers.

A GHOSTLY ENCOUNTER ON THE STAIRS?

What is the spirit world?

SUPERNATURAL PHENOMENA involve powers or spirits that do not belong to the natural world – ones that are literally "above nature". This is in contrast to paranormal phenomena, which are usually believed to be the result of some sort of natural power that is not yet known, but which will fit into the natural universe once we understand it better.

Reality check

The phenomena of the spirit world are extremely diverse – from hauntings, to witchcraft, to weeping statues – so it's difficult to give a blanket judgement on their plausibility. Your own judgement on the plausibility of the spirit world may depend on your personal beliefs.

For instance, a devout Catholic might be less sceptical about the reality of a vision of the Virgin Mary, while a practising Wiccan (a type of pagan religion associated with witchcraft) would probably believe that magical spells really work. A scientist, on the other hand, would probably find it harder to accept the reality of any supernatural phenomena, because the existence of the supernatural largely contradicts the scientific view of the universe.

■ **Seeing is believing:** *coming face to face with a ghost is the only way many people will allow themselves to believe in the supernatural.*

From the scientific viewpoint, a major problem with accepting the reality of supernatural phenomena is that most of them cannot be tested under controlled conditions, in other words, in a laboratory.

Almost all of the evidence for the supernatural is anecdotal.

But anecdotal evidence is often unreliable and is not generally considered to be convincing by scientists.

Possible explanations

If supernatural powers are not behind amazing tales of ghosts, levitation, spells, and visions, then what is? Sceptics have come up with a barrage of alternative explanations for why people might believe they have seen or experienced something supernatural. The most common explanation for stories of ghost and other visionary sightings is that people only thought they saw something weird. In other words they imagined it. There are several ways this could happen.

■ **When you're drifting off** *to sleep or waking up your mind can sometimes play strange tricks on you.*

- **Hallucination** This may sound like an extreme explanation, but hallucinations (experiences that seem real but happen entirely in the mind) are not restricted to the insane. As you fall asleep or wake up you pass through a slightly altered state of consciousness, known as a hypnagogic (while falling asleep) or a hypnopompic (while waking up) state. Fleeting hallucinations are common during these periods.

We may spend up to 5 per cent of our sleeping time in a hypnagogic or hypnopompic state, and as much as 64 per cent of people may have experienced hypnopompic imagery at least once.

- **Wishful thinking** An alternative psychological theory is that people who experience supernatural phenomena are more likely to have a "fantasy prone personality". This type of person has a rich imaginary life but a weak grip on reality, and is much more likely than others to have elaborate or vivid fantasies.

- **The cultural source hypothesis** Many supernatural phenomena seem to be heavily influenced by the culture in which they occur. Ghost sightings, for instance, seem to vary with culture. Native Americans often report that the spirits of the departed return in animal form, whereas the typical modern European ghost is an anonymous, shadowy human figure. Visions of the Virgin Mary appear almost exclusively to Roman Catholics. These patterns have led some researchers to suggest that supernatural experiences derive from the cultural background of the people who have them. So, for instance, both a Protestant and a Catholic might see a bright white light, but only the Catholic would interpret it as a vision of the Virgin Mary.

- **Misidentification** The senses are not as reliable as is often thought, and it is easy to mistake something innocent, such as a dim reflection in a distant window, for something sinister, such as a ghost. Misidentification is particularly common if the viewer is expecting to see something – a phenomenon known to psychologists as expectant attention. For instance, if you visited a house that someone had told you was haunted, you would be much more likely to misinterpret ambiguous sensations, like a harmless draught, as supernatural ones.

- **Fakers** One of the most obvious explanations for supernatural events is fraud. Sceptics argue that once one incidence of a type of phenomenon has been proved to be fake, we can assume that all the other instances are also fake. So, for instance, once one medium is shown to be a fraud we can assume that they're all frauds. This is an example of faulty logic, however, and ignores the fact that many reports come from honest witnesses who have nothing to gain, and who often risk ridicule by coming forward.

An innocent draught *can be easily misinterpreted as something more sinister if you're led to believe that a house could be haunted.*

Ghostbusters

The world of supernatural phenomena is very diverse, and also very popular. This means that there are an enormous number of organizations and individuals involved in practising, studying, and investigating it. Ghost-hunting societies can be found in dozens of countries all over the world. The oldest psychical research society in the world is Britain's Ghost Club, still going strong today after nearly 140 years. Previous members of the Ghost Club include Charles Dickens and the poet W. B. Yeats, as well as some big names in the field of psychical research, including Harry Price and Sir William Crookes. Harry Price is probably the most famous ghost researcher ever, while Crookes was a major figure in the scientific investigation of spiritualism in the 19th century.

The US has dozens of ghost-hunting societies, mostly operating at a state level. National organizations include the American Ghost Society and the International Society for Paranormal Research, a team of professional ghost hunters much in demand by the media. Ghost hunting/research is also one of the major activities of the Society for Psychical Research (SPR) and its American sister organization. Another big name is the Association for the Scientific Study of Anomalous Phenomena (ASSAP).

Spiritualists and miracle watchers

Spiritualism may not be as popular now as in its 19th-century heyday, but it is a widespread religion nonetheless. In the US, for instance, there are dozens of churches affiliated to the National Spiritualist Association of Churches. These churches all practise "modern spiritualism", which is essentially Christian in nature. Some spiritualist organizations play down the Christian element and there are plenty of people who practise mediumship and hold séances independently of any churches.

The Roman Catholic Church has been gathering information on supernatural phenomena for nearly two millennia, making them the undisputed experts in the field. On the whole, though, the Catholic Church is very wary of hoaxes, fakes, and impostors and has set up a special division – the Congregation for the Causes of Saints – to investigate and pass judgement on claims of miracles and wonders.

The magic circle

There is currently a resurgence of interest in magic and the occult, particularly through the rising popularity of the new pagan religion Wicca. Wicca is a mish-mash of pagan beliefs and medieval witchcraft, and although there are groups such as the Pagan Federation, Wiccan "magicians" by their nature tend to favour independence, practising on their own as "hedge witches".

The type of magic phenomena that most people will come into contact with are astrology, tarot cards, and other methods of telling the future.

Anyone can set themselves up as a "qualified" astrologer or tarot card reader because there are no licensing laws, but there are also societies and organizations such as the American Tarot Association that provide a way of finding a reputable practitioner.

Accepting the inexplicable?

If you have a scientific mind that finds it hard to accept phenomena that can't be tested under controlled conditions, read the following chapters in Part Two to see if there's anything that may challenge this point of view. Remember, not everything can be explained.

Chapter 7

Ghosts

GHOSTS ARE THE MOST COMMON, widely reported supernatural phenomenon, coming in a bewildering variety of shapes and sizes. In this chapter I'll introduce the main types of ghost, look at theories about the origin of ghosts, and explain how to do a spot of ghost hunting yourself.

In this chapter...

- ✓ What are ghosts?
- ✓ Inhuman ghosts
- ✓ Ghosts of the living
- ✓ Haunted houses
- ✓ Poltergeists
- ✓ Ghost hunting
- ✓ Making sense of spooks

What are ghosts?

A GHOST IS A SPIRIT, ***apparition****, or presence of something or someone that isn't really there. Ghosts have been reported by every culture throughout history. The stereotypical ghost is the spirit of a dead person that appears as a transparent image, but there are many other types of ghost – they don't have to be of people (they don't even have to be dead). Ghosts typically, but not always, haunt a specific location or person.*

DEFINITION

An **apparition** *is a visual presence – something that can be seen.*

The classic ghost

One of the most famous ghost stories is the tale of Athenodorus, as told by Roman writer Pliny the Younger (61–113 CE). According to Pliny, there was a house in Athens haunted by the spectre of an old man in rags, who would moan and rattle his chains. This terrible apparition frightened off all potential tenants until a visiting philosopher, named Athenodorus, decided to spend the night. A few hours after dark, Athenodorus duly heard the clanking of chains and saw the ghost. He followed it to a spot in the courtyard – digging the next day revealed a human skeleton in chains. The bones were given a proper burial, and the ghost was never seen again.

The rattling chains *of Pliny's ghost have become a ghost cliché – for instance, Dickens used it for the ghost of Marlowe in* A Christmas Carol.

Pliny's classic tale illustrates many of the elements of the stereotypical ghost. The typical ghost is the spirit of a dead person, which appears as a pale or transparent version of its living self. Usually the apparition is wearing clothes and if it interacts with living people at all it does so in a limited way (it may not be able to speak, or it may only be able to repeat a few words).

Often a ghost seems to have a motive in appearing – to get the living to perform whatever ritual or process is necessary to let the ghost rest in peace. This is known as "laying a ghost". In Pliny's tale, the ghost's original body was not properly buried, so its spirit was condemned to haunt the night. This motif is found in ghost stories as far back as the ancient Assyrians and Egyptians, and as far afield as Japan and South America.

Re-enactment ghosts

Not all ghosts act with a purpose. In fact many of them seem oblivious to the real world or living people, and display no form of intelligence or consciousness. An example of this sort is the ghost that re-enacts a sequence of actions when it appears, passing through walls and closed doors and sometimes appearing to stand above or below the level of the floor.

Re-enactment ghosts are thought to be following a route they took in life. They are usually linked to violent or traumatic events – battles, murders, executions, accidents, or suicides.

A famous example is the Treasurer's House in York, England. Witnesses have described troops of Roman soldiers in full armour marching through the cellars of this historic building. Crucially, the soldiers appeared to be knee-deep in the cellar floor – at the level of an original Roman road through the area.

Cyclic ghosts

Many ghosts are said to appear "cyclically" on significant anniversaries – these are known as "cyclic ghosts". Famous examples include Catherine Howard, one of Henry VIII's wives, who is supposed to be seen running screaming through the halls of Hampton Court Palace on the anniversary of her sentencing to death.

Trivia...

Ghosts do not have to be apparitions. They can be noises, smells, changes in temperature or simply invisible forces with no personality at all.

Respected psychical researcher and author Ian Wilson regards such claims with scepticism, pointing out that if ghosts really did reappear that predictably a ghost hunter's job would be extremely easy. Another problem is that the calendar was changed in Europe in 1582 (1752 in England), with the loss of 11 days, so that if Howard really does appear she will effectively be 11 days late.

■ **A misty figure in Tudor dress,** *thought to be Queen Catherine Howard, was sighted in the grounds of Hampton Court in the 1960s. Screams are said to be heard coming from the palace gallery on the anniversary of her death.*

Inhuman ghosts

ONE MAJOR PROBLEM for the theory that ghosts are spirits or personalities that survived death is that there are many reports of the ghosts of animals and even inanimate objects (mainly vehicles).

INTERNET

www.ghostclub.org.uk

This is the web site of the UK Ghost Club, the oldest psychical investigation society in the world. It provides a wealth of national and international information on cyclical, re-enactment, and all other types of ghost.

Creepy critters

Belief in animal spirits is common in hunting cultures – hunters sometimes perform elaborate ceremonies after killing an animal so that its spirit will not be vengeful. In arctic Siberia, for instance, hunters hold a festival in honour of each whale they kill, so that its ghost will not frighten off other whales.

Ghost dogs are a common feature of western folklore, especially large black dogs with glowing eyes, known as barguests, devil dogs, gyrtrash, or shuck-hounds. Barguests are usually thought to be bad omens, but can be helpful, protecting travellers in lonely places.

Other animal ghosts include the White Devil, a ghost stallion said to haunt the American prairies; Gef, the talking mongoose, who haunted a farm on the Isle of Man during the 1930s; and a giant bear that scared the wits out of a Beefeater in the Tower of London in 1816. The latter is thought to have been the ghost of one of the bears kept in the Tower by Henry III in the 13th century.

■ **Conan Doyle's large black dog** *in* The Hound of the Baskervilles *is a classic example of the use of a motif from folklore – the barguest – in a fictional context.*

Planes, trains, and ghost ships

Probably the best known ghost vehicle is the *Flying Dutchman*. This legendary vessel is said to be a 17th-century sailing ship crewed by dead men, whose captain is doomed to sail the world forever as punishment for his sins. Many sailors have reported encounters with the ship, which is usually described as glowing red or ghostly pale.

THE PRINCES AND THE FLYING DUTCHMAN

The most famous sighting of the ghost ship occurred in 1881 when the 15-year old Prince George (future king of England) and his brother Prince Albert were at sea. The incident was recorded in the princes' logbook and is often quoted: "At 4 a.m. the Flying Dutchman crossed our bows. A strange red light as of a phantom ship all aglow". The princes, however, did not actually see the apparition themselves, and it has been suggested that the ghost ship was a magic lantern projection from one of the other boats that was travelling with their ship. Slides of the *Flying Dutchman*, which fit the princes' description exactly, were popular entertainments at the time.

This painting *by Albert Pinkham Ryder reflects the ambiguity of sightings of the Flying Dutchman. Could it be the eerie glow of mast and sails or simply a strange cloud formation in a stormy sky?*

Another ghost ship was a Maori war canoe, which appeared with a full crew on Lake Tarawera in 1886, apparently presaging an eruption of the supposedly extinct Mount Tarawera. There are also ghost trains, such as Lincoln's funeral train (said to be crewed by skeletal musicians, in what sounds suspiciously like a fanciful embellishment), and the ghost of the Tay Bridge disaster train, which carried more than 80 people to their deaths in Scotland on 28 December 1879; and ghost aeroplanes, such as the biplane that appears during thunderstorms over Weybridge, in south-east England.

Ghosts of the living

AN IMPORTANT CLASS OF GHOSTS are apparitions of people who are still alive (although in many cases not for long). These ghosts have been called "passing callers" because they tend to appear only once, rather than haunting a place or person.

Crisis apparitions

Ghosts of the living usually involve people who are experiencing or approaching a crisis – hence they are known as crisis apparitions. Typically a friend or relative, possibly many miles away, will see the person, who may look quite real and appear in an unremarkable fashion (for example, popping in to say "hi"). Later they discover that their friend died or experienced a crisis at the same time or very shortly afterwards, and couldn't have been anywhere near where they were sighted. Crisis apparitions do not fit into most theories about ghosts – the people are still alive, they are far away, and they don't seem to have much purpose.

Many people argue that crisis apparitions are actually telepathic projections of some sort, in which sudden physical crisis boosts psi power for a moment.

Doppelgangers

Another type of living ghost is a double – an apparition that looks exactly like the witness. These ghosts are known by their German name – doppelganger. The appearance of a doppelganger can often be a bad omen, but not always.

Many people argue that doppelgangers, like crisis apparitions, are actually telepathic projections, not ghosts. There is also a rare medical condition, known as autoscopy, that causes people to hallucinate a transparent mirror image of themselves.

Trivia...

In Celtic lore, a doppelganger is known as a "fetch". In Iceland they are known as Fylgja, and in Norway as Vardogr. These Scandinavian doubles announce someone's arrival by appearing a few minutes before the actual person.

Haunted houses

A FAVOURITE ELEMENT of popular ghost lore, the haunted house dates back at least as far as the story of Athenodorus, which incorporates many of the classic haunted house motifs: a creepy house, residents who are scared off, and a brave individual who dares to stay the night. The truth about haunted houses, however, often turns out to be disappointingly mundane.

Organizations like the Society for Psychical Research (SPR) find that most phantom phenomena have non-supernatural causes.

The most haunted house in the world

The title of the world's most haunted house is usually awarded to Borley Rectory, a house built in 1863 in the village of Borley, in Essex, to the north-east of London. The site was said to have been haunted by a phantom nun for centuries. Until it burned down in 1939 (1948 according to some sources), over 200 sightings were said to have been reported, including a phantom horse and coaches, spirit writing, strange fires, invisible assailants, unexplained footsteps and more. Harry Price, a famous psychical investigator and ghost hunter, and a leading light of the SPR, rented the whole house for a year in 1937, building up a huge file of spooky incidents. However, it has since come to light that Price and a couple of others faked almost all of the "supernatural" phenomena, and that historical reports of Borley Rectory's ghosts were invented or exaggerated.

■ **For almost 80 years,** *Borley Rectory was allegedly the site of hundreds of mysterious phenomena; ghosts, objects moving by themselves, whisperings, strange voices, footsteps, and the ringing of bells were all reported to have taken place here.*

THE MOST COMMON MUNDANE CAUSES OF GHOST PHENOMENA

In most cases, a house that is reputed to be haunted will be old. A sceptic would argue that this is because old houses are more likely to make strange noises as they settle, have faulty plumbing and wiring that can cause "ghostly" phenomena, let in draughts, and affect suggestible residents. Below are some of the less exciting reasons why things can go bump in the night.

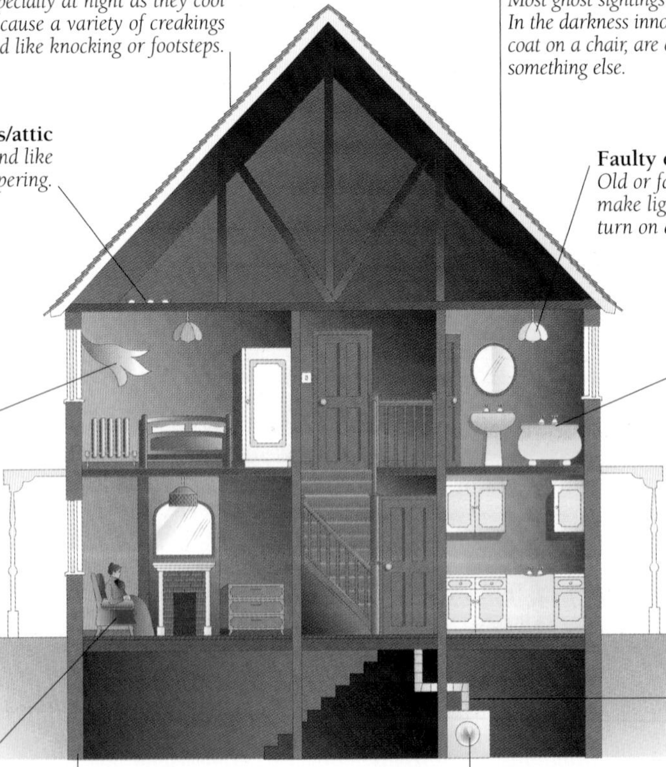

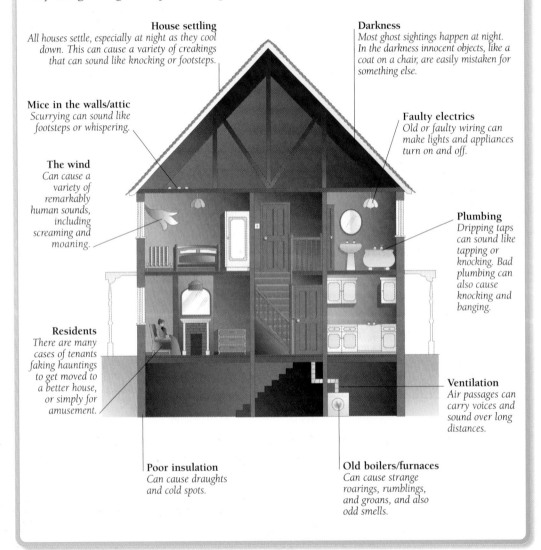

House settling
All houses settle, especially at night as they cool down. This can cause a variety of creakings that can sound like knocking or footsteps.

Darkness
Most ghost sightings happen at night. In the darkness innocent objects, like a coat on a chair, are easily mistaken for something else.

Mice in the walls/attic
Scurrying can sound like footsteps or whispering.

Faulty electrics
Old or faulty wiring can make lights and appliances turn on and off.

The wind
Can cause a variety of remarkably human sounds, including screaming and moaning.

Plumbing
Dripping taps can sound like tapping or knocking. Bad plumbing can also cause knocking and banging.

Residents
There are many cases of tenants faking hauntings to get moved to a better house, or simply for amusement.

Ventilation
Air passages can carry voices and sound over long distances.

Poor insulation
Can cause draughts and cold spots.

Old boilers/furnaces
Can cause strange roarings, rumblings, and groans, and also odd smells.

Poltergeists

THE MOST CONVINCING type of haunting – the poltergeist – may not be caused by a ghost at all. The word poltergeist is the German term for "noisy ghost", and is the name given to a type of haunting in which the ghost, if there is one, is invisible, manifesting itself through a variety of physical phenomena.

Bad behaviour

Common symptoms of a poltergeist haunting or infestation include: objects being moved or thrown about; banging, rapping and knocking; small fires that start mysteriously; appliances going haywire; inexplicable wet patches; and foul smells. Generally poltergeists are more of a nuisance than a danger, although in at least one case – the infamous Bell Witch of Tennessee, which tormented the Bell family between 1817 and 1821, and eventually poisoned John Bell, the head of the family – a man has been killed.

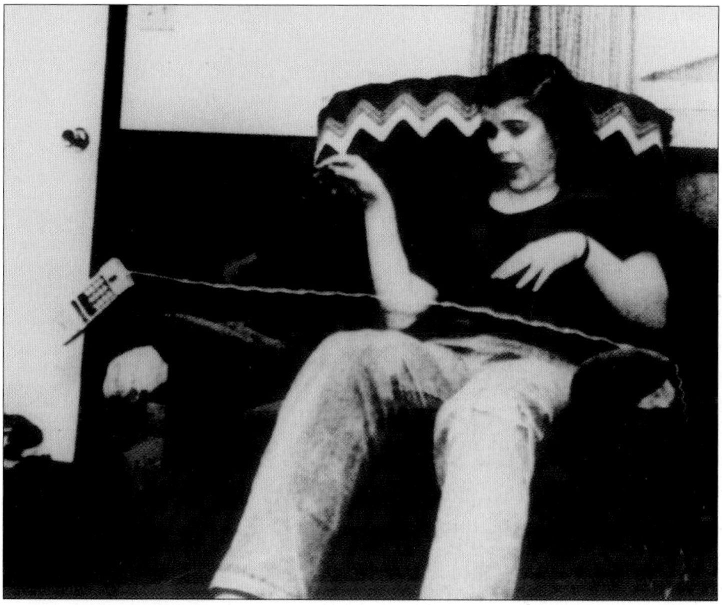

■ **Poltergeist activity** *generally centres on one member of the household – usually a teenager.*

The epicentre

The other distinguishing feature of a poltergeist haunting is that it tends to be centred on one person, and often follows that person if he or she attempts to move house, for instance.

The focus of a poltergeist haunting is known as the "epicentre". Epicentres are most commonly children or adolescents.

All in the mind

The things that happen in a poltergeist infestation are very similar to the phenomena produced by psychokinetics and their close relations the physical mediums. This, and the fact that an epicentre is usually involved, have led many people to argue that poltergeists are not ghosts at all, but instances of psychokinetic powers that are not under conscious control, technically known as "recurrent spontaneous psychokinesis" (RSPK), produced by the epicentre. One of the theories behind RSPK is that puberty triggers the sudden development of uncontrolled mental powers.

■ **Steven Spielberg's successful film *Poltergeist*** *explored the disturbing phenomena affecting a very ordinary family, in which the youngest daughter was plagued by evil poltergeist activities.*

The real McCoy?

Poltergeists provide convincing evidence that something unusual is really happening, whether it is supernatural or paranormal, for two reasons. Poltergeist hauntings follow the same pattern in most cases, wherever and whenever they occur. This undermines the cultural source explanation, and suggests a genuinely supernatural or paranormal phenomenon. Secondly, investigators have exposed many poltergeist hauntings as hoaxes, in many other cases they have observed inexplicable phenomena at first-hand.

Trivia...

Famous church reformers Martin Luther and John Wesley were both terrorized by poltergeists.

SPIRIT PHOTOGRAPHY

It is notoriously hard to obtain decent pictures of ghosts, but a number of "spirit photographs" have surfaced since photography began in the 19th century. Unfortunately these photos are easy to fake through a variety of means. The most popular is double exposure, in which a faint initial exposure overlays a second exposure of the same piece of film – you can try this yourself if your camera doesn't automatically wind on. Almost every purported spirit photograph has turned out to be a hoax, a mistake, or a processing error. However, this doesn't stop publishers from printing discredited photos and claiming they are genuine.

The "Rynham Hall Ghost" *photograph was taken in 1936. The photographer claimed to have seen a veiled ghostly figure coming down the stairs. On closer inspection, however, it is easy to see that the photograph could have been made up of two images. For example, look how the patch of reflected light at the top of the right-hand banister appears twice.*

Ghost hunting

ANYONE CAN TRY THEIR HAND at ghost hunting, but doing it properly can be difficult and requires expensive equipment. It is also notoriously unrewarding. Bill Bellar, general secretary of the Ghost Club, once said, "When a ghost hunter enters through the front door, the ghosts hurriedly leave through a back window." If you fancy having a go at ghost hunting yourself, follow the steps below.

INTERNET

www.hauntings.com

This site takes you to the home page of the International Society for Paranormal Research, where you can hire some professional ghost busters for the low, low price of $7,500 (£5,300) basic, plus expenses.

Step 1: Choosing a site

If you are not lucky enough to live in a haunted house or know someone who does, try your local library, or history or folklore society, where you may be able to pick up some leads. Alternatively get online and access a relevant ghost "gazetteer" – a listing of haunted places. The trickiest part may be getting permission to conduct an investigation – not everyone wants strange people tramping through their property all night.

Step 2: The stake-out

Once you've got the go ahead, meet up with the owner and get a detailed history of the haunting, together with a careful tour of the location. Make a plan of the house and agree which areas you can access. Assemble some helpers – some people you can trust, who will not think it's a laugh to hoax you or fake anything. Assuming that your investigation is to be an overnight operation, pack the owner off and choose a central room as a base. Set up your equipment (see Step 3) in likely spots (in other words, where spooky stuff has been reported), and arrange a rota of patrols to check the sites and watch for ghosts. Remember to keep detailed notes and record exactly when and where anything happens. Use a piece of chalk to mark the locations of objects so that you can tell if they've moved.

Step 3: Assemble your equipment

The minimum equipment that you need for a ghost hunt is a watch, a pen and paper, a torch, a tape measure, a thermometer (for measuring sudden changes in temperature and local cold spots), a compass (to check for sudden changes in the local magnetic field), a camera with a flash, and a tape recorder (for recording ghostly sounds). Experts recommend several other items: extra cameras with black-and-white and infra-red film; video cameras, with low light adaptors if possible; thread to stretch across doorways or corridors; and containers for interesting substances. Professional outfits use expensive apparatus such as instruments for measuring pressure, humidity, vibration, electromagnetic forces, and possibly even a Geiger counter (for measuring radiation levels).

CAMERA WITH FLASH

TORCH

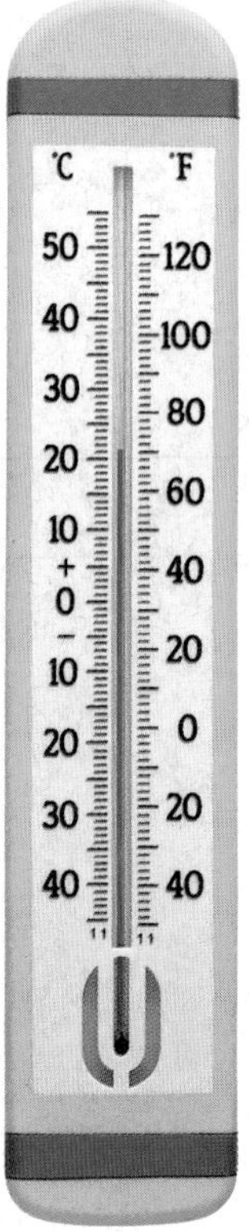

THERMOMETER

TAPE MEASURE

These items make up *part of the basic ghost-hunting equipment – essential when staking out a possible haunted location. Try to use the ghost-hunting tools together, since a lone photograph without supportive evidence will not carry much weight with the professionals.*

Step 4: What to do if there is evidence of a haunting

If you should find evidence of a haunting the chances are the owner of the house won't be too happy about it. There are a number of ways of getting rid of a ghost. You could ring your local church or temple and ask about ***exorcism*** – most religions perform some form of exorcism, and many have specific departments and full-time exorcists. Alternatively you could call in a psychic, who may be able to visualize and even communicate with the ghost, and convince, help, or force it to leave. Or you could attempt to "lay" the ghost by finding out why it is haunting this particular house, and redress any wrongs it may have suffered; for example, it may have been improperly buried.

DEFINITION

Driving out a ghost or evil spirit by means of prayer and holy ritual is known as **exorcism**. *The priest or other person who performs this process is called an exorcist.*

Trivia...

The Matumba people of central Africa believed that ghosts would cling to people, but could be dislodged by running water.

Ghost expert Ian Wilson points out that if ghosts really do exist because they are trapped on Earth by the trauma of an unhappy end, forcing them out by exorcism, and even chasing them round with cameras, is cruel and unnecessary. He argues that all that may be required is a simple prayer or blessing, which you can say yourself.

Making sense of spooks

BY NOW IT SHOULD be fairly obvious that there are lots of different types of ghost, which behave in lots of different ways. The variety of reported hauntings spells trouble for theories about where ghosts come from, because any theory that claims to be able to "explain" ghosts also has to explain a mass of contradictory "ghost facts".

The unquiet dead

The most usual theory is that ghosts are the souls of the departed, trapped on Earth for some reason. This theory explains why ghosts might appear, and also why they disappear when laid, but it doesn't explain ghosts of the living, ghosts of inanimate objects, or "boring" ghosts that seem to have no purpose.

The stone tape theory

Many ghosts seem to be linked to traumatic or significant events, and this has led to the theory that people and events can somehow leave an impression on their surroundings, as if they were recorded in the stones of a house – hence the "stone tape" theory. Hauntings are replays of these recordings. This theory explains why some ghosts seem not to be conscious – for example, re-enactment ghosts – but not ones that interact with the living, or ones that are seen away from where they lived and died.

■ **This photograph** *shows a ghostly figure in an old London church. Could this person have left their impression in the very fabric of the building only to reappear centuries later? That's just one ghost theory!*

The witness projection scheme

Perhaps ghosts are created by the people who see them, by some method of psi projection not yet understood. This theory works well for some types of ghost, but doesn't explain how some ghosts seem to know things that the living witnesses don't.

The sceptical viewpoint

The sceptical explanation is that ghost sightings are the result of a complex mix of sensory confusion, faulty memory, cultural influence, and exaggerated or false reporting. In other words, ghosts exist only in the mind. Sceptics claim that their theory is the only one that accounts for the whole range of "ghost facts", and that the huge variety of ghost reports results from the individual and cultural variety of the witnesses. But the sceptics can't explain the hard core of reports of ghosts experienced by more than one witness, or cases where ghosts know things that living people do not.

INTERNET

www.ghostweb.com

Go to the International Ghost Hunters Society web site for loads of convincing pictures to test your scepticism.

A simple summary

- ✓ Belief in ghosts is universal to all cultures, and ghost stories around the world have similar elements.
- ✓ Ghosts come in many varieties. Some seem to have a purpose and can interact with the living, others act like mindless recordings. There are also ghosts of animals and inanimate objects.
- ✓ Ghosts of the living may be telepathic projections caused by crises.
- ✓ The haunted house is a popular feature of ghost lore, but there are many mundane causes for the phenomena of a haunting.
- ✓ Poltergeists are the most convincing ghostly phenomenon, but may actually be caused by involuntary psychokinesis.
- ✓ Ghosts can be driven out in a number of ways, particularly exorcism, but if ghosts really do exist this may be cruel and unnecessary.
- ✓ There are several theories about how and why people experience ghosts, but they each have problems explaining all the data.

Chapter 8

Spiritualism

SPIRITUALISM IS A MOVEMENT based on the belief that the human personality, soul, or spirit survives death and can communicate from the Other Side. Since it began in the 19th century it has had a profound effect on the development of all areas of paranormal and supernatural enquiry.

In this chapter...

- ✓ Speakers for the dead
- ✓ The séance
- ✓ Exposed!
- ✓ Keeping the candle burning
- ✓ Astral travellers
- ✓ Let's go round again

Speakers for the dead

SPIRITUALISM WAS BORN in Hydesville, New York, on 31 March 1848. Two young members of the Fox family – Margaret, aged 10, and her sister Kate, aged 7 – began to communicate with a spirit that apparently haunted their house. The Fox sisters would ask the spirit questions and it would reply by means of a rapping or knocking sound, which became known as "spirit rapping".

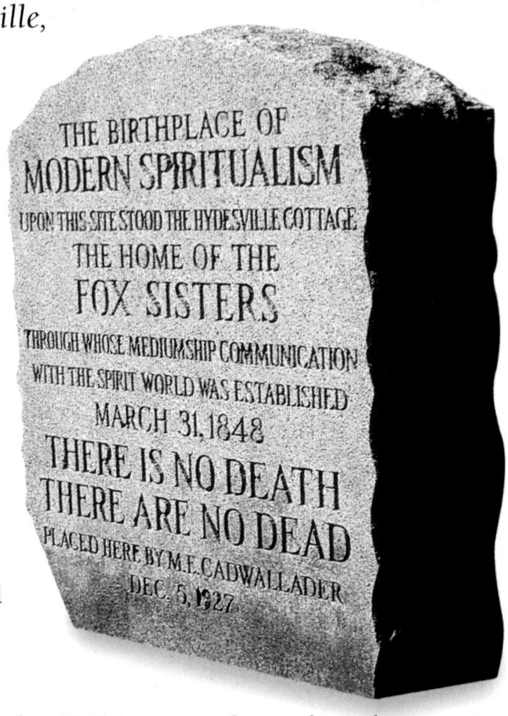

THE BIRTHPLACE OF
MODERN SPIRITUALISM
UPON THIS SITE STOOD THE HYDESVILLE COTTAGE
THE HOME OF THE
FOX SISTERS
THROUGH WHOSE MEDIUMSHIP COMMUNICATION
WITH THE SPIRIT WORLD WAS ESTABLISHED
MARCH 31, 1848
THERE IS NO DEATH
THERE ARE NO DEAD
PLACED HERE BY M.E. CADWALLADER
DEC. 5, 1927

This memorial stone *bears the poignant inscription "There is no Death, There are no Dead" in memory of the Fox sisters and the birth of spiritualism in Hydesville, New York.*

The Fox sisters identified their friendly spirit as the ghost of Charles Rosma, a 31-year-old peddler who had been murdered in the house 5 years earlier. A human skeleton accompanied by a peddler's box was indeed found in the basement, as the sisters predicted.

The sisters became celebrities and soon devised an alphabetical code for communicating complex messages from other spirits, who exhorted them to spread the word about spiritualism.

Spirit crazy

Enthusiasm for spiritualism spread like wildfire across the US and then Europe. By 1851 there were over 100 practising mediums in New York alone. The movement grew in popularity until, by the time it reached its peak just after World War I, there were tens of thousands of spiritualists on both sides of the Atlantic. Spiritualism became an organized religion, based on an attempt to merge Christian beliefs with the phenomenon of the ***séance***.

DEFINITION

In a **séance**, *a group of people gather together to help summon the spirits and watch the medium. The word is French for a sitting or meeting, derived from the Latin* sedere *– to sit.*

Spiritualists believe that the soul survives death but that there are no such things as heaven or hell.

■ **Eternal flame:** *the survival of the spiritual body after death continues to be one of the fundamental beliefs held by spiritualists all over the world.*

Celebrity mediums

Some mediums became celebrities, drawing huge crowds to their lectures and famous patrons to their séances. Many mediums wowed their audiences with physical feats such as levitation, an aspect of spiritualism known as physical mediumship. Mental mediumship involved communication with and messages from the spirits. Celebrity supporters became almost as important as the mediums themselves. One of the most famous was Sir Arthur Conan Doyle, creator of Sherlock Holmes and an ardent spiritualist who spent a lot of time promoting the new religion.

The séance

AT THE HEART OF SPIRITUALISM is the séance. Here we take a look at what would have taken place during a typical séance right up until the 1930s.

The set-up

A typical séance would be conducted in a quiet, comfortable room, often prepared by the medium with drapes and hangings to enhance the atmosphere. Usually the séance would take place in dim light or near darkness – to this day, very few mediums perform in fully lit conditions. Sceptics argue that mediums insisted on conditions such as darkness and heavy drapes because it made fraud much easier.

The guests (known as sitters) and the medium would sit round a table (sometimes there were things on the table, such as musical instruments). Often they would hold hands or place their hands on the table with their little fingers touching their neighbours'. Physical contact in this way was thought to help amplify individual psychic energies and thus boost the medium's own powers. Again, sceptics argue that it meant that sitters could not use their hands to check what was happening around them.

■ **Séances usually took place around a table,** *where the sitters joined hands in the belief that this would combine their psychic energy, boosting the medium's ability to contact the spirits.*

Mental mediumship

The role of the medium was both to summon or activate the spirits and to communicate with them. Typically the medium or a sitter would enquire whether such-and-such was "present", and then the sitters could pose questions. The medium would pass on the spirit's answers. Often the medium would go into a trance to allow communication with the spirit world, but not all mediums did this.

DEFINITION

When a spirit enters the body and mind of a living person and takes partial or complete control, that person is said to be **possessed**.

Sometimes a spirit would ***possess*** the medium, using his or her body or voice. This is known as channelling. Spirits could make use of the medium's hand to write or draw. This phenomenon is known as automatic writing, and can also be produced during hypnosis. Some mediums apparently produced writing in languages they didn't speak, which was hailed as proof that the information came from spirits.

Psychical researchers soon realised that mental mediumship might be explained by some form of ESP on the part of the medium, rather than genuine communication with the dead. This is known as the super-ESP theory of mediumship.

Ouija boards and planchettes

A more direct method of communicating with the spirits was provided by the Ouija board. The most important element of a Ouija board is a pointer that can move about on a surface with rollers or simply by sliding. An upturned glass can be used as a pointer if the table is slippery enough. A popular variant of the pointer was the planchette, a heart-shaped piece of wood on two rollers with a pencil stuck vertically through it, so that it could trace out shapes and letters.

The word "Ouija" *is actually a trademark. The boards were (and still are) manufactured as games, and "ouija" derives from the French and German words for "yes" – one of the words marked on the board.*

To use a Ouija board, the questioner puts one or two fingers on the pointer. In response to questions the pointer moves about and points to letters, numbers, and words marked on the Ouija board. (Alternatively these can be marked out on the table or any other surface.) The sequence of letters is supposed to spell out answers to the questions.

Table turning

During the 1850s, one of the most popular forms of communicating with the dead was table turning, where the spirits answered questions by rapping, knocking, or moving a table. Sometimes the table would even lift into the air.

Trivia...

Abraham Lincoln and Queen Victoria and Prince Albert all experimented with table turning.

INTERNET

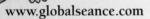

www.globalseance.com

Read what the British spiritual healer Helen Parry-Jones has to say about her experiences of the spirit world.

Physical mediumship

The most spectacular phenomena were, like table turning, physical. A huge variety of effects were produced, many of them similar to the claims of today's psychokinetics. People and objects would levitate, ghostly figures, limbs, and even pets would appear, and musical instruments would sound when no one was playing them. Sometimes objects would materialize out of nowhere – these were known as apports. Some mediums produced a strange substance, called ectoplasm, that was said to be from the spirit world. It would stream from their orifices, and sometimes it would form into shapes.

Haunting tunes: *piano keys playing on their own were one of the supernatural highlights of the séance.*

Exposed!

RIGHT FROM THE BEGINNING the extraordinary claims of the spiritualists attracted the attention of the scientific community. Many prominent men of science went on record to say that they believed the phenomena were genuine, and that the mediums could not be faking. Many others, however, caught mediums in the act of fraud or found mundane explanations for spiritualist phenomena.

Faraday turns the tables

It was a well-known physicist, Michael Faraday, who conducted one of the earliest investigations into spiritualism. He looked at table turning, devising a simple apparatus that could tell whether the table was moving "on its own" or under pressure from the hands of the sitters. The apparatus conclusively demonstrated that the sitters were moving their hands. When sitters knew what the device was for, no table turning occurred. It seems likely that table turning was caused by unconscious muscle twitches and movements made by the sitters – Ouija boards and planchettes probably work the same way. Also, many mediums were caught lifting tables with their feet or hands.

CON ARTISTS?

Mediums pulled off some amazing hoaxes at the expense of gullible sitters, many of whom were desperate to believe that spirits existed. Tricks could be performed using a free hand or foot under cover of darkness. Others needed accomplices – dressed all in black to move about undetected in the dark séance room. Glowing paint could then be used to create a disembodied hand or face. Muslin could be swallowed and vomited up on cue to produce ectoplasm.

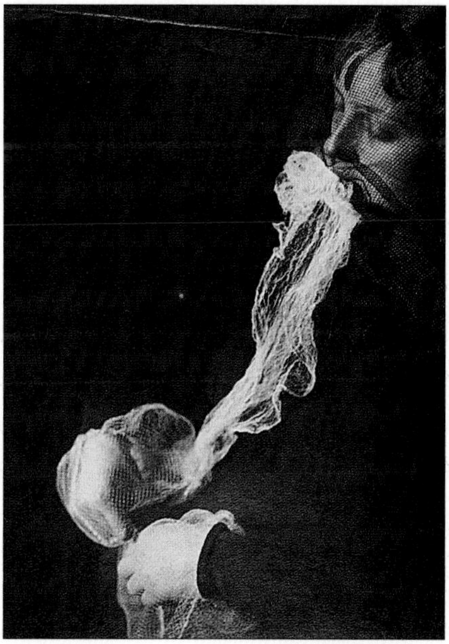

■ **Although ectoplasm** *caused much excitement during séances, its uncanny resemblance to man-made material meant few researchers could take it seriously.*

Mediums unmasked

Psychical investigators went to great lengths to test mediums. Mediums might be strip-searched before the séance and have their feet tied to a chair and their hands held by sitters on either side. They might even be gagged to prevent them from throwing their voice.

Some mediums were pronounced undeniably genuine by one researcher, but were caught in the act by another.

The Italian medium Eusapia Palladino (1854–1918), for instance, produced many phenomena that convinced researchers of her powers. She would rise into the air despite being strapped to a chair and held on either side. She could impress her features into putty kept in a sealed box on the far side of a room. But she was also caught red-handed on several occasions. In 1895, for instance, she was discovered to be using her foot to raise a table and a free hand to produce other effects. Palladino's supporters claimed that sometimes she had to resort to trickery because her powers varied and she didn't want to disappoint sitters.

Eusapia Palladino's *supposed feats of mediumship included the power to levitate tables during a séance. Some researchers insisted she was genuine – but she was caught cheating by others.*

The Fox sisters confess

In 1888 the mothers of spiritualism, Kate and Maggie Fox, publicly confessed to having hoaxed their spirit rapping through a combination of cracking the joints in their toes and rigging simple noise-making devices. They went on a public lecture tour debunking their own claims, proclaiming "spiritualism is a humbug from beginning to end". Several commentators have pointed out that by this time the Fox sisters were practically destitute alcoholics, who needed the money the "confession" brought in. Maggie retracted her confession a year later.

The Home controversy

Equally confusing is the career of the most celebrated medium of them all – Daniel Dunglas Home (1833–86). Home was never proved to be a hoax, but fell into disfavour after accusations of homosexuality and being found guilty of defrauding an elderly admirer. Many prominent researchers were absolutely convinced of his powers, which were often demonstrated in good light. Home could apparently float, levitate other objects, summon strange lights, handle red-hot coals, and physically elongate.

Home's most celebrated "miracle" happened on 13 December 1868, when he floated out of one third-storey window and into another, at a séance attended by three highly respectable witnesses.

The history of this tale is a fascinating illustration of the dangers of taking claims that you read in books at face value. Many things have been written about this feat – that the witnesses saw him float in and out, that they saw him hovering outside, and even that he was seen from the street below, hovering in mid-air. Careful research has shown that none of these claims are true.

The séance took place in a darkened room, and Home supposedly "flew out" through a window in a neighbouring room, so that no one saw him leave. Basically, none of the sitters saw anything that suggests Home could not easily have faked the levitation.

D.D. Home often performed *impressive feats such as levitation in good light, and was never proved to be a fake despite the best efforts of his implacable enemy Harry Houdini, who offered to duplicate many of his "illusions".*

Trivia...

One sitter, Lord Adare, claimed to have seen Home standing on a small balcony outside one of the windows, but one sceptical writer has suggested that Home never left the building and simply slipped back into the séance room under the cover of darkness.

Keeping the candle burning

IN SPITE OF THE CONTROVERSIES and revelations of the 19th century, spiritualism still survives to the present day. Spiritualist churches can be found all around the world, and groups still meet for séances.

The Scole Group

An excellent example of modern spiritualism is the case of the Scole Group. Between 1996 and 1999, the British SPR investigated the claims of a group of mediums from Scole in Norfolk, England. The Scole Group claimed to be in contact with a group of scientists from the "Other Side", and had witnessed a variety of phenomena – apports, strange sounds, levitation, thoughtographs, and dancing points of light.

But it seems that little has changed in the world of spiritualism. The Scole mediums insisted that the séances be conducted in a dark room, and it was they who determined the type and extent of controls that could be set up to prevent fraud. Ultimately the SPR investigation was inconclusive because of these drawbacks.

Electronic Voice Phenomena

■ **Konstantine Raudive (1906–74),** *one of the pioneers of EVP, captured hundreds of spirit voices on tape under strict laboratory conditions.*

One modern form of spiritualism is the use of technology to communicate with the dead. Messages can be received by phone or e-mail or simply recorded from the ***ether*** by any form of electronic recording device. The general term for this is Electronic Voice Phenomena – EVP.

DEFINITION

When electricity was first described it was thought to exist in the **ether** *– the space between particles of matter. Although physicists eventually concluded that the ether did not exist, spiritualists had already adopted the notion to explain where spirits resided.*

The most common form of EVP is the white-noise phenomenon. EVP enthusiasts record white noise, usually by tuning into a radio frequency between stations, onto a blank audio tape. When the tape is played back, distinct voices emerge from the background noise, speaking words, short phrases, and occasionally sentences. EVP experimenters claim that the voices identify themselves as real people and often sound like deceased friends and relatives. Even more controversially, they claim that the voices will answer questions recorded on the same tape.

Talking rubbish?

EVP enthusiasts insist that the voices are genuine, but the main problem is the lack of coherence or intelligence to the messages, which tend to be a mixture of gibberish, inane waffle, and slightly ominous warnings.

The sceptical view is that EVP is an example of the psychological phenomenon of pareidolia – a tendency to perceive a pattern when exposed to random sounds (or other sensations). In other words the brain naturally imposes meaning where there is none. The same phenomenon explains why we see shapes in the clouds, or patterns in the static on an untuned TV picture. This explanation is supported by the fact that different people tend to interpret the same EVP sounds differently.

INTERNET

www.alphaland.com/evp.htm

This is a weird site that claims that EVP voices have proved the existence of a place called the Kingdom of Alphaland. Click here to learn more!

Phone calls from the dead

Other forms of EVP include phone calls from the dead – instances in which a person has a perfectly ordinary telephone conversation with someone who later turns out to have been dead at the time – and e-mails from ghosts. In the latter type, mysterious files are found on computers. The files turn out to contain messages from a long dead person. Sceptics have dismissed these as misremembered dreams or hypnagogic hallucinations and hoaxes, respectively.

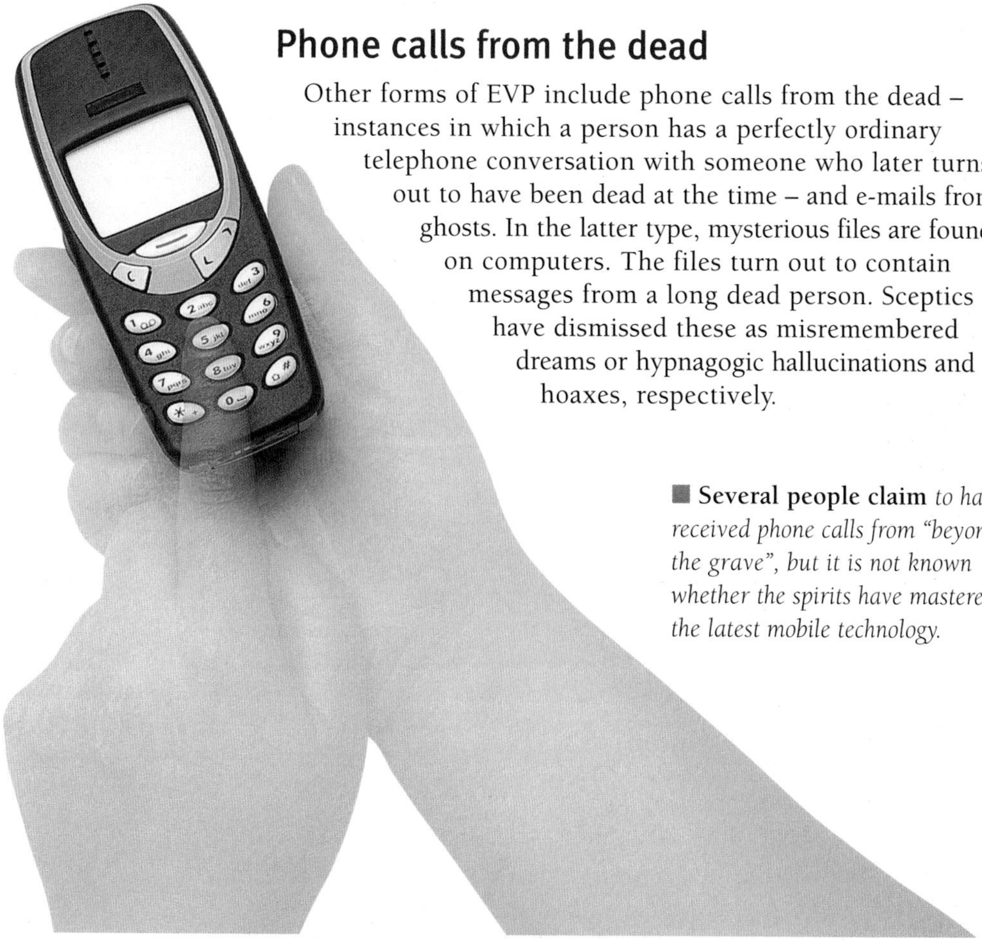

Several people claim *to have received phone calls from "beyond the grave", but it is not known whether the spirits have mastered the latest mobile technology.*

Astral travellers

A CORE BELIEF OF SPIRITUALISM is that we all have souls or spirits that inhabit our body but are separate from it. Known as the separable soul hypothesis, this belief explains how the soul can survive bodily death, and also allows the possibility that the soul might separate from the body during life, for instance during sleep or trance states. This was an early explanation given for dreams, and was also used to explain the psychic or spiritualist phenomenon of astral travel.

Spiritualists believe that the soul, or astral body, *can temporarily leave the physical body in moments of deep meditation, sleep, or during a near-death experience.*

Astral travel is closely related to the more common type of experience known as an out-of-body experience, or OBE, in which people find themselves looking at their own bodies from a distance.

Out-of-body experiences

An OBE is a bizarre phenomenon in which a person's consciousness seems to leave their body and look about independently. Sometimes the person finds that they can move about, fly, or pass through walls. Often they can see themselves going about their business. The experience typically lasts for under a minute but can go on for hours. Psychologist and OBE expert Sue Blackmore has found that around 10 per cent of the population have experienced an OBE at one time in their lives. Psychics and spiritualists claim to be able to have an OBE at will – it is known as astral projection, because it involves projecting the astral body beyond the physical one.

Near-death experiences

A closely related phenomenon is the near-death experience, or NDE, reported by many people from around the world who have come close to death before being revived – for example, after their hearts have stopped and then been restarted with an electric shock. A near-death experience consists of the sensation of leaving the body, observing it as people try to resuscitate it (in other words, having an OBE), and then travelling down a tunnel towards a bright light.

A glimpse of heaven? *The bright light that is common to many NDEs is believed to be the effect of oxygen starvation of the visual cortex – the part of the brain that generates images.*

The essential elements of the NDE are very similar around the world, but the interpretations vary. For instance, Christians may identify the bright light as heaven, and report seeing and even meeting Jesus.

Often a near-death experience is accompanied by a sense of wellbeing and joy. Both OBEs and NDEs tend to leave people with an altered outlook on life.

All in the mind

Psychics and spiritualists see OBEs and NDEs as evidence that we do have separable souls, and that there is life after death, but Blackmore and other researchers argue that there are psychological and neurological (involving the nervous system) processes that can explain all the different elements of these experiences.

Let's go round again

SOME SPIRITUALISTS BELIEVE that the soul not only survives death, but can return to life by inhabiting a new body – in other words through reincarnation. Belief in reincarnation is a feature of many religions, including Hinduism, Buddhism, and the religions of the Zulus and Australian aborigines.

Reincarnation in the West

Modern Western interest in reincarnation was mainly sparked by the 1956 publication of *The Search for Bridey Murphy*, a book that detailed the hypnosis of a Colorado housewife Virginia Tighe. Under hypnosis, Tighe recalled a former life as an Irish woman named Bridey Murphy, who lived in Cork and Belfast between 1798 and 1864.

The book was a bestseller and there was a flood of similar cases, many of which produced such an amazing wealth of period detail that it was argued they must be genuine. How else could ordinary men and women know obscure facts about times and places they claimed to know nothing about? However, careful investigation of the Tighe case revealed that while growing up she had lived next door to an Irish woman named Bridey Murphy, from whom she had borrowed nearly all the elements of the story. Since the Bridey Murphy case, other hypnotic regression cases have been similarly linked to exposure to books, films, radio plays, or other sources that, while not consciously recalled by the "reincarnated" person, had somehow surfaced under hypnosis. This phenomenon is known as cryptomnesia, or hidden memory.

This artwork depicts the Buddhist *doctrine of* Samsara *– the continuous cycle of birth, death, and rebirth.*

Reincarnation in the East

Better evidence for reincarnation comes from the research of parapsychologist Ian Stevenson, who investigated claims from India, Sri Lanka, Alaska, and elsewhere. His cases centred on children who spontaneously recalled past lives as deceased family members or people from nearby villages.

Stevenson's research uncovered many correspondences between the children's stories and the dead people. For example, Ravi Shankar, who was born in 1951, claimed to remember a past life as a 6-year-old who was killed and beheaded by a relative. Shankar even had a scar on his neck that corresponded to the fatal wound. Stevenson argued that his cases could not be due to cryptomnesia, because the children involved were too young, but critics argue that his verification of the crucial correspondences was sloppy.

Regional differences for reincarnation?

Differences between the past lives recalled by people in the West and those in the Asian countries (for example, people in Asia hardly ever change gender, and normally reincarnate close to their village) suggest that the cultural-source hypothesis is a good explanation for reincarnation. As writer Mike Dash says: "It seems more probable that these differences are the product of cultural and religious influences than it does that reincarnation [...] works differently for Western souls than it does for Indian and Sri Lankan ones."

A simple summary

✓ Spiritualism had humble beginnings but quickly caught on in the public imagination – it has influenced the way that all of us think about the afterlife and other aspects of the paranormal and supernatural.

✓ The central element of spiritualism is the séance, which commonly involved a range of mental and physical phenomena, including messages from beyond the grave, table turning, and ectoplasm.

✓ The rapid spread and enormous popularity of spiritualism soon brought it under intense sceptical scrutiny, and all in all it hasn't fared too well – most aspects of spiritualism have been discredited at one time or another.

✓ Spiritualism lives on in several forms, including the intriguing but ultimately unconvincing phenomenon of EVP.

✓ Other phenomena associated with spiritualism include astral projection, OBEs, NDEs, and reincarnation. Sceptics argue that known psychological processes, such as pareidolia and cryptomnesia, can account for all of these.

THE HERMIT.
SUN
THE MAGICIA

Chapter 9

Magic and the Occult

MAGIC IS A TOPIC steeped in history and secrecy, and therefore mystery. Everyone knows a little bit about magic, but generally only enough to think that it's scary or weird. In this chapter I'll explain what magic is, where it came from and how it's done, and hopefully dispel some of your wilder notions.

In this chapter...

- ✓ What is magic?
- ✓ Practical magic
- ✓ Telling the future
- ✓ World magic

THE DARK WORLD OF MAGIC HOLDS MUCH MORE THAN YOU CAN SEE

What is magic?

*MAGIC IS A SYSTEM of beliefs and practices that allows man to control nature through supernatural means. Most magic involves special knowledge and rituals, which are hard to learn and used to be revealed only to **initiates**. Nowadays most magical rites are available for anyone – in books or on the Internet – but they are still difficult to follow, and the world of magic remains mysterious and exclusive.*

DEFINITION

In occult terms, an **initiate** *is someone who has been introduced to secret knowledge – usually by being admitted, or initiated, into a secret society.*

■ **Lucky charms,** *whether a horseshoe on the wall or a four-leafed clover, are forms of low magic that have survived to this day.*

High and low magic

Humans have always tried to understand, explain, and control the world around them. In the modern world we use science and technology for this purpose, but in the past magic was a system for making sense of the world and trying to change it. For thousands of years, magic was a way of explaining and controlling the world, in much the same way as science is today. This is still true of some cultures around the world.

At one time, everyone probably practised magic to some extent, but some individuals were thought to have special knowledge or power. These people became shamans – priest-magicians – and the practice of magic became organized, with the development of spells and rituals.

By the time civilization developed, there were two types of magic – high and low magic. Practically anyone could practise low (or folk) magic, which involved simple charms and superstitions such as touching wood or spitting to ward off the ***evil eye***.

Only a few elite priest-magicians with special training, often involving secret initiation rites, could practise high magic, which had become a complex system too hard for most people to learn or understand. High magic involved knowledge of the movement of the sun, moon, stars, and planets, the properties of herbs and minerals, and the memorization of complicated rituals.

DEFINITION

The belief that a person can bring misfortune to another human by giving them a look is known as the **evil eye**.

Pagans and witches

Until the coming of Judaism and Christianity there was little or no difference between magic and religion. Pagan religions included many magical beliefs and practices. The ancient Greeks and Romans, for instance, were very keen on divination, a branch of magic used for predicting the future.

■ **Since the Middle Ages,** *witches have been portrayed as evil old women who practise their witchcraft under cover of darkness. Henry Fuseli's painting of the three witches from Shakespeare's* Macbeth *epitomizes this stereotype.*

The early Christians, however, drawing on their Jewish roots, were keen to draw a line between religious practices, which were good, and magical ones, which were evil. From now on, in the West, magic became the occult – hidden, dark, secret – and was associated with the Devil.

Belief in low magic lived on among the common people as a combination of medical and herbal knowledge and superstitious belief – witchcraft. People who were particularly good at it were known, among many other names, as wise women, wart charmers, or hedge witches. During the Middle Ages they became the target of witch-hunting crazes.

Kabbalists and alchemists

High magic also lived on in the West, where it remained the preserve of a few highly educated scholars. Despite its dark associations – it was often referred to as "black magic" – many of these scholars were holy men, and high magic involved a lot of religious theory.

During the Middle Ages, Jewish scholars and mystics developed a system of magic known as kabbalah (from the Hebrew word for "tradition"), which was enormously influential on all subsequent magical systems. Drawing partly on the kabbalistic tradition, and partly on Roman and Greek philosophy, medieval Western scholars developed their own tradition of magical research, which centred on the art and science of alchemy.

INTERNET

www.kabbalah.com

Go to this web site for the latest in kabbalistic thought.

The Philosopher's Stone

Alchemy was the science of the Middle Ages – a mix of religion, philosophy, experimentation, and magic. It centred on attempts to find an elixir (potion) of immortality and the ability to turn lead into gold – a process known as transmutation.

These aims could be achieved with the help of a magical substance or artefact known as the Philosopher's Stone (nobody was exactly sure what it looked like). Alchemists tried to make the Philosopher's Stone by mixing chemicals and following magical rituals.

ALCHEMIST'S EQUIPMENT

Secret societies

During the 17th and 18th centuries, science, in its modern form, began to develop, and alchemy and magic fell out of favour. Around the same time a number of secret societies sprang up around Europe, with names like the Rosicrucians, the Egyptian Rite Freemasons, and the Illuminati. Alchemy effectively turned into science, but magical beliefs and practices lived on in the secret societies of Europe.

The aims of these societies were to bring about political and religious change, and they offered their members – who were drawn from the educated artistic and aristocratic elite – secret knowledge and magical power.

The Age of the Irrational

In the 19th century there was a lot of interest in all things paranormal and supernatural, including the occult. So many societies and orders sprang up at this time that the historian James Webb called it the Age of the Irrational. One of these societies was the Hermetic Order of the Golden Dawn (HOGD), founded by MacGregor Mathers. Its members included W.B. Yeats and Constance Wilde, wife of Oscar Wilde.

Trivia...

America's founding fathers may have been involved with secret societies such as the Illuminati. To this day there are Illuminati symbols on the American dollar, including a pyramid with an eye.

MacGregor Mathers was the father of modern magic, and most occult societies today are related to his Hermetic Order of the Golden Dawn.

The HOGD was highly organized, with complicated secret rules, rituals, ranks, clothing, and paraphernalia. Mathers claimed that the rituals and magical writings of the HOGD were of ancient origin, but the truth is that he invented most of them himself by mixing and reinterpreting older sources, under the guidance, he claimed, of telepathic immortals called the "Masters".

The HOGD was relatively short-lived, lasting from 1888 to 1900 before breaking up into a number of spin-off groups. The most infamous ex-member was Aleister Crowley, who in later decades became known as a ***Satanist*** and referred to himself as "the Beast". The newspapers called him "the wickedest man in the world".

DEFINITION

A **Satanist** *is a person who worships the Devil. In medieval times witches were accused of being Satanists.*

Modern magic

Various societies still practise the magical systems of MacGregor Mathers and Aleister Crowley, and the study of the kabbalah is fashionable at the moment (devotees are said to include Madonna and Jeff Goldblum). Witchcraft has made a big comeback, with the growth of Wicca, a modern form of paganism. Wiccan magicians practise white (good) magic and call themselves witches, whether they are male or female.

Dawn worship. *Modern-day witchcraft, or Wicca, is closely related to the principals of pre-Christian religions, in which the forces of nature are revered and the natural powers of healing followed.*

Practical magic

BY NOW YOU MAY BE WONDERING what a magician or witch actually does. How do you cast a spell? Do they actually work?

Principles of magic

Most magic is based on a few basic principles, which are found in magical systems around the world. Two of the most important principles of magic are outlined below.

1. **The Law of Association** says that objects or words that are or have been associated with other things have power over those things. For instance, your name or a lock of your hair have power over you because they are or were associated with you. This means that if a magician gets hold of some of your hair he can cast a spell on you by performing magic on the hair.

2. **The Doctrine of Correspondences** says that there is a secret order of correspondences throughout nature, which links things that might not ordinarily seem to be linked. For instance, according to the doctrine, there are correspondences between the sun, certain types of plant such as sunflowers or vines, certain types of mineral such as gold, the colour yellow, and even certain names, places, animals, and birds. This means that by using, say, sunflowers in a magical ritual you can tap into the spiritual and magical power of the sun. Principles like these also form the basis of many systems of complementary medicine, including herbalism and homeopathy.

■ **According to one** *law of magic, you can harness the power of the sun by creating a spell or magical ritual using corresponding natural elements, such as sunflowers.*

Casting a spell

Spells can be simple or complicated. Some involve nothing more than repeating a short phrase, but, in general, serious magicians rely on complicated ceremonies to gain access to the right energies or powers. For instance, a typical ritual might involve taking a bath, putting on special robes decorated with magic symbols, lighting candles, and burning incense in a specially prepared and decorated room, repeating a complicated formula, walking around the room in a set pattern, using chalk to mark a figure on the floor, mixing together and burning a collection of obscure ingredients, and then reciting some more phrases.

■ **The candle** *is one of the basic elements required for casting many types of magical spell.*

Magic objects

Magic involves heavy use of symbols, and objects decorated with symbols, or with symbolic value themselves, are an integral part of many spells. For instance, HOGD members would make their own wands, wear badges (known as lamens), and use ornate daggers (known as athames) in a magical ritual (known as a working).

Does magic work?

Many intelligent, educated people claim to have successfully performed magic, and there is an ancient tradition of practical magic around the world. In many parts of rural Europe, for instance, people still visit wart charmers, who use simple rituals or phrases to cure warts, and claim that they routinely succeed where conventional medicine fails. However, controlled studies on magic have not been done, and are unlikely ever to be conducted.

There is at least one way in which magic might have a genuine effect – the power of suggestion. If the subject of a spell is aware that a spell has been cast and also believes in the power of magic, the spell might become a sort of self-fulfilling prophecy. For instance, if you knew that someone had cast a spell to make you ill, and you believed in magic, you might make yourself ill by worrying about it. A lot of magic is about personal and spiritual growth and self-discovery, and in this sense magic can certainly produce real results.

Telling the future

THE MOST WIDESPREAD and popular form of magic is probably divination – telling the future. There are dozens of forms of divination, but the best known are cartomancy (telling the future by reading cards) and astrology (telling the future by the stars and planets).

The Tarot

The Tarot is a pack of 78 cards, 56 of which (the Lesser Arcana) are similar to familiar playing cards and 22 of which (the Greater Arcana) are decorated with special motifs and have names like Death, The Tower, and The Wheel of Fortune. The Greater Arcana were the first playing cards used in Europe, and the Tarot is the forerunner of modern playing cards.

The origins of the Tarot are shrouded in mystery. It first appeared in Europe in 14th-century Italy, but was probably based on much older models from Asia or the Middle East (or ancient Egypt, according to some legends). Over the years, each card has built up a host of associations and meanings, and this allows the Tarot to be used for divination.

■ **Tarot readers** *use the symbolic meaning of selected Tarot cards to catch a glimpse of what the future may hold. The cards are placed face down and then turned over before a "reading" can be made. Above is a selection of French Tarot cards.*

Reading the stars

Millions of people around the world read their stars every day, and astrology is practised by different cultures all over the world. The basic principle of astrology is that human personality and fate is linked to the motions and positions of the sun, moon, stars, and planets.

Trivia...

There are dozens of forms of divination, including some very odd ones. Gallomancy, for instance, is telling the future by the pecking pattern of chickens. Ichthyomancy is telling the future by looking at fish entrails.

In Western astrology, everyone belongs to one of 12 zodiacal signs, determined by the position of the sun in relation to the 12 zodiacal constellations on the date of their birth. Astrologers believe that your character is determined by both your zodiacal or sun sign and your ascendant (the sign of the zodiac that was rising on the eastern horizon when you were born).

Does astrology work?

Astrologers claim that there is a mass of evidence that astrology works, but almost all of this evidence is anecdotal. The few controlled studies or statistical analyses of astrology that have been carried out have given almost entirely negative results. French mathematician Michel Gauquelin performed the best statistical study of astrology in the 1950s. He tried to find some kind of link, or correlation, between people's sun signs and their occupations.

Gauquelin investigated dozens of possible correlations but found only two significant ones, which are now collectively known as the Gauquelin effect. He discovered that successful scientists were more likely to have been born with Saturn in the ascendant, and successful soldiers and athletes with Mars in the ascendant. However, sceptics point out that if you search for enough correlations you will always find one or two.

World magic

SO FAR I'VE CONCENTRATED on the Western magical tradition, but belief in magic is universal. In other cultures high and low magic are sometimes more mixed together, particularly in those cultures where magic remains a day-to-day part of life.

Africa

Belief in magic penetrates to every level of society in many African countries (although Christian churches and Islamic states tend to disapprove of magic). Day-to-day misfortunes, such as illness or poor harvests, may be put down to malicious witchcraft, in which case a witch doctor is called in to provide charms and spells to counteract the evil sorcery.

This mask *is worn by the Yoruba people of Nigeria to counteract the evil doings of witches in the local community.*

The Americas

Native Americans have extensive shamanic traditions, but because of colonization and the slave trade, the Americas have also been exposed to the magical traditions of both Europe and Africa. This can be seen most clearly in the voodoo traditions of Haiti and the Santeria religion of Brazil. Both involve the fusion of elements of Catholic belief – the saints and the Virgin Mary, for instance – with elements of African magic and religion.

Trivia...

In 1997 panic struck several countries in West Africa, including Ghana, Nigeria, Gabon, Cameroon, Togo, and the Ivory Coast, when rumours of penis-snatching sorcerers started to spread. Mobs beat and killed several people suspected of being evil magicians who only had to touch their victims to make their penises disappear. Over forty suspected sorcerers were lynched in Senegal.

Asia

India and China have complicated magical systems that are similar to Western high magic – the latter contains many elements of oriental magic. The Chinese have a particularly strong tradition of divination, including the famous *I Ching* ("Book of Changes"), a book of ***oracles*** that is at least 3,200 years old.

DEFINITION

An **oracle** *can be both something that gives prophecies or advice and the actual prophecy given. Usually oracles are not simple predictions – they tend to be ambiguous, and the questioner must interpret them for himself.*

ZOMBIE NATION

Haitian voodoo sorcerers are famous for their ability to create zombies – reanimated corpses used as mindless slaves. American anthropologist Wade Davis discovered that Haitian sorcerers really can use a combination of suggestion and paralysing and mind-altering drugs (derived from the toxic puffer fish, the cane toad, and plant sources) to turn living people into sluggish, malleable servants.

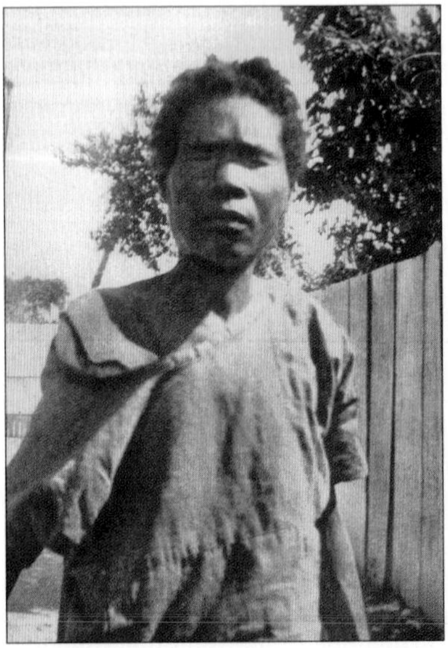

■ **Living proof?** *In 1936 Felicia Felix-Mentor was found wandering in a confused state in Haiti. Her father recognized her as the daughter who had died of fever 29 years earlier.*

Oceania

Australian aborigines blame some cancers and other illnesses on spells cast by enemies. Magic also plays a strong part in Pacific island communities. In the Trobriand Islands off New Guinea, for instance, it is an everyday part of life, regularly used in farming and at home.

■ **In the Trobriand Islands,** *agricultural yields are influenced by the garden magician, whose magical rites are believed to control the forces of nature. Here, young men celebrate the yam harvest festival.*

A simple summary

✓ Magic is a universal phenomenon in human history and culture. Its original function was similar to the role played by science today – to explain and help control the world.

✓ There are two types of magic – high and low. In the West, low magic became witchcraft and high magic became alchemy, kabbalah, and other complicated systems.

✓ Magic may not be literally real, but it can produce spiritual and psychological effects.

✓ Modern forms of magic claim to be directly descended from older forms, but are usually reinterpretations of previous systems.

✓ Tradition, ritual, and symbolism are vitally important to magic.

✓ Divination is the most popular form of magic, and astrology and Tarot reading are the best-known forms of divination.

✓ Magic remains a vital, everyday part of life in many cultures around the world.

Chapter 10

Religion

RELIGION IS BASED ON A BELIEF IN THE SUPERNATURAL, so it's hardly surprising that it is associated with supernatural and paranormal phenomena. In this chapter I'll introduce some of these phenomena, focusing mainly on the Catholic Church, which provides the richest store of miracles, powers, and wonders.

In this chapter...

- ✓ The exorcist
- ✓ Demons and angels
- ✓ Saints alive!
- ✓ The Turin Shroud
- ✓ Stigmata
- ✓ Visions and miracles

THE CROSS IS A HOLY SYMBOL IN MANY RELIGIONS, NOT JUST CHRISTIANITY

The exorcist

RELIGION IS A SYSTEM OF BELIEFS based around the worship of supernatural powers. Magic and religion are not exactly the same but there are very large overlaps. Although there are hundreds of religions around the world and each one is associated with many marvels, miracles, and wonders, I'll be dealing largely with Christianity, which is associated with enough incredible phenomena to fill several books.

Evil spirits within

One of the best known religious phenomena is ***possession***. Typical symptoms include convulsions, swearing and shouting, grimacing, foaming at the mouth, and talking in a lower, deeper voice than normal.

DEFINITION

Possession *is the apparent inhabitation of someone's body by another spirit or intelligence.*

Possession is found in many religions and cultures, but can be viewed very differently in each.

Christians normally believe that possession is a bad thing, caused by evil spirits such as demons and devils. In voodoo or Santeria, however, possession is a normal part of worship, and possessed people are said to be "ridden by divine horsemen".

Exorcising the Devil

The Christian response to possession is to drive the evil spirits out of the possessed body by using exorcism – a combination of prayer and sacred symbols. This is usually carried out by a trained priest, who will use a crucifix, holy water, repeated appeals to God, and specific prayers to drive out the evil spirits.

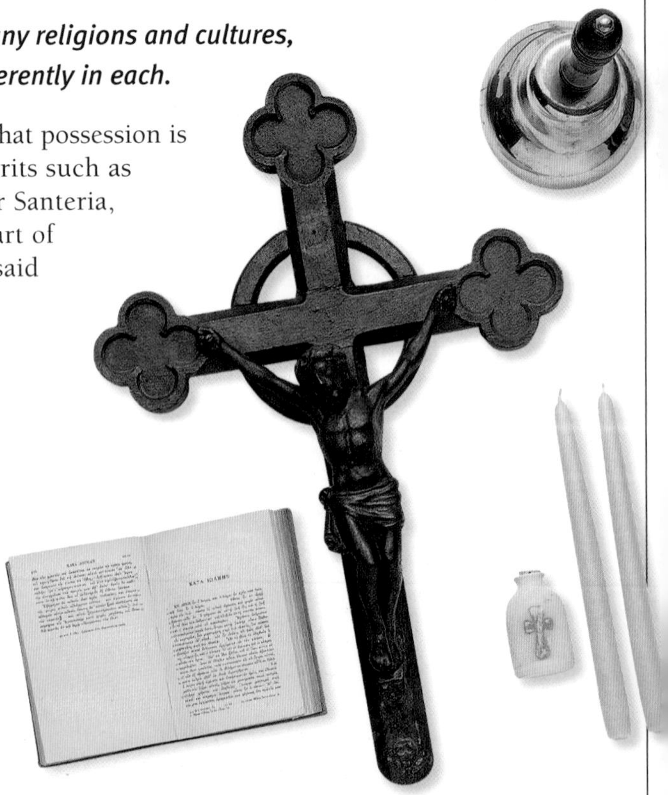

■ **Exorcising tools:** *during the rite of exorcism the priest will read from the Greek New Testament, light candles, ring a bell, hold the crucifix over the victim, and apply holy water.*

Inner demons

Although the process of exorcism can be long and harrowing – the possessed person may resist, screaming obscenities and vomiting – some exorcisms do seem to work. In successful cases the possessed person appears to be "cured" and their personality returns to normal. But is possession a genuinely supernatural phenomenon?

The symptoms of possession match those of recognized psychological and neurological disorders. For instance, epilepsy can cause convulsions and foaming at the mouth, while a neurological disorder called Tourette's Syndrome causes the sufferer to swear uncontrollably.

■ **Jesus himself was an exorcist,** *famously driving a large number of devils, who collectively called themselves "Legion", out of a man and into a herd of pigs (Mark 5:1–20).*

Even in medieval times, the Church recognized that many cases of apparent possession were caused by hysteria and mental delusion rather than evil spirits.

In the West today, a parishioner who is worried about possession is likely to be directed to a doctor or psychiatrist rather than an exorcist. Exorcism can be horribly misused, with vulnerable or sick people being subjected to distressing verbal and physical abuse in the belief that they are possessed.

THE TURBULENT PRIEST

In some parts of the Christian world, possession and exorcism are still taken seriously. In the late 1970s the Archbishop of Zaire (now the Democratic Republic of Congo), Emmanuel Milingo, performed mass exorcisms on a regular basis. In 1982 official disapproval from the Papacy led to Milingo being called to Rome, where Church authorities hoped he could be kept quiet and out of sight. Milingo, however, soon attracted a following among Italian Catholics and began to hold mass exorcisms at open air masses all over the country. Milingo continues to embarrass the Papacy with his colourful antics, and has been suspended from his duties and denounced by one cardinal as a sorcerer and an "African clown".

Demons and angels

ACCORDING TO MANY OF THE WORLD'S FAITHS, there is a class of beings between man and the gods – creatures of supernatural power who are not fully divine. In Judaism and Christianity these creatures are called angels and demons, depending on whether they are good or evil. In the Christian tradition, demons were angels who took part in Lucifer's revolt against God, and were cast into the fiery pit of Hell alongside him.

Army of darkness

According to tradition, there are thousands of greater and lesser demons living in Hell, arranged into an army of evil with regiments and captains ("Princes of Hell", such as Eurynome, the Prince of Death). When not preparing for the Final Battle of Good and Evil predicted in the *Book of Revelation*, demons spend their time torturing the souls of the damned and attempting to gain control of the souls of the living. To this end they would sometimes appear on Earth to living people.

A common element of black magic rituals *was the inverted pentacle – a potent magical symbol drawn upside down to direct its energies to evil ends.*

Demons hardly appear on Earth any more – people are more likely to see ghosts or aliens these days – but in the Middle Ages it was believed that they were regularly summoned by black magicians and witches.

For instance, evil sorcerers might draw a pentacle (five-pointed star) on the floor and then summon a demon. The demon would be trapped inside the pentacle, and could be made to do the sorcerer's bidding. Sometimes a **Faustian bargain** would be struck.

DEFINITION

In a **Faustian bargain**, *a person trades their immortal soul for power and success on earth while still alive.*

Guardian angels

According to Jewish and Christian tradition, the angels are ranked in Heaven like the demons in Hell. The two highest ranks are the Cherubim and the Seraphim, which include the Archangels such as Gabriel and Michael. It was believed that angels very rarely visited Earth, but since the 1990s there has been an explosion of angel sightings, often very similar to sightings of alien beings.

■ **The idea of a guardian angel** *protecting us on our journey through life is one that goes back to the days of the Old Testament; here an angel brings food to the prophet Elijah, exhausted in the desert.*

Angelic visions usually follow a similar pattern, appearing as serenely beautiful humans bathed in white light. Sometimes they have wings, although bizarrely they are sometimes dressed in suits or seen wearing turbans.

Angels can play a guardian angel role, appearing during moments of crisis (for example, a car crash) and miraculously averting danger, or they can offer prophecies, words of wisdom, and feelings of love to people feeling very vulnerable.

Few paranormal researchers seriously believe in the reality of angelic visions. They are normally explained as hallucinations brought on by moments of physical or psychological crisis.

Religious people interpret the hallucinations as angels; people with an interest in UFOs interpret them as aliens. However, there are plenty of people who claim that an angelic vision has changed their lives, and there is a thriving subculture of books, magazines, and web sites devoted to angelic visions.

INTERNET

saints.catholic.org/angels.html

Click here to find out more about angels from the Bible as well as real-life encounters.

Saints alive!

IN CHRISTIAN BELIEF a saint is someone officially recognized by the Church as an especially holy person, by virtue of their deeds in life and miracles attributed to them after death.

During the Middle Ages writings about saints and their lives – known as hagiographies – were one of the most popular forms of literature. Many legends grew up about the saints, and the veneration of relics (worshipping the remains of saints and items connected to Jesus himself), such as finger bones, was a major feature of religious life.

Strange powers of the saints

A variety of strange powers were attributed to saints. A common one was levitation – the ability to lift off the ground. Usually this happened involuntarily during intense prayer or concentration – for example, St Ignatius Loyola (died 1556), founder of the Jesuits – but St Joseph of Cupertino (died 1663) could sometimes fly at will, swooping up to the roof in front of hundreds of witnesses.

Many saints were said to glow or radiate light, sometimes while levitating. Others could appear in two places at once (bilocation), travel great distances instantaneously (teleportation), survive burning and other tortures, handle hot coals, or talk to the animals.

St Francis of Assisi *was not only famed for talking to the animals, he was also said to float and glow.*

Trivia...

Although the body of St Anthony of Padua rotted away, his tongue was discovered lying on the bottom of the coffin, "red, soft and entire".

Heaven scent

Many saints have continued to show miraculous powers after death, giving off sweet smells (known as "the odour of sanctity") and refusing to rot (known as the incorruptible corpse phenomenon). For instance, St Cecilia died in 177CE, but in 822 and again in 1599 her corpse was supposedly discovered in perfect condition, giving off the scent of flowers.

Relics of the saints

Various body parts claimed to be the remains of saints, including fingers, knuckle bones, shin bones, hearts, and whole mummified hands have long been treasured possessions of many churches, cathedrals, and monasteries. They are often kept in ornate and valuable containers known as reliquaries. Healing miracles are associated with some saints' relics.

■ **The dried blood of St Januarius** *liquefies when handled. Sceptics believe this is due to the fact that the blood contains thixotrophic substances, which can change from solid to liquid when shaken.*

It is, of course, practically impossible to verify the authenticity of a relic, and this leads to some disputes. For instance, both the Blessed Duns Scotus church in Glasgow and the Whitefriar Street church in Dublin claim to own the true relics of St Valentine.

A well-known miraculous relic is the blood of St Januarius, kept in the Santa Chiara basilica in Naples. Stored in dried form in phials, the blood appears to liquefy when handled and held aloft on festive days. Failure to liquefy is seen as a sign of bad luck.

THE DEVIL'S ADVOCATE

Making someone into a saint is a two-stage process. First comes beatification – when there is evidence for the candidate's virtuous life and associated miracles. Then canonization – after the evidence has been challenged by a specially appointed priest, the *Promotor Fidei* ("Promoter of the Faith", commonly known as the Devil's Advocate), and there is evidence of further authentic miracles.

The Turin Shroud

MORE POWERFUL AND SACRED than the relics of the saints are those of Jesus himself. These include dozens if not hundreds of splinters of wood said to come from the cross on which Christ was crucified (known as splinters of the True Cross), nails from the crucifixion, and the lance used to pierce Christ's side while he was on the cross (known as the Spear of Destiny or the Spear of Longinus).

Probably the most famous relic in the world is the Turin Shroud, a cloth that bears the image of a bearded man, said to be the sheet that was wrapped round Jesus when he was taken down from the cross.

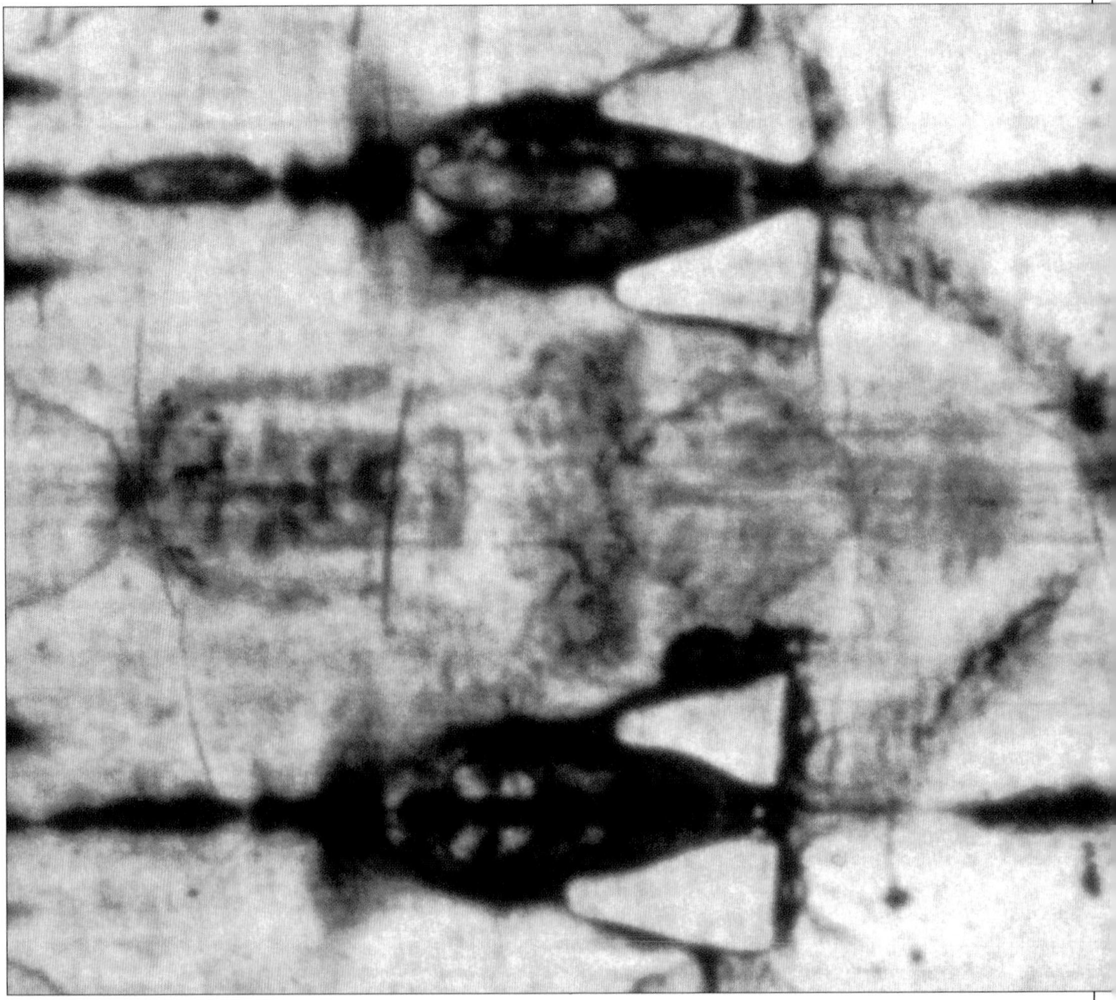

Shrouded in mystery

According to sindologists – those who believe in the authenticity of the shroud – the divine power radiating from Jesus caused his image to be miraculously imprinted on the cloth. However, there are a number of problems with this claim. The image on the cloth resembles a Western European, not someone from the Middle East. The proportions of the picture on the cloth are more like a photograph or painting than the distorted image that would be obtained by direct transfer from a body. The image on one side of the shroud is larger than on the other, and the head image seems to be separate from the body.

■ **The body of Christ?** *Tests carried out in 1988 suggest that the Turin Shroud – the best-known Christian relic in the world – actually dates back no further than the 13th century.*

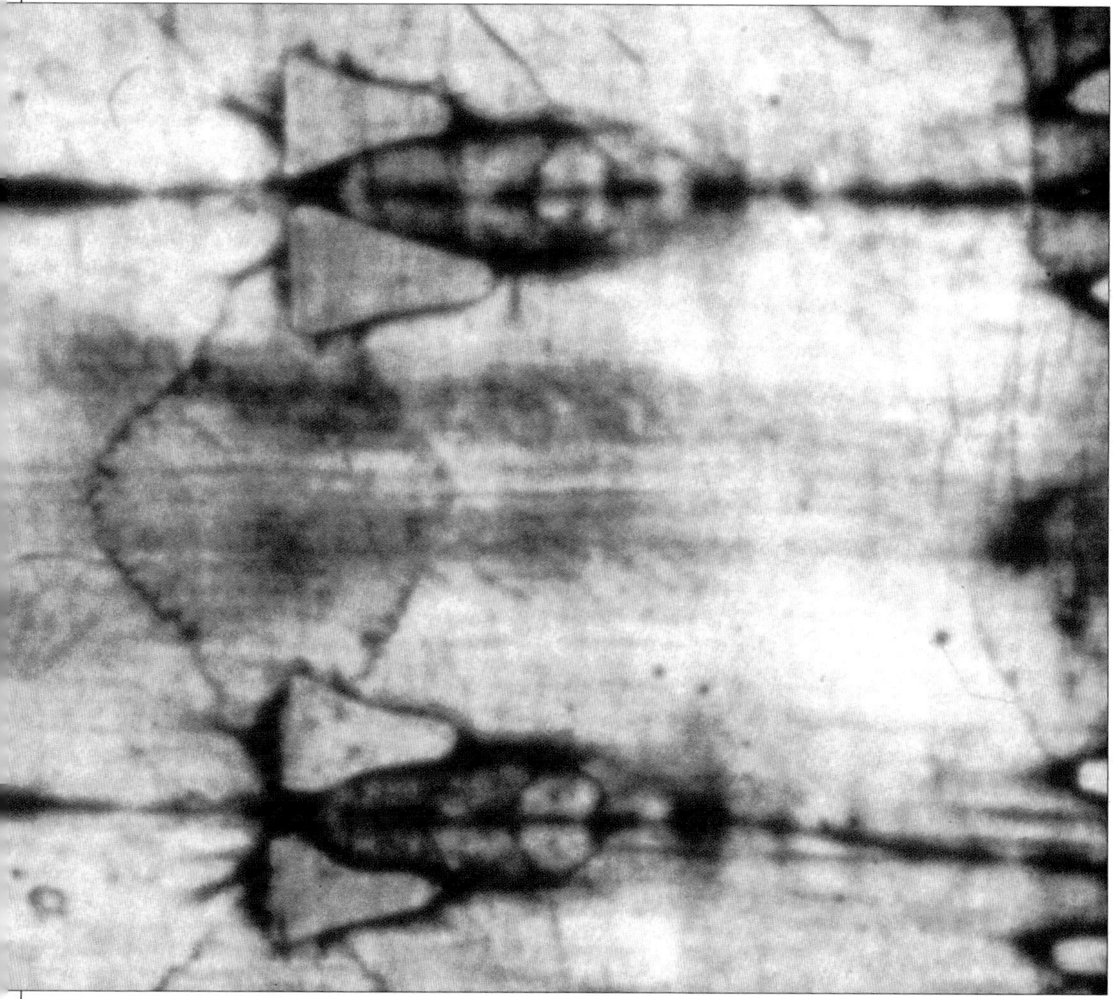

The history of the Shroud is also very uncertain. There is no concrete record of it until around 1350, when it was described as a crude fake, suggesting a different item from the eerily convincing image familiar today.

In 1988 a piece of cloth from the Shroud was carbon dated by three separate laboratories to between 1260 and 1390.

Although controversy has raged over the dating process, sceptics saw this as proof that it was a fake (albeit a brilliant one). The real question now seems to be how was such an amazing image produced in medieval times?

INTERNET

www.shroud.com

Go to this web site for the latest research and news about the Turin Shroud.

A technological breakthrough

The traditional sceptical position was that the Shroud was a clever forgery produced by painting, but now the most popular idea is that it was produced by an early form of photography. Researchers have shown that it is possible to make a close photographic replica of the Shroud using only technology that was available in the Renaissance.

Stigmata

STIGMATA ARE MARKS ON THE BODY that correspond to Christ's crucifixion wounds. Usually they take the form of open, bleeding wounds that don't become infected and close up of their own accord leaving no trace. Sometimes stigmata are extremely painful, and people bearing them, known as stigmatics, have been known to lose up to 0.5 litres (1 pint) of blood in one day. For believers, the appearance of stigmata is a miracle bestowed upon the especially devout.

The blood of Christ

The first stigmatic was St Francis of Assisi (died 1226), who received the wounds after having a vision of Christ on the cross. Since then there have been around 400 stigmatics.

Most stigmatics display the same five wounds as St Francis – one in the palms of each hand, two in the soles of the feet, and one in the side.

Some also bleed from the forehead, as if from a crown of thorns. Others bleed as if they've carried a heavy cross or been whipped.

In this haunting painting by Albert Bouts, *Christ displays the wounds of his crucifixion; stigmatics exhibit corresponding wounds on their hands, feet, side, or brow, often accompanied by intense pain.*

Suspicious wounds

Almost all stigmatics develop wounds that match those shown in most paintings and statues of the Crucifixion. But in real crucifixions nails are hammered through the wrists and ankles, or the nails would not support the weight of the body. If stigmata are not true miracles, what could they be?

Fraud is one possibility – several famous stigmatics were suspected of or caught inflicting wounds on themselves.

The most likely explanation of stigmata is that they are psychosomatic – in other words, self-induced through suggestion.

Hypnotic suggestion can induce similar effects, such as raising welts and causing wounds to start or stop bleeding. It may be that stigmatics work themselves into a sort of trance state similar to self-hypnosis (see Chapter 2) – many of them are psychologically disturbed and the wounds often appear during moments of religious ecstasy.

INTERNET

skepdic.com/stigmata.html

Go to this site from Robert Carroll's excellent Skeptic's Dictionary and see what you make of his argument that (almost) all stigmata are self-inflicted.

PADRE PIO

The most famous modern-day stigmatic is Padre Pio, an Italian monk who died in 1968. Pio received the five typical wounds in 1918 while celebrating the anniversary of the stigmatization of St Francis. Pio was also credited with powers of healing, levitation, and bilocation, and is currently a leading contender for canonization.

■ **For years, Padre Pio** *tried to conceal his open wounds in order to avoid the public eye. Despite this, people flocked to see the modest cleric whose bleeding palms were never proved to be fake.*

Visions and miracles

VISIONS HAVE PROBABLY been a central element of religious and mystical experience for as long as mankind has existed. Shamans used drugs, music, and dancing to induce them; Christians used music, fasting, and scourging. Most saints had at least one vision during their lives.

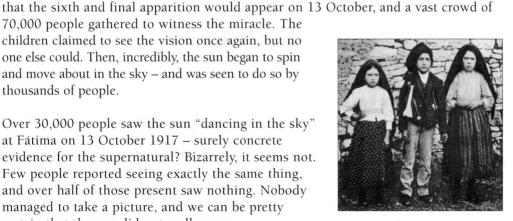

A VISION OF THE VIRGIN AND CHILD OR SIMPLY CLOUDS?

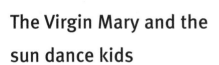

Visions seen by only one person are easily dismissed as hallucinations, but those seen by more than one person – shared vision – could be proof of the the supernatural.

The Virgin Mary and the sun dance kids

Probably the most common subject of religious visions, particularly amongst Catholics, is the Virgin Mary. Thousands of people in the 20th century alone claim to have seen the Virgin Mary, and she was the subject of two of the most famous shared visions of all time – the vision at Lourdes in 1858 and the one at Fátima, in Portugal, in 1917. The Fátima visions started in May 1917, when three peasant children had a series of visions of the Virgin Mary. The children predicted that the sixth and final apparition would appear on 13 October, and a vast crowd of 70,000 people gathered to witness the miracle. The children claimed to see the vision once again, but no one else could. Then, incredibly, the sun began to spin and move about in the sky – and was seen to do so by thousands of people.

THE FÁTIMA CHILDREN

Over 30,000 people saw the sun "dancing in the sky" at Fátima on 13 October 1917 – surely concrete evidence for the supernatural? Bizarrely, it seems not. Few people reported seeing exactly the same thing, and over half of those present saw nothing. Nobody managed to take a picture, and we can be pretty certain that the sun did not really move.

Various explanations have been offered. One is that anyone trying to stare at a fixed object will experience unnoticed involuntary movement of the head, which might make the sun appear to move.

The most likely explanation for the apparition at Fátima is that some of the witnesses were so desperate to see something that their fantasy took over for a few moments, so that in a sense they really did see the sun dance.

Other witnesses may have convinced themselves after the event, swept up in the excitement.

Weeping icons

Statues that move, bleed, or weep are another popular class of religious phenomena, drawing huge crowds. Usually the statues are of the Virgin Mary, but in September 1995, all over the world, statues of the elephant-headed Hindu god Ganesh began to drink milk. Photos, paintings, and icons of various figures from Jesus to Jimi Hendrix have also been observed to weep tears or blood.

The Church itself is usually suspicious of such claims, and a weeping or moving statue can turn a poor village into a rich pilgrimage destination. Apparent movement of statues is normally explained as the result of unnoticed involuntary movements of the head, as with the Fátima visions. The most widely accepted explanation for weeping or bleeding statues is the capillary action theory of Italian chemist Luigi Garlaschelli.

This statue of the Virgin Mary, *displayed by the devoutly Catholic Rosa Mystica group, began weeping tears of blood in September 1982.*

Crocodile tears

Dr Garlaschelli found that a glazed statue made of porous material such as plaster or ceramic will soak up fluids (including milk) by capillary action, but that the glaze will stop it from flowing out. If an imperceptible scratch is made in the glaze, in the corner of the eye for instance, the fluid will leak out in drips.

The fluid itself can be stored in a tiny space inside the statue, and Garlaschelli found that a type of Virgin Mary statue involved in several weeping cases has exactly such a space because of the way the mould is made.

A simple summary

✓ Religion is associated with many supernatural and paranormal phenomena, and Catholicism seems to have a particularly rich store of them.

✓ Demon sightings and demonic possession, which is probably a misidentification of neurological or psychological problems, have become less common since the Middle Ages, but exorcism is still routinely practised, and sometimes horribly misused, around the world.

✓ Angel sightings are increasingly popular, and often seem to be related to alien sightings or New Age experiences.

✓ Saints and their relics are associated with an amazing variety of supernatural and paranormal phenomena, including levitation, bilocation, and incorruptibility.

✓ The Turin Shroud is almost certainly a forgery, but a wonderfully advanced and impressive one.

✓ Stigmata are physically real, and are probably caused by some sort of poorly understood psychosomatic process.

✓ As with stigmata, the true value of visions is what they reveal about our psychology and the power of belief.

✓ Most miraculous "weeping" statues can probably be explained by capillary action.

PART THREE

Natural Mysteries

THIS SECTION OF THE BOOK deals with an amazing range of mysterious phenomena from the natural world, including dowsing and ley lines, strange objects falling from the sky, and mystery animals.

Chapter 11

Natural Mysteries – the Basics

THIS CHAPTER INTRODUCES the complex and varied topic of natural mysteries, explains how they challenge the views and assumptions of mainstream science, and presents some of the important figures who have studied and written about them. It will introduce several concepts using examples that will be explored in greater depth in Part Three, and will raise questions such as: what is the difference between a bigfoot and a yeti; what is the real origin of crop circles; does the Bermuda Triangle really exist; and is there sufficient evidence to support the theory of spontaneous human combustion?

The natural forces of the unexplained are many and varied, challenging the laws of nature and defying physics. These mysteries don't fit neatly into categories, so I have divided the subject into four groups: human mysteries; earth mysteries; mad world; and mysterious creatures.

What are natural mysteries?

NATURAL MYSTERIES are ***anomalies*** *of nature. They often involve elements of the natural world that are familiar to science – such as electricity or animals – behaving in ways that are unfamiliar.*

DEFINITION

Anomalies *are abnormalities – things that are out of place or irregular, and not as expected.*

Because natural mysteries are anomalous, they tend not to fit into neat categories, so if the way that I've grouped them into chapters seems a bit arbitrary, it's because it is!

■ **A unicorn** *is a mythical one-horned horse, supposedly endowed with magical powers.*

Natural mysteries are phenomena that do not seem to be supernatural, but at the same time cannot be explained by science. The umbrella of natural mysteries covers four main categories:

1. **Human anomalies** such as combustion and dowsing, that don't fit into other human categories
2. **Earth mysteries**, which cover aspects of landscape, geology, folklore, crop circles, prehistoric monuments, and strange lights that appear to come from nowhere
3. "**Mad world**" **mysteries**, which incorporate a range of extraordinary natural anomalies, including strange things falling from the sky and animals appearing or behaving strangely
4. **Mysterious creatures** such as monsters and fairies, like the Loch Ness Monster, Bigfoot, vampires, mermaids, and leprechauns

The study of strange creatures is known as cryptozoology – a fascinating blend of science, history, and folklore.

Reality check

The term "natural mysteries" covers such a diverse range of phenomena that it's hard to make generalizations about this category, but it's safe to say that natural mysteries are among the best reported and verified of unexplained phenomena. They include several types of phenomena that have been proved to exist, as well as many others that may be proved to exist in the future.

Once damned ...

The scientific establishment has a history of ignoring or denying the existence of phenomena that do not fit into accepted models of the world. Writer and researcher Charles Fort – the most influential figure in the field of natural mysteries – said that it was as if this sort of information was "damned", because of the way it was shunned and reviled. However, there have been several notable cases where "damned" phenomena have come to be accepted by mainstream science.

Until Western explorers *returned from Africa with photographic evidence of gorillas, sightings were dismissed as tall tales.*

... now accepted

These days everyone has heard about meteorites – lumps of rock from outer space that fall to earth. There are movies and books about them and they regularly make the news.

However, until the beginning of the 19th century the suggestion that these rocks came from outer space was regarded as scientific heresy, and you would have been laughed at for suggesting it. People who reported seeing meteorites actually falling from the sky were dismissed as liars or idiots, in much the same way that people reporting UFOs today are often treated.

The coelacanth, *a prehistoric fish thought to have been extinct for more than 70 million years, was discovered in 1938 off the coast of south-east Africa.*

The gorilla is familiar to us from TV programmes and zoos, but the reports of early African explorers were dismissed as travellers' tales until a specimen was actually brought back. Cryptozoologists often point to the story of the gorilla when defending their claims about Bigfoot or the yeti.

The coelacanth, a large, armour-plated fish, is now famous around the world as an example of a living fossil. Previously known only from fossils, it was thought to have been extinct for 70 million years. However, the discovery of a live specimen off the coast of south-east Africa in 1938 thrilled the scientific community and proved that ancient species can survive undetected until the present day.

Bermuda Triangle

There have been some notable cases where a combination of factors give life to a mystery that may not really exist. One example is the Bermuda Triangle, an area of the Atlantic Ocean that, according to popular belief, has a spooky effect on ships and planes.

According to some researchers, careful re-examination of the disappearances said to have taken place in the Bermuda Triangle reveals that many of them have either been solved, were never mysterious in the first place, or simply didn't happen at all. In other words there may not be anything strange about the Bermuda Triangle whatsoever.

Mistaken identity

Natural mysteries present a real challenge to the scientific establishment. Many examples even leave clear physical evidence, and this makes it hard to dismiss them as hallucinations or flights of fancy on the part of the witness. But there are also many natural mysteries where evidence is absent and the reality of the mystery rests on shaky foundations.

We've already seen in this book just how easy it is for witnesses to make mistakes when it comes to mysterious events. Natural mysteries are no exception.

Rocky the dog, *shaved for an operation, gave rise to reports of lion sightings in Barnsley, UK.*

A significant proportion of cases of mysterious lights or strange animal sightings turn out to be the result of simple misidentification of things like distant headlights or large domestic cats.

A historical view

People have been investigating and writing about anomalous phenomena throughout history. Since the 19th century one man in particular stands out for the breadth of his interest and the extent of his influence. The leading figure in the field of natural mysteries, as I mentioned earlier, is Charles Hoy Fort (1871–1932).

The Fort that counts

Fort was an American researcher and philosopher who spent many years trawling through the great libraries of the world in New York and London, searching for reports of oddities and anomalies that were excluded from mainstream science.

Fort had a very open-minded approach. He collected information on a huge range of topics and was interested in anomalies that resisted neat or convenient explanation. Of particular interest to him were natural mysteries, such as fish falls or out-of-place animals, and he invented the concept of teleportation as a possible explanation for these strange occurrences. Fort worked by making notes on small cards, and at his death he left a collection of more than 40,000 of these.

■ **Charles Hoy Fort** *was a prominent 19th-century researcher of mysterious natural phenomena. Many of his theories are still relevant today.*

***Charles Hoy Fort's name is now used to describe the whole field of unexplained phenomena, which are collectively termed* forteana.**

DEFINITION

Forteana *are events, occurrences, or things that are strange, unexpected, or inexplicable. People who study such things are called forteans.*

Fort's unique approach to the world of the unexplained has had an enormous influence on subsequent writers and researchers. Since his death, like-minded researchers have continued his work. The *Fortean Times* is the journal of record for modern forteans, and has recently helped to set up the Charles Fort Institute, a resource and research centre for all aspects of the paranormal, supernatural, and fortean world.

Examining the evidence

In the following chapters, we will be looking at several of the natural mysteries that have baffled scientists and fascinated followers for centuries. There is a remarkable amount of credible evidence for reports of sometimes incredible events, although whether or not you trust its authenticity is up to you!

Chapter 12

Human Mysteries

HUMAN MYSTERIES exist right on the border between the known and the unexplained – between science and the paranormal. In this chapter we'll explore some of the best known human mysteries – spontaneous human combustion, electric and magnetic people, and finally the mystery of dowsing.

In this chapter...

- ✓ Spontaneous human combustion (SHC)
- ✓ The body electric
- ✓ Dowsing

Spontaneous human combustion (SHC)

THOUSANDS OF PEOPLE die in fires every year. Normally these deaths are not mysterious and the fires have an obvious cause. But there are cases where people seem to have been burnt alive in a very odd fashion, by a fire with no apparent source. This phenomenon is known as spontaneous human combustion, or SHC.

Ashes to ashes

Spontaneous human combustion involves the reduction to ashes of some or all of a human body by a fire of unknown origin, which damages only the body and areas in immediate contact with it.

SHC entered the popular imagination with the case of Countess Bandi of Casena, an Italian noblewoman whose head and fingers were found arranged around a pile of ashes in June 1731. Since then upwards of 300 cases of SHC have been reported, some of which have been investigated in great detail.

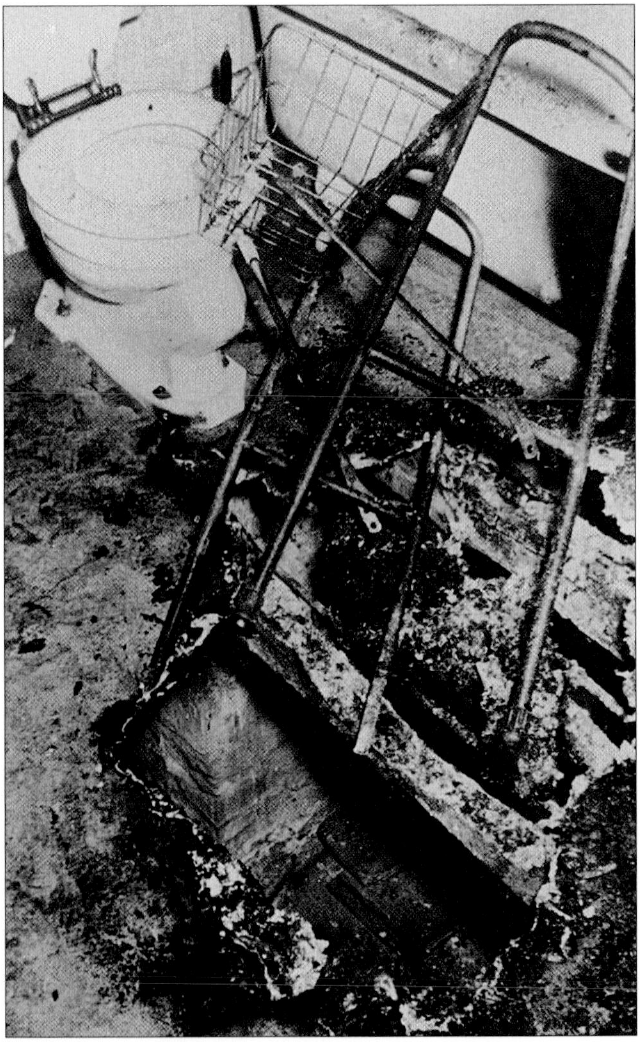

■ **This is a typical scene** *of spontaneous human combustion. The victim's body has been reduced to nothing more than a pile of ashes, while the intense but localized heat it produced has burnt a hole in the floor.*

Well-known cases of SHC include that of Mary Reeser of Florida, whose remains were discovered in July 1951 – only her shrunken skull, liver, and a foot inside a slipper remained, but papers just a few feet from the body were untouched. In November 1964, the remains of Helen Conway of Pennsylvania were found, completely reduced to ashes above the knees.

There are consistent features in most cases of SHC:

- *a* The ends of the legs and arms may be left intact while the rest of the body is completely reduced to ashes, including the bones
- *b* If the room where the body burned was not ventilated there may be heat, and greasy soot covering all surfaces
- *c* A particularly puzzling feature of SHC is that victims do not seem to cry out, seek help, or struggle, despite suffering what should be an agonizing death. It has been suggested that they fall into some sort of trance, although this is not always the case – when the body of an English tramp, named Bailey, was discovered in a stairwell on September 1967, his teeth were sunk into the mahogany banisters. This case is also one where witnesses saw the body still burning. As with other cases of SHC observed in action, there was an intense blue flame issuing from the abdomen

Trivia...

Humans aren't the only things that spontaneously combust. In November 1999, a Northumberland Yucca plant spontaneously burnt a hole in its pot.

Burning questions

These grisly details raise a host of questions. Completely incinerating a body, and in particular the bones, is very difficult. A crematorium burns bodies at 1371 °C (2500 °F) for hours but may still use crushers to pulverize the bones. Somehow the bodies of SHC victims reach temperatures higher than this without charring slippers and socks just centimetres away from the zone of incineration.

The most important question raised about spontaneous human combustion is how a body can be reduced to ashes and only affect materials in immediate or very close contact.

Other mysteries include the source of the fire – not all SHC victims are smokers – and the speed at which it burns – in some cases the victim was apparently burnt to ashes in just a few minutes.

INTERNET

www.castleofspirits.com/shc.html

This site has good coverage of the basics of SHC, a list of cases, and a sceptical review of the evidence.

Infernal combustion

The traditional theory of SHC was that it afflicted alcoholics and moral degenerates whose flesh was somehow infused with flammable substances. This probably had more to do with Victorian morality than scientific fact.

In modern times the most popular theory of SHC is the "reverse candle effect". According to this theory, the fat of the victim's body acts like the wax of a candle and the clothes act like a wick around the outside (hence "reverse").

Experiments have shown that this process can produce an intense localized heat that reduces the body to ashes without burning surrounding materials. Because the flames burn upwards and the body fat is concentrated in the torso, the legs and arms can escape damage.

According to the reverse candle theory SHC is not really spontaneous – apparent victims of SHC are actually killed by a conventionally caused fire operating in an unusual way.

Spontaneous outbursts

There are several flaws in the reverse candle theory. Not all SHC victims are smokers and in several cases no source for the fire could be found. Also the candle process takes a long time, contrary to reports of SHC taking just minutes. And what about the trance state of victims and the blue flame sometimes witnessed issuing from the victim's abdomen?

An early scientific theory proposed that SHC is caused by the combustion of intestinal gases such as phosphane and diphosphane, highly flammable substances that may spontaneously catch fire on exposure to oxygen.

In Charles Dickens's *19th-century novel* Bleak House, *the character Mr Krook dies of suspected SHC.*

However, only traces of these are found in the human gut and it would be rare for them to come into contact with oxygen inside the body. In summary, no theory yet proposed can explain all the strange features of SHC, which remains a gruesome mystery.

The body electric

FOR SOME PEOPLE electricity is not just something that turns on the lights. These people interact with ***electromagnetic (EM) energy*** *in some very strange ways.*

DEFINITION

Electricity and magnetism are two types of energy or force that are closely related. Each can produce and affect the other, and therefore they are sometimes collectively referred to as **electromagnetic (EM) energy.**

Since the 19th century there have been cases in which people have apparently become electrically charged or magnetized, causing them to have an EM effect on objects around them. These people are called electric or magnetic people.

Attraction and repulsion

One of the earliest electric people on record is Angélique Cottin. Cottin was a 14-year-old French girl whose strange condition manifested itself on 15 January 1846. For 10 weeks the hapless Angélique found that she repelled objects – even heavy furniture. She only had to touch an item to send it violently spinning or jumping away. Compasses went haywire near her, and she suffered convulsions.

Subsequent electric people have caused fuses to blow, turned electrical equipment on and off and given people static electricity shocks strong enough to knock them down. In 1976 12-year-old Vyvyan Jones from near Bristol in England became electric after breaking his arm. He was powerfully charged with static electricity and could even light up a light bulb simply by holding it in his hand.

The phenomena produced by electric people are similar to many poltergeist phenomena. Perhaps some poltergeists are actually EM effects caused by electric people.

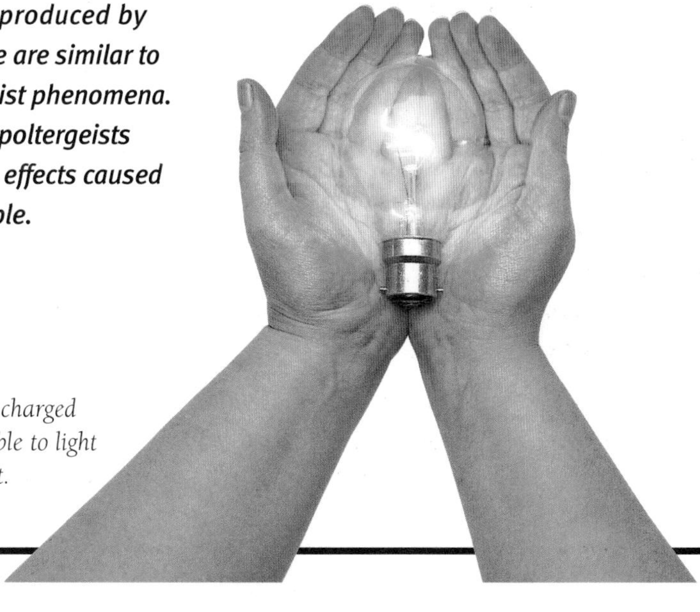

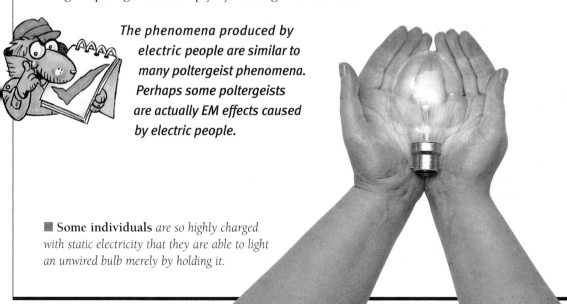

■ **Some individuals** *are so highly charged with static electricity that they are able to light an unwired bulb merely by holding it.*

Electric allergies

As well as becoming charged or magnetic, people can also become allergic to electricity and electromagnetic fields. Having an adverse health reaction to electromagnetic forces is known as electrosensitivity. According to some estimates up to 0.5 per cent of the population suffer from this condition.

Electrosensitive people cannot bear to be near sources of EM energy, including TVs, fluorescent lights, computers, mobile phones, or overhead power lines.

■ **Fluorescent lighting** *and the microchips found in modern electrical equipment in offices today can have a devastating effect on the health of electrosensitive people.*

Exposure to these causes headaches, nausea, and fatigue, and depresses the immune system. These people may even become highly charged themselves.

The causes of electrosensitivity are unclear. Sufferers blame mobile phones, phone masts, and overhead power lines, but no one knows how any of these could cause someone to become sensitive or charged. Whatever the cause, the effects can be devastating. Sufferers may even have to leave work, restrict travel, and take special steps to insulate their homes and themselves from electricity. Some sufferers have to use old-fashioned electrical equipment that does not contain microchips.

Explaining electric people

Bioelectricity is still poorly understood, and none of the conditions described here can be properly explained by scientists. Some of the reports of electric, and in particular magnetic, people are a bit suspect, but there is little doubt about the reality of electrosensitivity. Thousands of people around the world may suffer from this condition, so it is surprising that more research is not being done.

DEFINITION

Bioelectricity *is electrical energy in living things. Humans use bioelectricity to send messages between nerves; electric eels use it to shock their prey.*

Dowsing

DOWSING IS THE ABILITY to find hidden water or other substances using a forked twig, known as a divining or dowsing rod, or a similar tool. German miners used dowsing in the 15th century in their search for iron ore, and American soldiers used it in Vietnam to help find enemy booby traps.

The searchers

Known since ancient times, dowsing is still practised by thousands of people today, who use it to locate everything from hidden oil reserves or shipwrecks to lost pennies or pets. The basic process of dowsing involves the dowser walking around holding a branch of the dowsing rod in each hand with the point facing forwards horizontally.

The twitching or dipping of a dowsing rod indicates the location of hidden substances.

Traditionally dowsing was a means of locating underground water sources or veins of mineral ore, but it has been used to find many other substances, sometimes with spectacular success. One of the largest oil fields of all time was discovered in Oklahoma in 1944 by veteran oil prospector Ace Gutowski, using a form of dowsing.

INTERNET

www.dowsers.demon.co.uk

Home page of the British Society of Dowsers, with links to the American and Canadian Societies of Dowsers.

■ **How dowsing** *works is a mystery. But when environmental clues are removed, dowsers are less successful in their search for hidden substances.*

DIY DOWSING

Dowsing is something that anyone can try for free. All you have to do is follow these simple steps: make a rod, learn how to hold it, and get dowsing.

1 Make your rod

There are two main types of rod: forked twigs or pairs of L-shaped rods. The most traditional material is a forked hazel twig, but you can use any suitable wood. Look for a Y-shaped branch that's a bit thinner than your little finger (about 1 cm [½ in] across) below the divide and splits into two branches of equal length (about 30 cm [12 inches] each). Trim off any side branches.

To make an L-rod use pliers to snip a coat hanger in two places as shown. The short arm should be about 10 cm (4 in) long, and the long arm 40 cm (19 in). Straighten the bend to give a right angle. You'll need two of these.

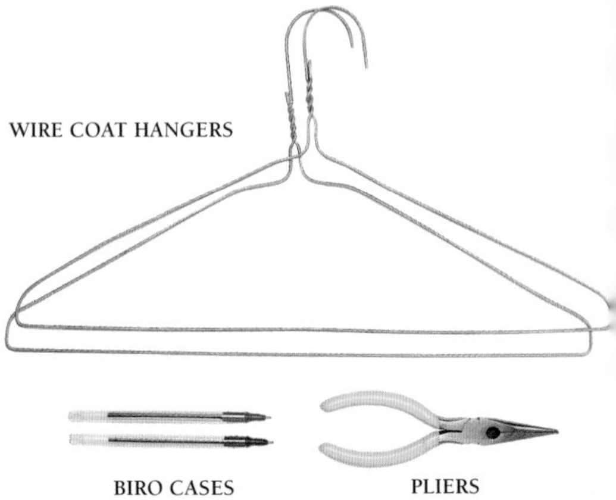

If you are making *your own L-rods, you will need two wire coat hangers, two biro cases, and a pair of pliers.*

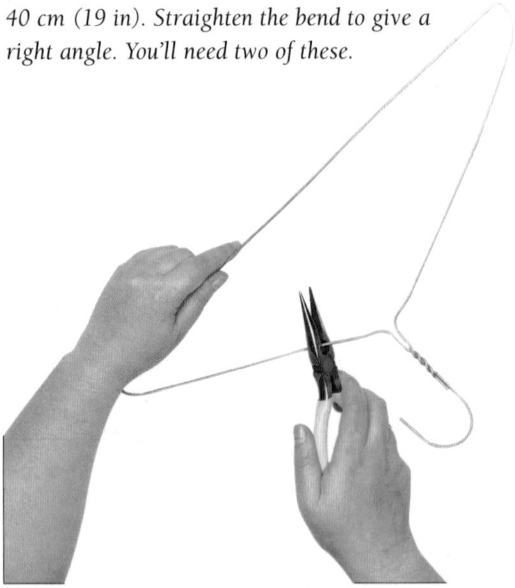

To make the short arm, *snip the hanger at least 10 cm (4 in) from the bend.*

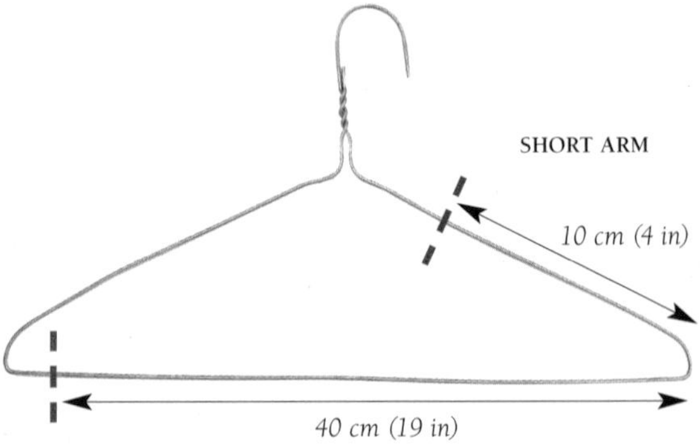

To make the long arm, *make another cut 40 cm (19 in) from the bend.*

2a The correct grip for a forked twig

With a forked twig, hold the ends of the branches in your hands with your palms up and your thumbs pushing the ends out so that the twig is in tension. The point should be horizontal.

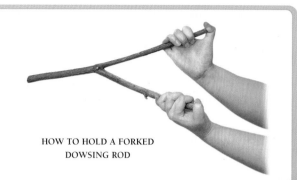

HOW TO HOLD A FORKED DOWSING ROD

2b Alternatively, the correct grip for L-rods

With L-rods, hold the short arms and point them forwards like pistols.

Hold the rods firmly but loosely enough so that they can swivel. With L-rods it can help to fit the short arms into cotton reels or empty biro cases.

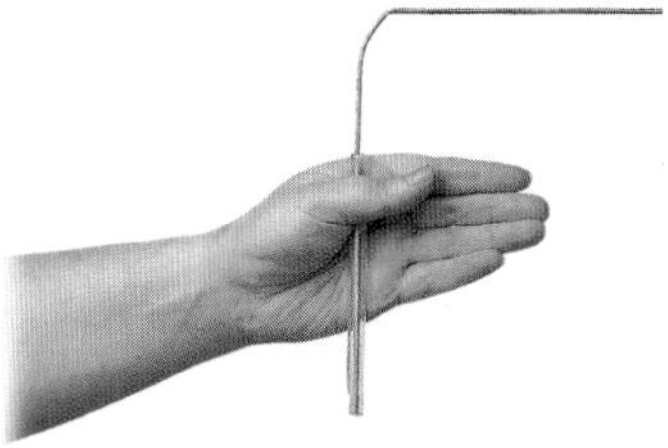

■ **Slot the short arm** *of the L-rod into a biro case, and hold it at right angles to your fingers directly in front of you.*

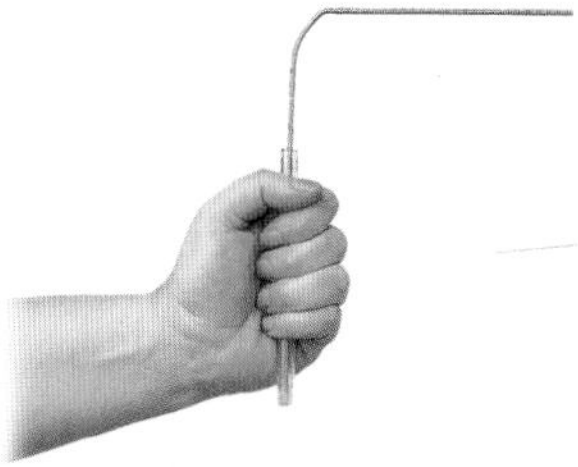

■ **Now wrap** *your fingers around the handle. The rod should swivel easily within the biro case.*

3 Get dowsing!

Now you need to practise walking around with your rod(s) and reading the response. Holding the rod(s) out in front of you, walk about (ideally outside). The twig may twitch or dip, while the L-rods should swing together or apart. Do not try too hard to make them move or to hold them still.

Try to get your rod to give you a consistent response to something you can see – for example a bucket of water. Walk up to the bucket and see if the rod responds. Keep practising until it does. Now you are ready to search for … anything.

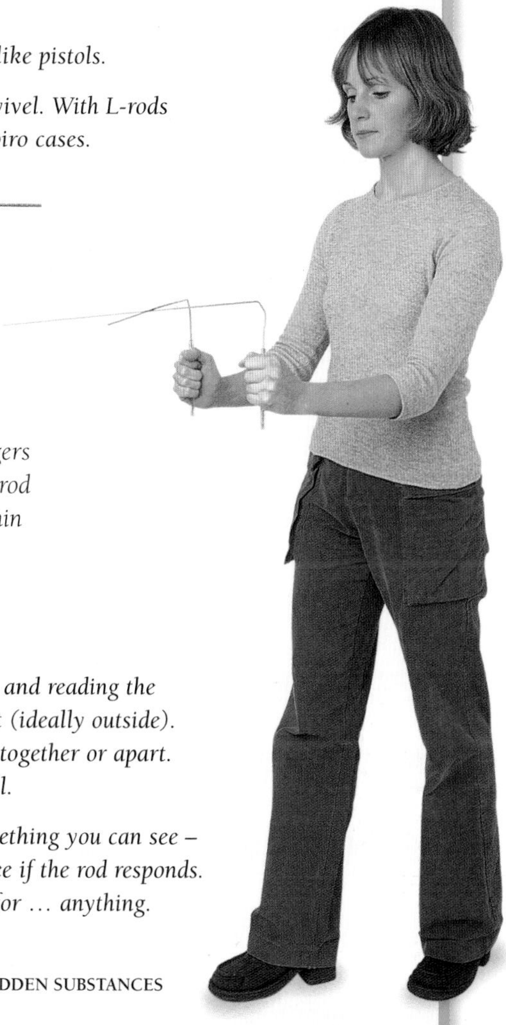

ASSUMING A DOWSING STANCE IN A SEARCH FOR HIDDEN SUBSTANCES

How does dowsing work?

Even avid dowsers don't claim to be able to explain exactly how dowsing works, but there are plenty of suggestions. The most widely believed explanation for dowsing is that the rods respond to magnetic fields.

Unfortunately this explanation is full of holes. Hazel rods and many other dowsing rod materials are not magnetic, so how can they respond to magnetic fields? While some dowsing targets are magnetic, the most traditional one, water, is not. Even large bodies of water have so little effect on magnetic fields that ultra-sensitive instruments cannot detect them. It's probably the dowser's hands that produce the movement. Dowsing rods are what scientists and engineers call "mechanical amplifiers".

Dowsing rods amplify invisible movements of the hand, such as twitches of the muscles, by translating them into visible movements.

In other words the dowser, not the target, is making the rod move, and this movement is subconscious. The real question is: why do the dowser's hands move?

I feel it in my fingers...

There are three main possible answers to the question of why the dowser's hands move:

1. Dowsers possess a natural but unknown ability to sense magnetic fields, similar to the ability that homing pigeons are thought to use. This special sense works only on the subconscious level
2. Dowsers possess some form of psychic ability or ESP, which allows them to sense hidden targets. Again, this ability is subconscious
3. Dowsers subconsciously read environmental clues, such as tiny changes in vegetation or humidity. The subconscious combines these with experience to make an educated guess, and this is translated into subconscious hand twitches

■ **Could it be** *that the intuitive ability of a dowser to sense a magnetic field is comparable to the homing instinct of a pigeon?*

The first explanation is unlikely, as it cannot explain how dowsers can find water and many other non-magnetic substances. Although there is a lot of anecdotal evidence that supports the theory that dowsers have some sort of ESP, the only way to tell for sure which of the other two answers is correct is through controlled experiments.

Experimental evidence strongly suggests that dowsers use subtle environmental clues to subconsciously make accurate guesses. When environmental clues are removed dowsers are no more successful at locating hidden targets than random guessing. Also, the best dowsers are those with the most experience. This doesn't mean that dowsers should not be employed. It simply suggests that there is nothing paranormal about dowsing.

Pendulums

Some people prefer to use a pendulum for dowsing, which is known as "radiesthesia". The direction in which the pendulum swings in a circular motion is then taken to mean either "yes" or "no". It probably works in the same way as a dowsing rod, by amplifying tiny hand movements. Pendulums are often used for map dowsing, where a pendulum is moved over a map, and its swing determines a target's location.

A simple summary

- ✓ In spontaneous human combustion (SHC), human bodies are reduced to ashes without damaging flammable materials just inches away.
- ✓ The most popular theory, the "reverse candle" theory, argues that SHC is not spontaneous.
- ✓ Electric and magnetic people become electrically charged or highly magnetic, can repell or attract objects, and affect electrical equipment or people.
- ✓ Electrosensitive people are allergic to electricity and have to take precautions to avoid sources of electromagnetic energy.
- ✓ Dowsers use dowsing rods or pendulums to find hidden targets such as underground water.
- ✓ The most likely explanation for dowsing is that dowsers subconsciously perceive environmental clues that help identify the target, causing hand twitching, which moves the rod.

Chapter 13

Earth Mysteries

EARTH MYSTERIES include a wide range of topics involving geography, landscape, and ancient monuments. Linking them together is the possibility that unknown forms of energy generated by the Earth's crust, atmosphere, or oceans might be causing paranormal phenomena.

In this chapter...

- ✓ Ley lines
- ✓ Pyramid power
- ✓ Mystery lights
- ✓ Crop circles
- ✓ The Twilight Zone?

DESPITE CENTURIES OF SPECULATION THE TRUE ORIGIN AND PURPOSE OF STONEHENGE REMAINS A MYSTERY

Ley lines

A LEY LINE IS A LINE ACROSS the landscape between points of historical or cultural significance (known as ley markers), such as prehistoric burial mounds, bridges, old churches, or crossroads. People who search for these lines on maps and in the countryside are known as ley hunters. Actually following a ley line, or ley, on the ground is known as "walking the ley".

The old straight track

The concept of the ley line was invented by an English countryside enthusiast, Alfred Watkins, in the 1920s. In his 1925 book, *The Old Straight Track*, he proposed that ancient landmarks and monuments were deliberately aligned in straight lines that criss-crossed the English countryside.

There is no doubt that lines can be drawn between many ancient monuments and landmarks, but whether these lines are significant or exist simply by coincidence is another question.

One of the best known leys can be found in the English county of Wiltshire. It runs for 29 km (18 miles), passing through Stonehenge, Salisbury Cathedral, and several ancient earthworks including a hill fort and a burial mound. Watkins's original theory was that ley lines were trade routes, marked out to help ancient merchants, pilgrims, and other travellers navigate the forests, valleys, and hills of prehistoric Britain.

■ **In Wiltshire, UK,** *a ley line runs through Old Sarum, Salisbury Cathedral, and Clearbury Ring.*

In the 1950s, some UFO writers believed that leys were flight routes for alien spaceships, a concept known as orthoteny. In the 1960s, ley lines became associated with New Age theories. Many people now believe that ley lines are channels of earth energy, and that ancient people deliberately built monuments along leys in order to channel or harness this power.

DEFINITION

Geomancy *means "earth magic". It refers to any system of belief or practice that uses geography or landscape (for example alignments of buildings or landmarks) to produce results such as predicting the future or bringing good luck.*

Leys around the world

Although the ley phenomenon is centred on Britain, mysterious lines in the landscape are found in many other countries. Alignments similar to leys were discovered in Germany in the 1920s, and the aborigines of Australia believe that a network of sacred paths, or "songlines", cover their country.

The Chinese have a system of ***geomancy*** known as feng shui, according to which *lung mei* ("dragon paths" of earth energy) circulate through the landscape – although these lines are curved, not straight. Lines in the landscape are also found in Bolivia, India, and Africa.

■ **Fault lines in the earth's surface,** *such as the San Andreas Fault in California, USA, are frequently the site of magnetic disturbances and ancient sacred sites. Some believe that mysterious phenomena are concentrated around natural fault lines, or even that ley lines cross or converge along the fault's path.*

The trouble with leys

There are several flaws in the ley line theory. Watkins's original theory of leys as trade routes makes little sense. Many leys are too short or do not run between likely trading posts, and critics point out that all other prehistoric trails known to us do not run in straight lines – they have to be bendy to avoid obstacles. The earth energy theory is also flawed. No one has suggested what type of energy might be involved, or how the energy is generated, and no one has been able to consistently detect earth energy with scientific instruments.

Careful statistical research has cast doubt on the existence of ley lines.

THE GIANT'S SKETCHBOOK

Among the most dramatic of landscape lines in the world are the immense line drawings (called geoglyphs) of the Nazca desert in Peru.

Between 400 BCE and 600 CE, the American Indians of Peru marked out a series of gigantic figures on the arid plains, including a spider, humming bird, monkey, whale, and many other animals, which have been described as a giant's sketchbook.

Some of these figures are more than 8 km (5 miles) long, and can only be properly made out from the air. How were they made, and who was meant to see them?

One theory was that the shapes were landing strips for ancient aliens. A more plausible theory is that the figures were meant to be seen by shamans on drug-induced "spirit flights", and that their construction was supervized from ancient hot air balloons.

In 1975 Jim Woodman and Julian Nott flew over the Nazca plain in a hot-air balloon constructed entirely from technology and materials available in 600 CE South America.

The enormous drawings did not meet public attention until 1939, as they were literally too big to be noticed other than from the sky.

■ **An aerial view** *of a Nazca geoglyph in the desert of Peru, which has been identified as a humming bird and a god.*

Pyramid power

THE ANCIENT MONUMENTS of Egypt have always inspired awe and a sense of mystery – as they were intended to do – and they were just as popular with tourists and sightseers in ancient times as they are now. Visiting the Pyramids and the Sphinx was a must for wealthy Romans.

The Pyramids

Since ancient times, monuments such as the Pyramids have inspired speculation about their occult significance and paranormal powers. The three great Pyramids of Ancient Egypt, the only survivors of the original Seven Wonders of the World, are found in Giza, just outside modern day Cairo. They were probably built between 2600 and 2500 BCE, as tombs for the pharaohs.

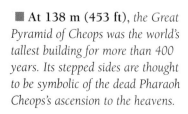

***The biggest of Egypt's three pyramids, the Great Pyramid of Cheops (aka Khufu), is also the most mysterious, inspiring a whole field of study known as* pyramidology.**

DEFINITION

Pyramidology *is the study of the secret wisdom that some people believe is encoded within the structure of the pyramids.*

Claims made for the Great Pyramid of Cheops include that its height divided by the area of its base gives the precise value of the mathematical constant *pi*, that its perimeter gives the length of the year, and that its height multiplied by 10^9 is equal to the distance between the Earth and the sun. Its dimensions have also been used to calculate the date of the end of the world and the Second Coming. In practice, claims made about the Great Pyramid have usually rested on fudged measurements, many of which are only approximate as the top of the structure is missing.

■ **At 138 m (453 ft),** *the Great Pyramid of Cheops was the world's tallest building for more than 400 years. Its stepped sides are thought to be symbolic of the dead Pharaoh Cheops's ascension to the heavens.*

Pyramids at the cutting edge

During the 1930s a French tourist discovered that the corpses of small animals inside the Great Pyramid seemed to be strangely well preserved. This observation has led to the discovery of "pyramid power" – the inexplicable effects that a pyramid, of any size, seems to produce on things placed inside it.

There is evidence that even small cardboard pyramids seem to be able to sharpen dull razor blades and preserve food. A Czech inventor, Karel Drbal, has been granted a patent for manufacturing styrofoam pyramids for use as razor sharpeners.

The Sphinx

The current academic consensus is that the Sphinx, the great statue of a human-headed lion that sits near the Pyramids of Giza, was probably built around 2,550 BCE, and that its face is that of the Pharaoh Khafre who ruled at this time. In 1991 Boston University geologist Robert Schoch sparked a raging controversy when he suggested that the Sphinx dated from at least 5,000 BCE, and was possibly much older.

Patterns of weathering on the Sphinx suggest that parts of it were eroded by water – but the area has been desert since before 3,000 BCE. Conventional Egyptologists (scholars who study ancient Egyptian civilization) have argued that Schoch is wrong about evidence of water erosion, but others have taken up his ideas enthusiastically, suggesting that the Sphinx dates back to 10,500 BCE, and was constructed by an advanced civilization – possibly by survivors of Atlantis.

■ **According to legend,** *the lost city of Atlantis lies beneath the Sphinx's paws at Giza. The real mystery of this awe-inspiring statue lies in the feat of its construction thousands of years ago.*

Mystery lights

MYSTERY LIGHTS are balls or blobs of light that appear from the ground or in the sky, hover, move about, and eventually disappear, with no apparent source or cause. Technically, mystery lights are a form of unidentified flying object (UFO), but this term is usually used to imply an alien spacecraft and mystery lights are not necessarily thought to be UFOs. Types of mystery light include ball lightning, earth lights, earthquake lights, and will o' the wisps.

Balls of fire!

Anecdotal reports of ball lightning have been made for centuries, but, as with meteorites and gorillas, mainstream science had denied their existence. Only when a leading scientist in the field, RC Jennison, was confronted with a glowing ball of light during a plane trip did the scientific community take notice. Ball lightning usually takes the form of a small (less than 30 cm [1 ft] wide) glowing ball of red, yellow, or orange fire that lasts for up to 30 seconds, and sometimes longer.

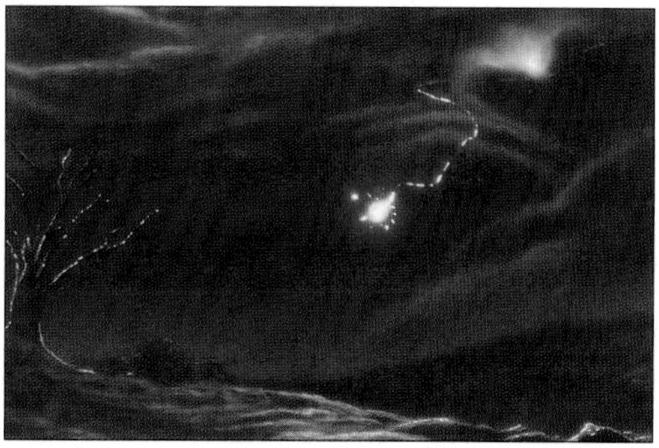

This is an artist's impression *of ball lightning. Sometimes, the ball explodes, damaging anything nearby, but usually it disappears without trace.*

Until recently it was thought that ball lightning was caused by spherical clouds of plasma (very hot, electrically charged gas), created by the massive energy of a lightning strike. This theory has recently been superseded.

The current leading theory about ball lightning is that lightning strikes soil to produce a cloud of highly reactive silicon gas, which then burns in mid-air, forming a glowing ball.

Will o' the wisp

Folklore from many cultures around the world tells of ghostly lights that lead unwary travellers to their doom in swamps and marshes. Known as will o' the wisps, they were previously thought to be either fairy creatures or the souls of the restless dead. They are also known as ghost lights, fairy lights, corpse candles, fox fires, or *ignis fatuus*. Will o' the wisps were believed to be burning pockets of marsh gas – a type of flammable gas produced by rotting vegetation – but are now thought to be a form of bioluminescence (light produced by chemical reactions in living organisms).

Earth lights

Earth lights are lights seen emanating from or disappearing into the ground, or are lights associated with other aspects of earth mysteries, such as crop circles or standing stones. The term was originally coined to distinguish between lights thought to be alien spacecraft and those thought to have an earthly source. Typically, an earth light is a ball of light seen at night, that appears to rise out of the ground, hover, and then disappear.

Some areas seem to be earth light hotspots – Marfa in the Big Bend area of south-west Texas, Hessdalen in Norway, and the Kimberley region of Western Australia (where local aborigines call them *min-min* lights). What are these lights and where do they come from?

The Northern and Southern Lights *are natural phenomena, occurring around Earth's poles as charged particles from the sun enter the Earth's magnetic field.*

Stress and tension

Many reports of earth lights – possibly the majority – probably result from misidentification of things like car headlights or people with torches, or even ball lightning or will o' the wisps. But there is a core of inexplicable reports. The leading earth lights' theory is Michael Persinger's "tectonic strain theory".

INTERNET

www.mysterylights.com

This site provides a good overview of the subject of mystery lights.

According to the tectonic strain theory, earth lights are caused by massive stresses and strains within the Earth's crust, which generate electrical energy that is discharged into the atmosphere, creating balls of plasma that give off light.

Mainstream science already accepts some parts of this theory. Rock subjected to high pressure, as in an earthquake, generates electricity that can be discharged as light. It is widely accepted that flashes of light, known as earthquake lights, sometimes accompany earthquakes. According to one radical theory, earth lights explain many UFO sightings, as well as other types of paranormal and supernatural experience.

Crop circles

A CROP CIRCLE IS A PATTERN IN A FIELD, formed by flattened plants. The stalks of the plants are mostly unbroken, and usually lie down in a uniform fashion, spiralling outward from the centre. When crop circles first started appearing in the 1970s, they took the form of simple circles, but since then patterns of increasing complexity have appeared.

Crop circle patterns now include rings, symbols, lattices of straight and curved lines, and even complex mathematically generated fractal shapes.

People who study crop circles are called cropwatchers or cereologists.

This incredibly intricate crop circle *appeared overnight in August 2001, on top of Milk Hill in Wiltshire, UK. It comprises more than 400 individual circles and measures 457 m (1500 ft) in diameter.*

The history of a mystery

The first modern crop circles appeared in Queensland, Australia, in 1966. They were small rough circles of flattened plants that local UFO investigators nicknamed "nests". In 1975 the first crop circles started to appear in fields in southern England, but very few people knew about them until 1980, when the media picked up on the strange phenomenon. There have been reports of strange phenomena associated with crop circles, including earth lights, tingling sensations and shocks big enough to knock people over, healing powers, UFO and ghost sightings, and strong effects on dowsing rods.

This "Flying Saucer Nest" *was one of the world's first crop circles. It was discovered in Australia by a local banana farmer, who claimed he witnessed a spinning saucer-shaped craft rising from the location of the circle and disappearing into the sky.*

A good crop of theories

The first theory was that UFOs were responsible – either the circles were the marks made by a spacecraft touching down, or they were intended as a message.

Meteorologist Dr Terence Meaden suggested that crop circles were made by small whirlwinds, or dust devils, formed by the wind eddying around the sides of hills.

As the formations of crop circles became more complex, Meaden elaborated his theory. Perhaps the small whirlwinds generated their own electric charge, becoming "plasma vortices" (tiny tornadoes of hot, electrically charged gas). Meaden claimed that such vortices could leave complex patterns of spirals and rings.

Meaden's theory received extensive media coverage in 1991 when a couple claimed to have been in the middle of a circle as it was created. They heard a high-pitched whine, and were pressed to the ground by a powerful wind as their hair stood on end – exactly as Meaden's theory predicted.

By now, though, patterns involving complex symbols were appearing. Clearly some sort of intelligence was behind the crop circles.

Trivia...

A 1678 pamphlet tells of the appearance of a strange circle in a field of oats, in the county of Hertfordshire, UK. Its construction was attributed to a "Mowing Devil" who came down from the sky in a chariot of fire to destroy the farmer's crops.

Circle makers come clean

In 1991 a pair of artists and UFO enthusiasts called Doug and Dave revealed that they had created all the initial circles in the UK as a joke.

Inspired by the Queensland saucer nests of the 1960s, Doug and Dave used their feet, and later a plank of wood with a rope attachment, known as a "stalk-stomper", to make the circles.

It soon became apparent that there were other circle-making groups, with names like the Bill Bailey Gang, Merlin and Co, and Spiderman and Catwoman. Their motives were mischievous and artistic. Between them the circle makers claimed responsibility for nearly every single circle in the UK. In November 2000, English computer technician Matthew Williams became the first circle maker to be fined for damage to crops. There is little likelihood that crop circles are the result of paranormal phenomena.

■ **Doug Bower and Dave Chorley** *were two British artists who, in 1991, claimed responsibility for the first crop circles to appear in the UK. There is now even a guide available on how to make these circles.*

Although it now seems likely that almost all crop circles are man-made, several mysteries still remain. Who or what created the original saucer nests? Why do man-made circles seem to produce paranormal phenomena?

The Twilight Zone?

THE BERMUDA TRIANGLE is an area of the Atlantic Ocean in which a large number of ships and aeroplanes have supposedly vanished under mysterious circumstances. According to some reports, since 1945 more than a hundred vessels have been lost in a triangular region of ocean situated between Bermuda, the tip of Florida, and Puerto Rico.

The disappearance of Flight 19

Perhaps the most famous victims of the Bermuda Triangle were the members of US Navy Flight 19, who vanished in their five Grumman Avenger torpedo bombers on 5 December, 1945.

According to the legend, the flight somehow became lost in fine weather, an hour after setting off from Florida. The flight leader Lt Taylor is reported to have complained that his navigational instruments, including the compass, were "going crazy" and that "everything seems wrong … strange … even the ocean doesn't look as it should".

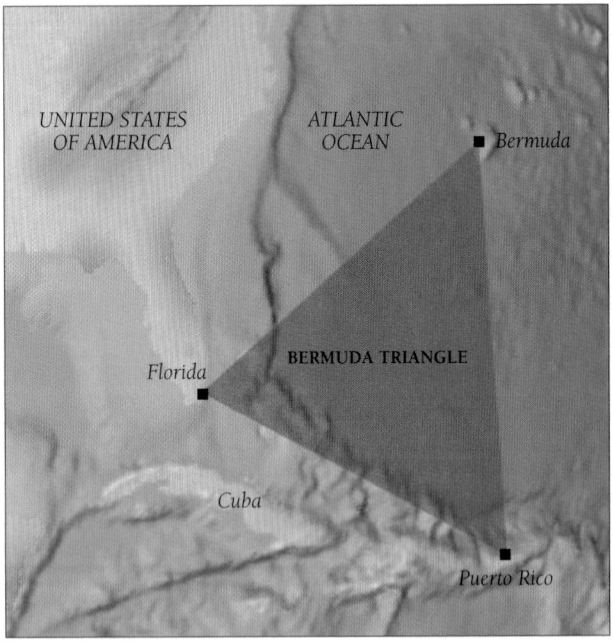

■ **The Bermuda Triangle** *is situated in the Gulf Stream, which is known for its propensity to strong currents and sudden local thunder storms.*

Radio contact was lost 45 minutes later. A search plane was sent after the distressed aircraft, but it was reported that this also vanished, supposedly without trace.

Theories proposed to explain the evil and mysterious effects of the Bermuda Triangle include interference by sea monsters, magnetic anomalies, giant crystals on the ocean floor, the release of gas bubbles from the sea bed, and even ancient technology from Atlantis.

Trivia...

The name "Bermuda Triangle" was invented by Vincent Gaddis in 1964, and popularized by a number of sensationalist books including Charles Berlitz's 1974 The Bermuda Triangle.

The mystery that never was

Careful research by American librarian Lawrence Kusche, detailed in his 1975 book, *The Bermuda Triangle Mystery, Solved!*, has revealed that there is nothing mysterious about the Bermuda Triangle, and offered alternative explanations. Most of the so-called mysterious disappearances either never happened or have rational explanations, and many cases said to be victims of the Triangle happened thousands of miles away. Most of the disturbing details about Flight 19, for instance, were simply invented. The radio conversation about things looking strange never happened and the weather was poor. Taylor's compasses were malfunctioning and he simply led his flight in the wrong direction with tragic consequences. The search plane did not disappear without trace – it was seen crashing into the ocean on fire. In my opinion there is little truth in the evidence of the mystery of the Bermuda Triangle.

Lloyds of London, the shipping insurers, say that there is nothing unusual about the number of ships lost in the Bermuda Triangle area, one of the world's busiest shipping areas.

A simple summary

✓ Ley lines are alignments of ancient landmarks. They were originally conceived as prehistoric trade routes, but are now popularly believed to be lines of earth energy.

✓ Statistics show that most ley line alignments are a matter of chance.

✓ Pyramidologists believe that ancient wisdom is encoded within the dimensions of the Great Pyramid of Cheops.

✓ Pyramid power may be able to sharpen dull razor blades placed in a pyramid.

✓ Mystery lights including ball lightning and earth lights may be created by electricity generated by storms or rock movements.

✓ All but the simplest crop circles are probably man made.

✓ The Bermuda Triangle is a myth that arose from faulty reporting.

Chapter 14

Mad World

THIS CHAPTER draws together a disparate variety of strange phenomena from the natural world, such as falls of animals from the sky, the appearance of out-of-place creatures or objects, and sightings of wild animals in inappropriate locations. Although very few of these natural anomalies can be properly explained, there is little doubt about their existence, and even evidence to support some of it.

In this chapter...

- ✓ Strange falls
- ✓ Cataclysm!
- ✓ Animal magic
- ✓ Out of place

Strange falls

FALLS OR RAINS OF STRANGE OBJECTS have been reported since ancient times, and were a favourite of Charles Fort. Reported falls from the sky range from excrement to rodents, but the most common rains are frogs and fish.

Dating from 1555, *this picture from historian Olaus Magnus's* Historia de Genibus Septentrionalibus *depicts a fall of fish. Such astonishing rains have been reported from the 1st to the 21st centuries.*

A hard rain's gonna fall

A frog or fish fall can involve anything from a few to a few thousand animals – normally small or juvenile forms. Sometimes the creatures are actually seen falling from the sky, but more often they are found scattered on rooftops, in gutters, and on the ground. Normally, but not always, the falls are associated with showers or storms.

Usually only one species of creature is found, and often they are all of the same size and stage of development. There are many reports of fish or frogs falling on only one small patch of land with peculiar precision and, strangest of all, the creatures are almost always unharmed by their fall.

Particularly odd characteristics of strange falls include their restricted range, selective content, and lack of damage caused to the animals that fall.

Spouting nonsense

The most popular theory to account for falls of fish, frogs, and other objects blames waterspouts, formed when a tornado touches down on the surface of water.

According to this theory, a waterspout picks up fish from the sea, or sucks up fish or frogs out of ponds or lakes, and then moves over land. When the spout collapses, a rain of water and creatures falls on land.

This theory cannot explain why strange falls are so selective – if a waterspout has sucked up the contents of a pond, why don't weeds and mud fall alongside frogs? It also cannot explain why the creatures are unharmed after their fall or how species not found anywhere near the area come to fall from the sky. There are few reports to support this theory.

From the ground up

Another common theory is that the fish or frogs only appear to have fallen from the sky, and have in fact come from the ground. According to this theory, a sudden shower of rain either drives hibernating creatures out of their holes or activates dormant eggs in the soil, which hatch out in the wet ground and grow remarkably quickly.

The result is hundreds or thousands of small creatures flapping about in puddles on the ground. The most obvious objection to this theory is that it cannot explain the dozens of cases where creatures have actually been seen falling from the sky.

■ **There could be** *a scientific explanation for the sudden appearance of hundreds of frogs during a downpour: migration, mating, and development of tadpoles after a lengthy dry spell are all natural possibilities.*

Trivia...

In Ecuador, in 1691, German explorer Alexander von Humboldt witnessed a shower of cooked fish, apparently blasted out of the hot vent of a volcano.

Out of thin air

Charles Fort argued that neither the waterspout nor hatching theory fitted the facts of the reports he'd collected from all over the world. He also dismissed the theory that creatures were dropped or regurgitated by birds flying overhead, as this would only explain falls of one or a few creatures.

Charles Fort suggested that strange falls were caused by a phenomenon that he called teleportation – instantaneous transportation from one place to another without covering the intervening space.

The most familiar example of teleportation is probably the "Beam me up" transporter device in *Star Trek*. According to Charles Fort, Mother Nature used teleportation to redistribute animals and other objects around the planet.

Trivia...

The terminal velocity (maximum speed reached when falling a long distance) of a small fish is roughly 50 kph (32 mph).

Fort's solution is too radical for most people to believe, but quantum physics now accepts the reality of teleportation at a very small scale, and strange falls are difficult to explain any other way.

Teleportation could explain many of the other phenomena in this chapter and in this book, including poltergeist activity, animals found where they don't belong, spiritualist apports, and frogs found inside stones. Exactly how or why it works isn't clear.

Lemmings, trolls, and angel hair

Although frogs and fish are the most common contents of a strange rain, dozens of other creatures and objects have been reported falling inexplicably from the sky. These include insects, mussels, rats, lemmings, worms, alligators, and even a small troll, which is supposed to have fallen on the Swedish town of Norrkoping in 1708. In the Arctic Circle, many peoples believe that lemmings originate in the stars and fall to Earth. Inuit tribes call them "mice from the sky". Another extraordinary substance reported to have fallen in a rain on numerous occasions is something referred to as angel hair.

Angel hair is a mysterious thread-like substance that falls from the sky and dissolves when handled. It was associated with UFO sightings in the 1950s, but since it was identified as threads of spider web, reports of it have become rare.

Even alligators *are reported to have fallen from the sky in mysterious rains.*

Cataclysm!

SURPRISINGLY, ALMOST NO ONE has ever been hurt by falling frogs, fish, or lemmings, but there are much more dangerous things up there in space. On three separate occasions in the past century, the Earth suffered cataclysmic collisions with random objects from outer space.

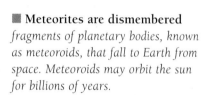

Meteorites are dismembered *fragments of planetary bodies, known as meteoroids, that fall to Earth from space. Meteoroids may orbit the sun for billions of years.*

Watch the skies

It is assumed that it was a massive meteor impact that helped destroy the dinosaurs 65 million years ago, and the possibility of another such strike is widely believed to be the biggest threat to human civilization today.

In 1930 and again in 1935, exploding meteors are believed to have devastated vast areas of South American rainforest. If either of these events had taken place over a populated area, millions of people would have died. The best known and most mysterious cataclysmic explosion also happened in a remote area – Tunguska, in deepest Siberia.

The Tunguska event

Just after midnight on 30 June 1908, a titanic explosion levelled over 2,150 sq km (830 square miles) of thick forest in a remote part of Siberia.

Witnesses reported an enormous fireball, known as the Tunguska Body, which detonated in a flash of intense light. Over 60 million trees were flattened like matchsticks and the resulting shockwave circled the globe twice.

NASA estimates that there are around 1,000 space objects big enough to cause planet-wide damage with trajectories that could collide with Earth's. About 50 Tunguska-sized asteroids pass between the Earth and the Moon every day.

INTERNET

www.tmeg.com/artifacts/tunguska/tunguska.htm

Visit this site for detailed exploration of every aspect of the Tunguska mystery.

■ **On 30 June 1908,** *a huge fireball, witnessed low in the sky over Tunguska forest in Siberia, flattened more than 3,000 sq km (1,158 sq miles) of trees. The catastrophic event is believed to have been caused by an exploding asteroid measuring over 50 metres (164 ft) in diameter.*

An asteroid is a celestial body, such as the remains of a comet, that orbits the sun. If it enters the Earth's atmosphere, it becomes a meteor, and when it falls to earth it is known as a meteorite.

It is now estimated that the Tunguska Body (TB) exploded with the force of a 10–20 megaton nuclear bomb, a thousand times more powerful than the Hiroshima bomb. Scientific expeditions to the area found no evidence of an impact crater, indicating that the TB had exploded in mid-air. Today the most widely accepted theory is that the TB was an asteroid (a large meteor) that vaporized explosively in the air before it impacted, but the Tunguska event has several mysterious features.

Big bangs

According to witnesses the TB was luminous and changed direction shortly before it exploded, and the blast itself bore all the hallmarks of a nuclear event. A bright flash of light, lack of meteor fragments in the blast area, and readings indicating a magnetic storm similar to that caused by a nuclear bomb were all reported. There are theories that the TB incident was actually an exploding alien spacecraft.

According to this theory the nuclear-powered spaceship's engine blew up after a fight with another spacecraft. Other candidates for the TB's identity include comet fragment, cloud of cosmic dust, exploding gas pocket, chunk of antimatter, or tiny black hole.

Animal magic

FORTEANS HAVE COLLECTED thousands of reports of strange phenomena involving animals or animal behaviour. Normally scientists are at a loss to explain what's going on, or why the animals in question are behaving in a way so far removed from their natural instincts.

Toad in the hole

One classic fortean phenomena is the frog found in a stone. During the 19th century reports regularly surfaced of rocks being broken open to reveal whole and often living frogs or toads.

Rocks containing frogs or toads usually show no signs of having been tampered with or stuck together – to all intents and appearances they were formed tens or hundreds of millions of years ago. How could a rock have formed around a frog, and how could the frog still be alive? But even stranger objects have been found inside stones.

Bizarre rock discoveries have included anomalous fossils – apparently human and sometimes modern artefacts, for example, embedded in rocks that are millions of years old.

In 1961, a spark-plug was found in a 500,000-year-old rock in California. Both frog and fossil phenomena challenge the normal scientific view of rock formation, and are usually dismissed as hoaxes.

■ **Reportedly discovered** *in a pile of flints in Sussex, UK, this toad in a stone was donated to a local museum by a known hoaxer.*

Trivia...

An orange bought in Cormierville, New Brunswick in Canada, on 10 September 1997, was opened to reveal a healthy orange frog living inside. It was later identified as a Pacific tree frog.

The birds

SCENE FROM ALFRED HITCHCOCK'S *THE BIRDS*

In Alfred Hitchcock's 1963 classic, *The Birds*, massed ranks of feathered fiends menace a small coastal community. Unknown to many, the film is based on real life incidents. For instance, in March 1997 the Romanian town of Turda was terrorized by hundreds of jackdaws attacking anyone who left their house.

Equally inexplicable is the phenomenon of bird parliaments, known from folklore since medieval times. Many witnesses, ancient and modern, tell of seeing a single bird surrounded by a ring of others (normally rooks or crows), which, after a period of squawking, fall on it and tear it to pieces. Other animals observed holding "parliaments" or animal courts include monkeys, turkeys, sparrows, mice, and storks.

The rat King

Apart from being a fairytale character, the rat King also appears to be a genuine animal phenomenon. A rat King is formed of a group of rats joined by their tails, which are knotted together.

They were reported from at least the 16th century, and one was found in the Netherlands as recently as 1963. A King may be made up of as many as 28 rats but usually seven or eight individual rats are involved.

According to reports the rat King "ruled" colonies of rats, and was tended by servant rats that brought food and water. Only black rats form Kings, and the phenomenon is found almost exclusively in continental Europe.

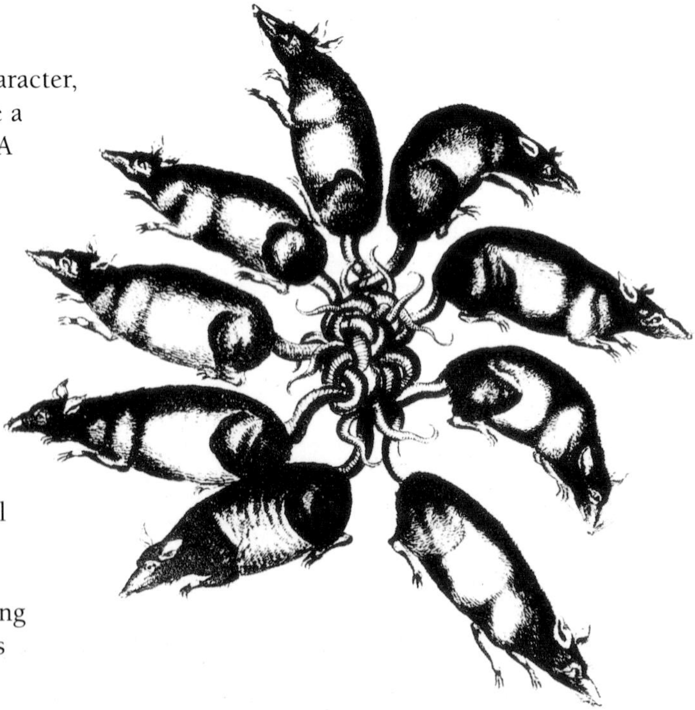

■ **Rat Kings were found** *to consist exclusively of black rats, inextricably tangled together by their tails. Reports are on the decline with the demise of the black rat population.*

Out of place

ANIMALS THAT ARE FOUND where they don't belong are called out-of-place animals, or OOPs. Probably the most common out-of-place animal is the Alien Big Cat, otherwise known as the ABC. ABCs are said to be alien because they are not native to the location where they are sighted. They usually have nothing to do with UFOs.

ABC sightings

The classic ABC report describes a black puma or panther-like animal far too large to be a domestic cat – normally about the size of a Labrador dog.

ABCs have been sighted in Europe, Australia, and the US, and some people claim to have been attacked by them. Farmers often blame dead livestock on ABCs, but official inquiries usually point the finger at dogs.

Despite numerous sightings and intensive searches, few Alien Big Cats are ever caught.

The true identity *of many out-of-place creatures remains a mystery. The animal shown here was captured on camera on Bodmin Moor in Cornwall, UK. "The Beast of Bodmin" is thought to be a big cat.*

Wandering wallabies

Kangaroos and wallabies are also favourite subjects of OOP sightings. A giant killer kangaroo terrorized Tennessee in 1934, and more recently, in May 1997, the Swedish province of Varmland experienced a flood of sightings. A frost-bitten kangaroo was captured in Belgium in the same year.

Giant killer, *or zoo escapee? An OOP's origin is rarely revealed.*

Other creatures found a long way from home include a coyote running loose in New York's Central Park in 1997, Tasmanian Devils in southern England, and cobras in Wales. As with ABCs, many of these reports are never cleared up – the animal is never caught and the stories simply dry up, or if it is caught its origin is never discovered.

Masquerading moggies

Sightings of and encounters with OOP animals are usually dismissed as misidentifications. This is probably true in many cases, as people are often much worse than they think at judging distances and relative sizes. Also, wild cats or hybrids between wild and domestic cats can be much larger than people expect.

Is it possible that the Beast of Gevaudan, *which is reported to have terrorized the French countryside in the 1760s, was actually just a feral cat? Locals at the time described a ferocious orange creature with a black stripe down its back and pointed ears, but there was no evidence to support this.*

When an out-of-place animal is actually caught or found dead, it is usually explained away as an escapee from a zoo, private collection (of which there are a surprising number), or circus. However, in many cases careful checking with local zoos, circuses, and collections reveals that no animal is missing.

Many reports of OOPs are genuine mysteries – where do the animals come from, where do they disappear to, and why are they so hard to find?

Do your eyes *deceive you? Mistaken identity can turn an amenable moggie into a massive marauder.*

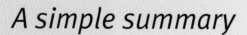

A simple summary

- ✓ There are many natural mysteries that although inexplicable are almost certainly genuine.
- ✓ Rains of frogs, fish, and other creatures are usually blamed on waterspouts or awakening of hibernating creatures by rain, but these explanations do not fit all the facts.
- ✓ Charles Fort suggested that teleportation was responsible for many unexplained phenomena, including strange falls.
- ✓ An asteroid falling from the sky is believed to have caused the Tunguska event, a huge explosion in Siberia in 1908.
- ✓ Bizarre animal phenomena include frogs found in stones, rat Kings, and killer birds.
- ✓ Big cats and other creatures are often reported in countries where they don't belong. Some reports are misidentifications and others are zoo escapees, but many are never accounted for.

Chapter 15

Mysterious Creatures

CRYPTOZOOLOGY – THE STUDY OF STRANGE ANIMALS – searches for evidence that monsters such as Bigfoot and the sea serpent really exist. Might other, more fantastic creatures, such as mermaids, fairies, or werewolves, have a basis in reality?

In this chapter...

- ✓ **Mythical monsters, actual animals**
- ✓ **Sea serpents and lake monsters**
- ✓ **Ape men**
- ✓ **Fairies**
- ✓ **Vampires and werewolves**
- ✓ **The goatsucker**

Mythical monsters, actual animals

CRYPTOZOOLOGISTS GENERALLY study creatures that might exist, avoiding ones that seem to be obviously mythical or fantastic such as dragons or mermaids. Some mythical monsters, however, may have their roots in reality.

Mermaids and unicorns

Mermaids are human above the waist and fishy below (male versions are called mermen or tritons). It may seem obvious that mermaids are creatures of make believe, but sightings have been reported as recently as 1957, and over the centuries hundreds of people claim to have seen and even captured one.

Mermaids were probably the result of a mixture of ancient folk belief in beautiful female water spirits and sailors' reports of manatees or dugongs. Also known as sea cows, these gentle marine mammals can, to someone with an active imagination, look a bit like women. They have swollen breasts (a common feature of mermaid reports) and flippers, in which they sometimes cradle their young in a human fashion.

■ **In this 19th-century illustration** *a manatee and a mermaid are juxtaposed. Mariners' stories of beautiful fish-tailed women emerging from the sea have often been attributed to manatee sightings.*

The legend of the unicorn may also have its roots in travellers' tales. Early reports of the rhinoceros may have given rise to the legend of the unicorn, a horse-like creature with a magic horn in the centre of its forehead.

Living fossils

Some mythical creatures may have been invented to explain early fossil finds. The fictional roc, for instance, was a giant bird of Arabian legend, most famous for its appearance in the tale of Sinbad the Sailor. It was supposedly so huge that it could carry away whole elephants.

The discovery of enormous fossil eggs from birds similar to the flightless New Zealand moa, which was up to 3 m (10 ft) high, may have helped start the legend of the roc.

The Cyclops was a huge one-eyed giant from Greek legend. In the story of Odysseus, the Cyclops lived in a cave on an island in the Mediterranean. It has recently been suggested that the legend of the Cyclops arose from the discovery of the fossil skulls of prehistoric elephants.

Prehistoric elephants – much smaller than surviving species – lived on several of the Mediterranean islands. Their skulls, discovered in caves, have a large central opening where the trunk attached, making them look uncannily like a Cyclops.

Dinosaur bones discovered in China were traditionally explained as the remains of dragons, and possibly gave rise to the whole idea of dragons.

■ **Fossilized dinosaur** *skeletons found in China may have inspired myths about Chinese dragons. These creatures are believed to control the elements and protect the gods, rather than breathe fire and wreak havoc like their European counterparts.*

Sea serpents and lake monsters

FOR MANY YEARS sea serpents were regarded as tall tales from sailors, but in 1848 a Royal Navy captain was brave enough to risk ridicule and report a sighting made by the entire crew of the HMS Daedalus.

His description of an 18 m (60 ft) long sea serpent triggered a flood of reports from other mariners, which have continued up to the present day. As recently as 1994 a creature known as Cadborosaurus was seen off the Canadian coast. Sea serpents are usually described as very long (up to 60 m [200 ft]), with undulating bodies and humps that stick up out of the water, and seaweed-like hair similar to a horse's mane.

This Great Norwegian *sea serpent was illustrated in Olaus Magnus's* Historia de Gentibus Septentrionalibus *in 1567.*

A closely related cryptozoological creature is the lake monster. The best known of these is Scotland's Loch Ness Monster, but other examples include Ogopogo, resident of Lake Okanagan in British Columbia, the monster of Lake Storsjo in Sweden, and the monster of Lake Van in Turkey. A typical lake monster report describes a V-shaped wake caused by a monster with a small horse-like head, long neck, and humped body.

Prehistoric survivors

The range of sea serpent and lake monster reports suggest that there could be several different types of strange creature beneath the world's waves. Cryptozoologists agree that most of them must be prehistoric survivors – ancient species that somehow escaped extinction. Creatures that have been suggested include plesiosaurs, pliosaurs (both types of giant aquatic dinosaur), zeuglodonts (prehistoric whales), giant otters, and long-necked seals.

Trivia...

Lake monsters have been reported from 250 of the world's lakes and rivers – 24 of them in Scotland alone.

Body of evidence

Unfortunately for the cryptozoologists, there isn't a shred of hard evidence to back up these claims. Occasionally a rotting corpse is discovered and heralded as a sea serpent carcass, but it usually turns out to be the remains of a shark.

The corpses of large sharks, such as the basking shark, rot in a way that makes them look like sea serpents, including even hair hanging from the "neck" (shreds of cartilage fibre).

Identity parade

If they're not plesiosaurs or another type of monster, then what are they? Suggestions include misidentified sturgeon (an extremely large fish), seals or otters, lumps of rotting vegetation from lake bottoms, giant conger eels, oarfish or dragonfish (rare types of deep sea fish that can be many metres long), or mini-waterspouts. Folklore probably plays a role, too. Scotland, for instance, has a long tradition of kelpies, a horse-like fairy creature that lives in lakes.

THE MYSTERIOUS LOCH NESS MONSTER

Loch Ness is a unique body of water with features that make it ideal for hiding a large monster. It is 38 km (24 miles) long and 1.6 km (1 mile) wide, and may have underwater connections to the sea. Use of sonar is difficult because of the great depth of the loch (up to 297 m [975 ft]), the canyons of its deeply ridged floor, and its overhanging sides, which create zones of sonar shadow. Using your eyes is equally difficult – the surface is frequently misty and the water is thick with particles of peat from the surrounding land, making underwater visibility close to nil. The region is frequently overcast and when the water is in shadow it is notoriously difficult to see below the surface or judge distances accurately. All in all, Loch Ness is one of the world's worst places to go monster hunting.

The famous "surgeon's photo" *of the Loch Ness Monster has been revealed as a hoax. It was actually a plastic model stuck onto a toy submarine.*

Ape men

APE MEN ARE LARGE, hairy, human-like creatures. The best known types of ape men are Bigfoot and the yeti, but dozens of other types have been reported from places as varied as New Zealand, Venezuela, Hawaii, and Africa.

The typical ape man report describes a 3 m (10 ft) high creature with a large head, heavy brows and long, ape-like arms, which is covered in brown or black fur and often smells repulsive.

Some types of ape men, such as the *orang pendek* ("little man") of Sumatra, are much smaller than humans – around 1 m (3½ ft) high.

Bigfoot

White trappers, hunters, and traders exploring America reported several encounters with "bushmen" in the 18th and 19th centuries, but the story of Bigfoot does not really start until 1958, when a huge humanoid footprint was discovered in Humboldt county, Northern California.

Although probably a hoax, the find prompted others to tell their stories and triggered a nationwide obsession with the creature swiftly christened Bigfoot. It is also known as *sasquatch* or *wendigo*, after creatures of North American Indian folklore.

Most Bigfoot reports come from the north-west states, but similar creatures have been seen all over the US. The Florida skunk ape gets its name from the terrible smell reported by witnesses.

Bigfoot and the yeti may be surviving examples of **Gigantopithecus,** ***a relative of early man thought to have died out 300,000 years ago.***

CAST OF BIGFOOT FOOTPRINT, CALIFORNIA, USA, 1967

The Abominable Snowman

Reports of ape men in the Himalayas date back at least as far as the 14th century, but the yeti only really hit the headlines in 1921 when a British explorer, Lieutenant-Colonel C.K. Howard-Bury, spotted some strange creatures in the Everest region.

When he discovered huge footprints at the same spot, his porters told him they belonged to a strange creature – the *metoh-kangmi*. This was later erroneously translated by a reporter as "Abominable Snowman". The word "yeti" derives from *yeh-the*, which loosely translates as "that-there thing".

Eric Shipton's 1951 photographs of a 33 cm (18 in) long footprint and the 1960 expedition of Sir Edmund Hillary (conqueror of Everest) stirred public interest to fever pitch, especially when Hillary brought back a skullcap purported to be made of yeti hide. It turned out to be goatskin. Definitive proof of the yeti's existence has yet to be discovered and there have been few recent sightings.

Early man

Some cryptozoologists believe that ape men are also prehistoric survivors, like the sea serpent or Loch Ness Monster, surviving undetected in wilderness areas.

Other ape men may be different types of living fossil. For instance, descriptions of "the alma of Mongolia" closely resemble Neanderthal man, *Homo neanderthalensis*, thought to have become extinct 30,000 years ago. The *orang pendek* of Sumatra could be a surviving form of *homo erectus*, the first ***hominid*** to leave Africa and settle across the globe.

DEFINITION

According to conventional scientific thinking, modern humans (Homo sapiens) *are the only surviving members of the* **hominid** *family (human-like ancestors), which included* homo erectus.

Missing links

Once again cryptozoologists are hampered by a lack of hard evidence for the existence of ape men. The best evidence for Bigfoot is probably the 1967 Patterson film supposedly showing a female specimen ambling across a clearing in Bluff Creek, California.

Patterson's 1967 footage *of Bigfoot in northern California, shows an ape-like figure, estimated to be 1.95 m (6 ft 5 in) tall, loping beside a creek. The footage has never been proved to be a hoax.*

Hoaxers and rabbits and bears

Sceptics claim that ape men sightings can be explained as hoaxes or misidentifications. Many Bigfoot reports and footprints have turned out to be fake. Sightings of bears rearing up on their hind legs probably account for many other sightings. One explanation for footprints in the snow is that they are created when prints left by small animals, for example rabbits, melt together in the sun to form larger marks.

On balance it seems unlikely that a population of ape men large enough to survive for tens of thousands of years could go almost undetected in the modern day.

Fairies

MOST CULTURES around the world have legends and folk tales about fairies or similar creatures. They are believed to have magical powers and to exist outside normal human time and sometimes in a different world. Types of fairy and related creatures include elves, trolls, dwarves, pixies, goblins, ogres, bogles, boggarts, brownies, hobgoblins, and pucks.

The Little People

In Celtic tradition it was dangerous to refer to fairies directly, so they were called the Little People or the Good Folk. Fairies could either be solitary or live in groups, in which case they were known as trooping fairies.

According to Irish legend, the fairies were originally known as the* daoine sidhe *(pronounced "theena shee") and were the first inhabitants of Ireland.

Later they were driven off the land and went to live in fairy mounds (natural hills or prehistoric earthworks). Other cultures have similar legends about fairies.

Away with the fairies

Fairy rings are circles of dark grass created by fungus growing out from a central point. In folklore it was believed that dancing fairies might carry you off to fairyland if you stepped into a fairy ring. When you returned years might have passed although it seemed like only minutes to you. Many scholars have drawn parallels between folklore like this and modern stories of alien abduction. Both involve abduction by small creatures, travel to other worlds, and lost time.

We were here first

Several scholars have suggested that fairy legends represent ancient memories of **aboriginal** races who were driven into wilderness areas by invading peoples.

If these original races were actually Neanderthals or *Homo erectus*, their appearance might have given rise to the stories of goblins, ogres, trolls, and dwarves. Other scholars dispute this theory, and argue that fairies probably developed from early belief in nature spirits – a form of religion known as animism.

DEFINITION

Aboriginal *means original inhabitants of an area – hence the Australian aborigines were the people who already lived in Australia when European settlers arrived.*

THE COTTINGLEY FAIRIES

In 1922 the famous author and noted spiritualist Sir Arthur Conan Doyle (creator of Sherlock Holmes) published photos taken by two young girls, Elsie Wright and Frances Griffiths, showing them playing with tiny fairies from the bottom of their garden. In 1983 one of the girls admitted to faking the photos and it now seems obvious that the tiny figures are crude paper cut-outs. At the time, however, the "Cottingley fairies" provoked intense public interest and were widely believed to be genuine.

■ **The two young girls** *who took the photos of the so-called Cottingley fairies later admitted to cutting out the fairy shapes and attaching them to the grass and flowers with long pins.*

Vampires and werewolves

VAMPIRES ARE UNDEAD HUMANS who feed off human blood and live by night. Werewolves are humans who transform into savage wolves or half-wolf creatures. Both of these monsters are reported all over the globe, although werewolves are were-leopards in Africa and were-jaguars in South America.

■ **Vampires have been** *the subject of literature, folklore, and more recently films, such as* Interview with the Vampire.

Living in fear

For people living in medieval Europe, vampires and werewolves were more than just horror stories or folk tales. They were real monsters to be feared.

A host of superstitions grew up about how to ward off vampires and werewolves. For instance, it was not unusual to see homes garlanded with garlic and the wolfsbane plant, while graveyards might be scattered with seeds, in the belief that vampires would feel compelled to spend all night picking up the seeds instead of biting people.

In medieval Europe, people were regularly tried and condemned for being werewolves.

Signs that indicate a person might be a werewolf include having a hairy body, eyebrows that meet in the middle, and index fingers that are longer than middle fingers. And as recently as 1924 a Transylvanian woman was buried with horseshoes nailed to her hands and feet, a wooden stake through her chest, and heavy stones on her coffin because it was believed that she was a vampire.

Children of the night

Many writers have assumed that vampires and werewolves have their roots in psychology. Fear of the night, the magical power attributed to blood, and the savage beast within are undoubtedly elements of the myth, but there are also a number of real phenomena that might have contributed.

Trivia...

In Greece, red hair and blue eyes were considered to be signs of the undead.

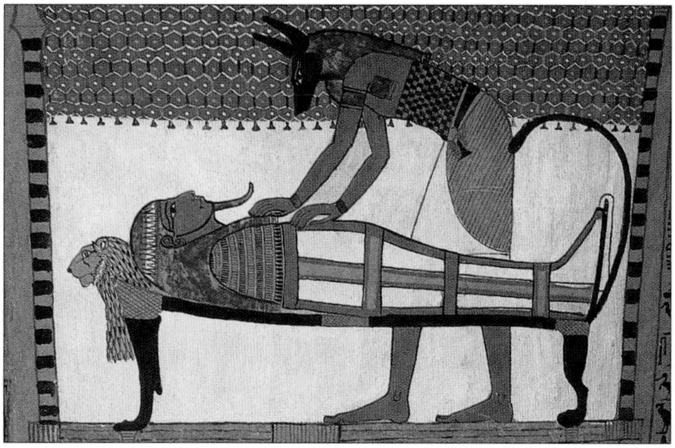

■ **The Egyptian god Anubis** *guided the souls of the dead into the next world. He had a jackal's head and dressed in wolf skins.*

In medieval times, for instance, no one knew about bacteria or viruses, so that the spread of disease was sometimes explained as the work of vampires. Poor medical knowledge meant that a number of diseases that produce death-like symptoms led to people being buried alive. When their coffins were later opened, they were found to have clawed at the lids and even bitten their own flesh in starved desperation. It's easy to see how stories of vampires arose.

Werewolf legends have been partly attributed to Viking berserkers – warriors dressed in bear skins – and ancient Egyptian priests of Anubis, the jackal-headed god, who wore wolf skins. The shamans of some North American Indian tribes also wear wolf skins for rituals.

Monstrous diseases

Some medical conditions might have contributed to belief in vampires and werewolves. Porphyria is a genetic disorder that can cause insanity and extreme sensitivity to sunlight. It has even been suggested that healthy blood might help alleviate the condition. Perhaps it contributed to legends of vampirism.

Lycanthrope is the Latin term for a werewolf, and lycanthropy is now used to describe a psychological disorder that leads people to believe that they are wolves. Some sufferers actually attack people. In earlier times their delusions might have been accepted as reality.

Another condition that might explain stories of werewolves is hypertrichosis, a genetic disorder that causes sufferers to grow hair all over their skin, including the face. During modern times, unfortunate sufferers have been exhibited as freaks.

■ **This family from Mandalay,** *Myanmar (formerly Burma), probably suffered from the genetic disorder hypertrichosis (excessive hair growth). Such individuals may have contributed to legends about werewolves.*

The goatsucker

A RECENT DEVELOPMENT in the world of cryptozoology is the emergence of the "chupacabras" *phenomenon. This vicious predator terrorizes livestock, and according to the dozens of people who claim to have seen it, has killed thousands of animals.*

INTERNET

www.princeton.edu/~accion/chupa.html

A chupacabras *folklore site, set up by Princeton University students.*

The *chupacabras* (Spanish for "goatsucker") is a horrible monster that has been plaguing Latin America since 1995. Described by some as a bat-winged kangaroo-like creature, the *chupacabras* drains the blood of goats, chicken, and other livestock.

The first reports of the *chupacabras* came from Puerto Rico in 1995, although this form of livestock mutilation dates back at least as far as medieval Europe.

The people's monster

After the initial report in 1995, *chupacabras* attacks spread alongside increasing media coverage. Not long after the Puerto Rican reports, similar stories showed up in Florida, Mexico, and other Hispanic areas. The authorities insist that all the attacks attributed to *chupacabras* are actually the work of dogs, cats, or other ordinary animals, and so far there is no hard evidence to support the existence of this fantastic beast.

■ **This artist's impression** *of the* chupacabras *is based on some eye-witness accounts. Mysteriously, other sightings liken the blood-sucking creature to a winged bat or kangaroo.*

Many reports of the *chupacabras* have paranormal elements – the creature dissolves into mist, or its attacks are linked to UFO sightings and government conspiracies.

Most cryptozoologists believe that the* chupacabras *is an* urban legend*– a modern expression of folklore traditions from Hispanic culture.

DEFINITION

*An **urban legend**, also known as a FOAF (friend-of-a-friend) tale, is a modern form of folklore.*

A simple summary

✓ Some mythical creatures may have been inspired by fossil finds, or grown out of reports of real animals. Some examples include dragons resulting from dinosaur fossils, mermaids from manatee sightings, unicorns from rhinoceros sightings, and Cyclops from pygmy elephant fossils.

✓ Sea serpents and lake monsters might be prehistoric survivors, but there is no hard evidence for their existence.

✓ Bigfoot, the yeti, and other ape men may also be prehistoric survivors – ancestors of modern humans thought to be extinct – but again there is little hard evidence for their existence.

✓ Legends of fairies may have arisen from folk memories of aboriginal races displaced by invading peoples, or from early beliefs in nature spirits.

✓ Vampires and werewolves may have their roots in real phenomena, including poorly understood diseases such as porphyria, lycanthropy, and hypertrichosis, or memories of Viking berserkers dressed in bear skins.

✓ The *chupacabras*, or goatsucker, is a recently reported monster that allegedly kills livestock in Hispanic communities. Most cryptozoologists believe that it is an urban legend.

PART FOUR

Aliens and UFOs

PART FOUR gives an insight into the mystery of aliens and UFOs – its history, popular theories, important cases, types of aliens, and much more.

Chapter 16

UFOs – the Basics

THE UFO ENIGMA is the biggest mystery in the world of the unexplained. More than 100,000 people have reported a UFO sighting over the last fifty years, and opinion polls consistently reveal that the majority of the population of the United States and other western countries believe that UFOs are alien spacecraft. However, despite the seeming willingness of much of the population to believe in aliens and UFOs, most of the "evidence" for their existence is anecdotal. What little physical evidence there is tends to be inconclusive, and as yet, there has been no definite indication that UFOs and aliens are anything other than a figment of our collective imaginations.

In this and the following chapters we'll look at how the mystery started, how it has developed, and what might be behind it. We'll examine some of the most famous UFO cases, look into reports of alien abduction, and delve into the conspiracy theories that cloud the UFO phenomenon – the truth is in here!

What are UFOs?

UFO STANDS FOR Unidentified Flying Object. In theory, simply classifying something as a UFO does not imply anything about its origin or purpose, but in practice, most people think of a spaceship or "flying saucer" when they hear the term UFO.

The theory that UFOs are spaceships piloted by aliens from another planet is called the "extraterrestrial hypothesis", or ETH. Supporters of the ETH are said to belong to the "nuts and bolts" school of ***ufology***.

DEFINITION

The study of UFOs is called **ufology**, *and the people who study UFOs call themselves ufologists.*

Birth of the flying saucers

The UFO enigma was born on 24 June, 1947. Although reports of what we would now call UFOs date back centuries, ufology did not really start until this fateful day.

Businessman and experienced private pilot Kenneth Arnold was flying his plane over the Cascade Mountains of Washington state. As he passed Mount Rainier, Arnold's eye was caught by a flash of light. Looking around for the source of the flash, he noticed "a chain of nine peculiar looking aircraft". The strange vehicles seemed to be moving at a fantastic speed, weaving in and out of the peaks. Observing them more closely he saw that they appeared to be bat-winged or crescent-shaped, and moved like "saucers skipping over water".

On landing Arnold reported his sighting to the military, and the press soon got hold of the story. An anonymous headline writer coined the phrase "flying saucers" and a phenomenon was born.

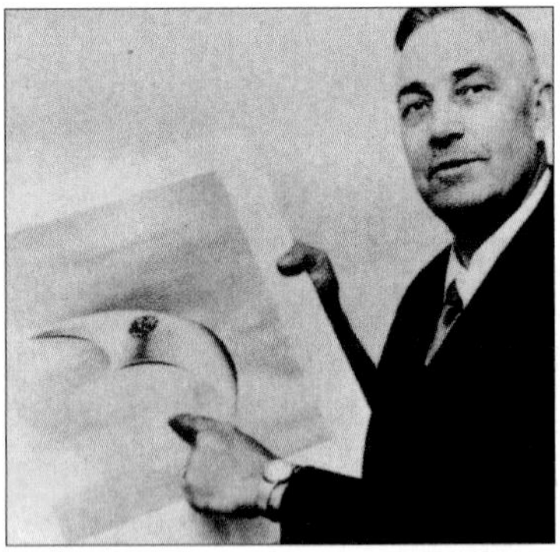

What did Kenneth Arnold *really see? Arnold stands above with an illustration of the "craft" he saw over Mt Rainier, and below is a flock of American White Pelicans in flight. Could he have been mistaken?*

It now seems likely that Arnold actually saw a flock of American White Pelicans, birds whose profile and flying style correspond exactly to his 1947 description.

Whatever the true identity of Arnold's "saucers", the widespread news coverage triggered a flood of similar reports from all over the country and around the world. Within 6 weeks of Arnold's experience, UFO sightings were being reported at the rate of 160 a day.

■ **Mt Rainier,** *site of Arnold's UFO experience, is seen here during the flush of the Northern Lights.*

Reality check

Ufology has been going for more than 50 years, but despite numerous claims of astounding discoveries and sensational evidence we are no nearer to proving that UFOs are alien spaceships or any other type of mysterious object.

The question remains – are UFOs a genuinely unknown phenomenon, or will they all turn out to be IFOs (identified flying objects)? All serious ufologists acknowledge one general truth about UFOs:

Nine out of ten UFO sightings can be explained – that is, nine out of ten UFOs become IFOs.

What interests ufologists are the 10 per cent of cases that cannot be explained. Sceptics argue that with enough detailed investigation almost all of these cases could be explained, and that the rest can be dismissed as hoaxes or delusions.

As with so many other paranormal phenomena, almost all the evidence for UFOs comes from eyewitnesses. Over the years it has been shown that even the most (theoretically) experienced, sober, reliable witnesses – people like fighter pilots, scientists, and policemen – can be very bad at observing, remembering, and reporting what they see.

Physical traces

Ufologists are most interested in the cases where a UFO leaves a physical trace of its presence, such as a radar return (a mark on a radar screen) or marks from a possible landing. There have been several such cases, but the physical evidence has always turned out to be ambiguous, inconclusive, or disappointing.

The most obvious type of physical trace is a photograph, film, or video, but after more than five decades during which thousands of photos and videos have been taken, there are only a handful of genuinely unexplained photographs.

On their own photographs and videos prove nothing, and in an age when digital manipulation of images is so easy, they are generally felt to be unreliable.

Alternative explanations

The investigations of the last 50 years have uncovered an amazing range of alternative explanations for UFO sightings. Remember, however, that nine out of ten sightings can be explained in one of the ways outlined below.

Is it a bird?... Yes

The majority of UFO reports turn out to be simple misidentifications, and there are dozens of objects or light sources that are routinely mistaken for UFOs. Here is a checklist of the most common:

- Celestial bodies (e.g., the planets, particularly Venus)
- Mirages (e.g., lights from vehicles over the horizon distorted by atmospheric conditions)
- Clouds
- Ground-based light sources (e.g., car headlights, spotlights, lighthouses)
- Conventional aircraft
- Camera artefacts (e.g., dirt on the lens, lens glare)
- Weather balloons
- Experimental aircraft/rocket launches
- Birds
- Lights reflected on windows

■ **It's easy to see** *how these lenticular (lens-shaped) clouds could be mistaken for UFOs. However, they are slow moving and obviously incapable of UFO-like bursts of speed.*

Liar liar

The explosive popularity of the UFO phenomenon brought with it plenty of incentive for hoaxers. Many of the early UFO photographs were simple but convincing fakes, made by hanging a hub cap or tossing a Frisbee in front of a camera.

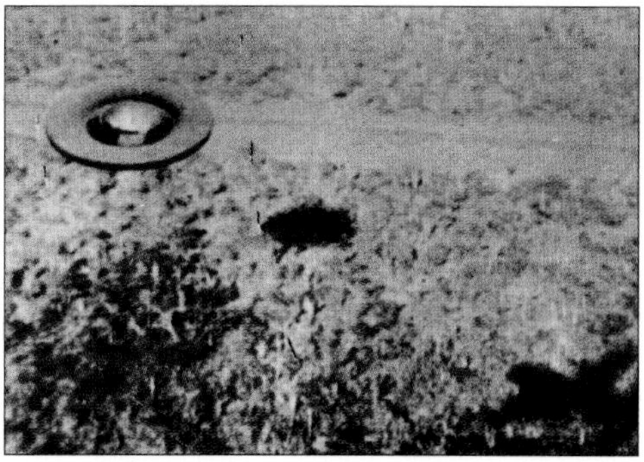

■ **This 1963 hoax** *photograph claimed to show a UFO flying over Venezuela. It was produced by an airline pilot, using a button as the "craft".*

The psychosocial hypothesis (PSH)

The PSH is the main alternative to the ETH. According to this hypothesis, UFO sightings have a psychological origin – for example, a hallucination or misidentification – and are then interpreted by the witness according to their social and cultural background.

Suppose for instance that someone sees a bright light of uncertain origin moving about in the night sky. A background of science-fiction movies and X-Files on television might lead them to interpret their sighting as a UFO. When they come to remember it later, this interpretation may lead them to add details, such as an intelligent pattern to the movement.

Supporters of the PSH draw parallels between historical stories of visions, demons, and encounters with fairies, with present day stories of UFOs and alien encounters.

In conclusion

Many scientists believe that there is life elsewhere in the universe, which means that the ETH is at least possible. But is the ETH a good explanation for UFO sightings, and is there any evidence to support it?

On balance the answer to these questions is probably no, but there are many strange aspects to the UFO mystery, and the ETH claims to be able to explain them.

In the final analysis, a theory is only worthwhile if it can be tested. "Nuts and bolts" ufologists insist that this is what they are trying to do – most other observers are sceptical.

The evidence that UFOs are alien spacecraft is very flimsy, but the extraterrestrial hypothesis should not be dismissed.

Over the next five chapters I'll take a look at the history of the UFO phenomenon, examine some of the "evidence" for the existence of UFOs and aliens, present some of the famous cases, and delve into the so-called conspiracies that are believed, in some circles, to cover up the existence of UFOs.

Chapter 17

The History of UFOlogy

THE HISTORICAL CONTEXT OF ARNOLD'S 1947 SIGHTINGS, together with the history of the UFO phenomenon before 1947 and its evolution since, are essential elements of the UFO mystery. By following this mystery from its earliest beginnings to the present day it is possible to notice patterns that may shed light on the true nature of UFOs.

In this chapter...

- ✓ Chariots of the Gods (Ancient times–700 CE)
- ✓ Fire in the sky (800–1900 CE)
- ✓ Invaders from Mars! (1900–1947)
- ✓ The Golden Age (1947–1969)
- ✓ War of the Worlds (1970–the present day)

ANCIENT ASTRONAUT? – A WANDJINA FROM AUSTRALIAN ABORIGINAL MYTH

Chariots of the Gods (Ancient times–700 CE)

MODERN UFOLOGY may have been born in 1947, with the famous Arnold sighting, but people have been seeing unidentified objects in the sky for thousands of years. Many of these sightings can be attributed to things like comets and meteors, but some of them sound a lot like modern UFO sightings. For instance, the Bible tells the story of Ezekiel's vision – "a great cloud, with brightness round about it, and fire flashing forth, and in the midst of the fire … gleaming bronze" (Ezekiel 1:4–7) – which sounds a lot like a UFO.

Ancient astronauts

In the 1960s and 70s the "ancient astronaut" movement gained popularity, led by the Swiss writer Erich von Däniken and his 1968 book *Chariots of the Gods.*

The "ancient astronaut" theory says that ancient peoples were visited by advanced spacemen who were responsible for the construction of the Pyramids and other wonders of civilization.

Evidence for this theory includes ancient Mayan drawings that appear to show men in rocket ships, and ancient rock paintings and carvings from Australia, Peru, and Italy that appear to show spacemen in helmets.

It has even been suggested that Jesus and other religious figures were spacemen descended to Earth. This theory explains the Star of Bethlehem as the flare from the jet engines of a landing spaceship.

A prehistoric rock carving *at Val Camonica, Italy, showing a figure known as "the astronaut".*

Modern disputes

Supporters of the extraterrestrial hypothesis (ETH) believe that ancient UFO sightings are proof that alien spaceships have been visiting the Earth for a lot longer than 50 years. However, the "ancient astronaut" theory is now largely discredited. Much of the so-called evidence has turned out to be fake or dubious.

For instance, von Däniken's reproductions of Mayan drawings, which seemed to clearly show a spaceship, were actually heavily edited versions of the originals, altered to promote his own interpretation. The rock paintings of "spacemen" are now believed to show humans in headdresses or masks.

Trivia...

The earliest recorded UFO sighting is usually said to be "the circle of fire that was coming in the sky", allegedly reported in an Egyptian papyrus from the reign of Thutmose III (c.1500 BCE).

Psychosocial hypothesis (PSH) ufologists believe that ancient reports of UFOs show that 20th century sightings are simply a modern expression of age-old superstitions and traditions.

Fire in the sky (800–1900 CE)

ONE STRANGE FEATURE of the UFO mystery is that UFO reports tend to involve vehicles or craft that are only a step ahead of current technology. In the 1940s, for instance, UFOs often took the form of rocket ships. In the 1990s reports of triangular black UFOs resembled advanced Stealth Bombers. This pattern also applied in medieval and Victorian times.

Fly the friendly skies

There are several reports from medieval sources of sky ships – vessels of similar construction to ordinary naval ships, but which floated in the clouds.

According to Dagobard, the 9th-century Bishop of Lyon, many people believed that there was a land in the clouds called Magonia, "from which ships, navigating on clouds, set sail". There were stories of captured "sky sailors" who had fallen out of their ships, and even of such "sailors" swimming down their anchor cables to the ground and being unable to breathe. These medieval stories have strong parallels with fairy folklore.

The PSH school of ufology, which believes that UFOs are not physically real, uses Magonia as a metaphor for the true source of UFOs – the realm of myth and folklore.

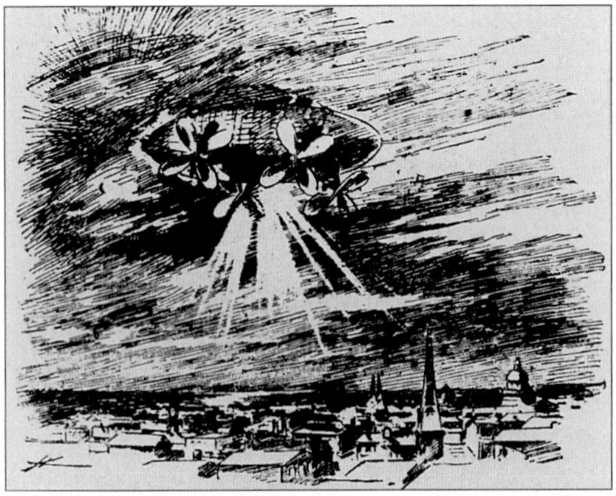

■ **This mystery airship** *with propeller-like appendages and bright lights was seen over Sacramento, California, during the 1896 flap.*

The great airship wave

By Victorian times the cutting edge of aerial technology was the airship (also known as a dirigible, blimp, or zeppelin), and in November 1896 America was struck by a wave of sightings of advanced airships.

The "great airship wave of 1896–97" featured reports from all over mid- and western America about gigantic cigar-shaped craft festooned with multi-coloured lights passing overhead.

The airships seemed to be of advanced design, larger and faster than any yet invented (there were none in America at the time). Sometimes their occupants were heard or seen, and were variously described as "Yankee inventors" or "Chinese dwarves". There was even a report from Aurora, Texas, of a crashed airship, whose Martian occupant had been buried in a local grave – a report that bears startling similarities to the notorious Roswell incident of 1947 (see Chapter 18).

The airship ***wave*** or ***flap*** died out by the end of 1897 and was forgotten about remarkably quickly. Diligent research has revealed that many of the reports were fakes or hoaxes, dreamed up by newspaper editors or local "liar's clubs", where gentlemen would gather to amuse one another with tall tales.

DEFINITION

Ufologists have noticed that while there may be a steady "background" rate of reported sightings, UFO sightings tend to come in **waves**. *A few reports build up rapidly into a rash from across an area, reaching a peak and then quickly subsiding. These incidents are also called* **flaps**.

Invaders from Mars! (1900–1947)

FOR MANY UFOLOGISTS the real question about Arnold's 1947 sighting is not "what did he see?" but "why did it have such an impact?" Was the Earth genuinely visited by a huge wave of UFOs in 1947, triggering the thousands of reports that followed the Arnold sighting, or was America, and the rest of the world, somehow primed for an explosion of UFO hysteria?

Pulp fiction

Flying saucers may not have arrived on the world scene until 1947, but spaceships and alien invaders had been around for decades. Science fiction had its roots in the 19th century, and writers like H.G. Wells had explored the topic of alien attack and advanced craft from other worlds way before the 1947 explosion.

During the 1930s science fiction enjoyed a "Golden Age", characterized by pulp fiction books and colourful magazines, like *Amazing Stories* and its sister magazine *Fantastic Adventures*. Edited by Ray Palmer, later an important early proponent of the ETH, these magazines featured tales of sex-mad aliens and visiting space ships, complete with lurid covers.

The June 1947 issue (that is, from the same month as the Arnold sighting) of *Amazing Stories* featured a round-up of reports of strange aerial phenomena – what we would now call UFOs. UFO sceptics argue that all the elements of the UFO mystery had already been circulating in American culture for decades by the time "genuine" UFO sightings began.

ORSON WELLES AND THE INVASION FROM MARS

On the night of 30 October, 1938, Orson Welles and the Mercury Theatre company broadcast a radio adaptation of H.G. Wells's 1898 novel, *War of the Worlds*. By setting the story in modern day America and using realistic staging methods, Welles fooled many people into genuine panic over an imminent Martian invasion. Although it is now thought that only a few hundred people were taken in, the newspapers quickly blew the story out of proportion, and it was widely believed that thousands of people in New Jersey and New York had run amok. UFO sceptics often draw a parallel between the reaction evoked by Welles's performance and the sudden UFO mania of 1947.

WELLES DURING THE BROADCAST

Foo fighters

During World War II, airmen of both sides reported seeing strange lights flying alongside them. Allied pilots nicknamed these UFOs "foo fighters". Foo fighters typically took the form of an amorphous light, but some sightings were of discs, globes, or cigar-shapes. They were reported from both the Atlantic and Pacific theatres. Each side thought they might be secret weapons developed by the other side.

The true nature of the foo fighters has never been explained and they remain a mystery.

Trivia...

The name "foo fighters" came from the catchphrase of a popular 1940s cartoon character, Smokey Stover: "Where there's foo there's fire". According to some sources the "foo" is a corruption of the French feu, *meaning fire.*

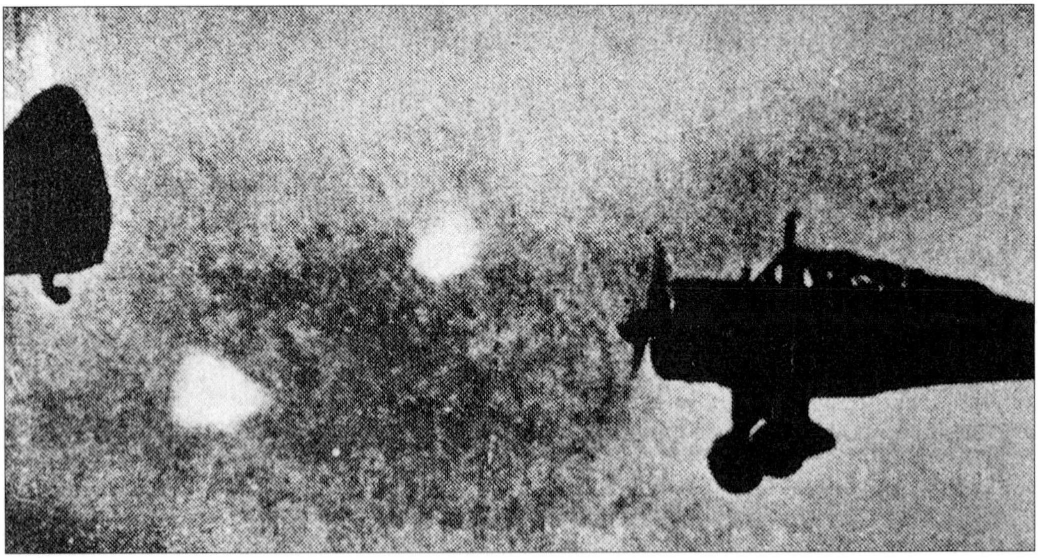

The fiery lights *known as foo fighters are shown here between the US Air Force planes during WWII.*

The Cold War hots up

In the post-war period relations between former allies the US and the Soviet Union quickly soured, and the Cold War began in earnest. There was uncertainty about the military capabilities of the USSR, and also a great deal of tension relating to the atomic bomb, which was poorly understood but greatly feared.

It was against a background of science fiction stories, Cold War tension, and nuclear menace that the UFO mystery was born. There is little doubt that the world public – particularly the Americans – were primed and ready for something.

The Golden Age (1947–1969)

THE PERIOD BETWEEN 1947 and the early 1970s is sometimes described as the Golden Age of ufology, a period when earnest enthusiasts genuinely believed they were about to prove the existence of alien spaceships.

Early on, the most common form of UFO sighting was the "daylight disc" – apparently metallic, structured craft seen during daylight. In later years, the strange light seen at night became the most commonly reported form of UFO sighting.

Saucer mania!

As we saw in the last chapter, Arnold's sighting on 24 June, 1947, triggered a wave of UFO reports and massive media attention. Well over a thousand UFO sightings were reported during June and July of that year, including an amazing story from Roswell, New Mexico.

According to reports on 8 July, initially confirmed by the US Air Force, a flying saucer had crashed at Roswell and its occupants had been taken into custody. The truth about what happened at Roswell is now extremely unclear (see Chapter 18), but that same day in July the Air Force claimed that the "crashed saucer" was nothing more than a weather balloon.

ALBUQUERQUE, NEW MEXICO, 1963

VALLEY HEAD, ALABAMA, 1969

■ **Typical "daylight disc"** *photographs from the Golden Age, with characteristic metallic UFOs.*

The official explanation for the saucer sightings seemed to satisfy both the media and the public, and the flood of reports slowed down to a trickle. The first great UFO wave was over, but a pattern had been set.

UFO reports tend to come in waves or flaps, roughly every 5 years – the first wave was 1947, followed by waves in 1952, 1957, 1964–68, 1973, and 1978.

The amateurs

The military originally took the lead in UFO investigations, but abandoned them in 1969 after spending most of its efforts in trying to debunk UFOs.

Public interest in UFOs quickly gave rise to a popular civilian ufology movement, with groups of amateurs collecting reports and making their own investigations. Almost all of these civilian groups believed that flying saucers were alien spaceships.

The key figure in the early history of civilian ufology was a journalist named Donald Keyhoe. Keyhoe had been a Major in the Marine Corps until injured in 1923. He had friends in high places including the first director of the CIA, Vice Admiral Roscoe H. Hillenkoetter.

In 1950 Keyhoe wrote *The Flying Saucers Are Real,* probably the first real UFO book. Keyhoe's books popularized the ETH hypothesis and the idea that the US government was engaged in a UFO cover-up.

In 1956 Keyhoe founded one of the first and largest civilian UFO organizations, the National Investigations Committee on Aerial Phenomena (NICAP).

The contactees

Among the early reports of sightings there were a few eccentric individuals who claimed to have had actual contact with aliens – they were known as the contactees. The most famous contactee was George Adamski, a hot dog vendor who claimed to have met a tall blonde Venusian in the Californian desert. He supported his story with photos that are now regarded as crude fakes.

INTERNET

ourworld.compuserve.com /homepages/AndyPage/

This site is a great launching point for UFO beginners.

Other contactees included George van Tassel, who arranged a series of Interplanetary Spacecraft Conventions at Giant Rock, California, Howard Menger, who claimed to have had sex with a beautiful Venusian, and Dorothy Martin, who channelled an extraterrestrial reincarnation of Jesus.

Although at the time many of the contactees had considerable followings, they are now regarded as a collection of con artists and eccentrics, a charming relic of the Golden Age of ufology.

The third *of George van Tassel's Interplanetary Spacecraft Conventions drew a crowd of enthusiasts to Giant Rock Airport, California, in 1956.*

Hooray for Hollywood

UFOs had plenty of entertainment value, and Hollywood wasn't slow to pick up on it. Soon UFOs had entered popular culture, and it became obvious that the stories of many witnesses had been more or less influenced by the movies.

Trivia...

The first UFO movie was 1949's The Flying Saucer.

During the 1950s a series of movies, such as *The Day The Earth Stood Still*, used the UFO threat as a metaphor for Cold War tensions. Subsequent movies have featured all the main elements of the UFO mystery, including alien abduction and government conspiracies.

The threat of alien abduction *has been a consistent theme in Hollywood films since the 1950s. This terrifying encounter comes from 1951's* The Man from Planet X.

PSH ufologists argue that the media is so pervasive that all sightings, no matter how sincere the witnesses, must be heavily influenced by the Hollywood version of UFOs.

War of the Worlds (1970–the present day)

DURING THE "GOLDEN AGE" (1947 to 1969) ufology seemed relatively straightforward. UFO sightings were either the result of misidentification or hallucination, or they were alien spaceships. All the ufologist had to do was find out which one was which, and sooner or later conclusive evidence for the extraterrestrial hypothesis would turn up. Of course things didn't work out as planned, and the conclusive evidence still hasn't arisen. Instead, ufology began to change in the latter part of the twentieth century as a host of new and often horrible UFO-related phenomena came to prominence.

Richard Hall, the chairman of the Fund for UFO Research, has described the period from the late 1970s to the 90s as "the weirding of ufology".

I'll be covering many of these latter-day developments in detail in later chapters – what follows is an overview.

High strangeness

Almost from the beginning there had been some paranormal aspects to the UFO mystery. Many of the contactees came from occult backgrounds, and communicated with their alien friends in paranormal fashion. Poltergeist phenomena or sightings of strange creatures (such as Bigfoot) accompanied some UFO sightings.

UFO reports that included paranormal or other weird elements were called "high strangeness" reports. As the UFO mystery evolved, more and more reports fitted into this category.

Paranoia rising

A parallel development was the increasing level of paranoia involved in ufology. Ufologists had begun to suspect that the government wasn't being completely honest from the early 1950s, but from the mid-70s secret, possibly governmental, forces began to figure in UFO reports.

These forces were marked by their use of unmarked black cars, vans, helicopters, and even suits. Mysterious, black-suited government agents are known as Men in Black (MIBs).

Cattle mutilation

Starting in the summer of 1973, and reaching a peak in 1976, a horrible wave of cattle mutilations spread across the American mid-west. Cattle mutilation is also known as "cattle ripping". It seemed to follow a characteristic pattern: genitals, eyes, and ears were missing, flesh was stripped off the jaw, and blood drained from the body. At first satanic cultists were blamed, but soon a more sinister array of culprits emerged.

Black helicopters and UFOs were seen in conjunction with the mutilations, and there were related stories of MIBs and alien abductions. Panic spread amongst the ranching community, and the stories were taken seriously enough for ranchers to start firing on ordinary helicopters.

Studies of the evidence concluded that the cattle had died naturally and then suffered from normal scavenging – the rest was the result of mass hysteria.

The media and most of the public lost interest after this, but a hard core of ufologists believed something much more sinister was going on. Gradually, out of a mixture of UFO sightings, witnesses' memories recovered under hypnosis and bizarre speculation, a terrible story emerged.

Investigators inspect the remains *of a mutilated cow carcase in Colorado. No culprit was ever found.*

Aliens, with the full knowledge and co-operation of the US government (hence the black helicopters), were mutilating cattle in order to obtain body parts for use in bizarre biological experiments.

No hard evidence in support of this fantastic tale has ever emerged, and although sporadic reports of mutilations have continued to the present day no one has ever been caught after nearly 30 years of cattle ripping.

The Dark Side

Probably the most significant development in the story of UFOs has been the abduction phenomenon.

In an alien abduction the subject is kidnapped, taken on board a UFO, experimented on, and returned with all memories of the event erased.

The first alleged abduction case occurred in 1957, but since around 1980 a core group of abduction researchers has used controversial hypnosis techniques to uncover what they claim is a massive conspiracy involving the nightly abduction of hundreds or thousands of people.

DEFINITION

The abduction phenomenon has been woven together with stories of government conspiracy to create a single conspiracy theory on a grand scale, known in ufology as the **Dark Side hypothesis**.

According to followers of the ***Dark Side hypothesis***, the governments of the world have established a secret pact with aliens. In return for advanced technology they help the aliens – who are established in secret bases all over the world – to abduct and experiment on humans and animals, with the intention of engineering alien–human hybrids who will then colonize the Earth.

Most serious ufologists try to distance themselves from this "lunatic fringe" but it remains the popular face of ufology – the books, films, and radio and TV programmes that attract the biggest audiences are those that subscribe to the Dark Side hypothesis.

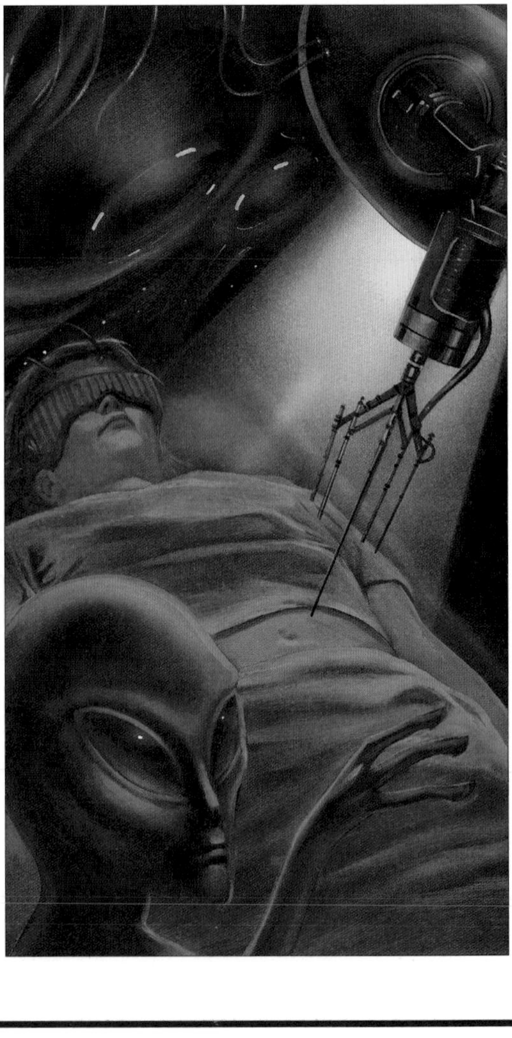

■ **A key component** *of the Dark Side hypothesis is state-sanctioned human abduction/experimentation.*

The latest developments

The late 1980s and 90s saw some more additions to the UFO mystery. Crop circles, which were originally known as "saucer nests", are now inextricably linked to UFOs despite admissions that they're practically all man made.

By the 1990s, many sightings involved black triangular UFOs in place of the traditional flying saucer.

In summary, ufology has changed a lot since 1947, but there's one thing that remains the same – a lack of convincing proof that UFOs are alien spaceships.

A simple summary

✓ People have been seeing unexplained phenomena in the sky since ancient times. According to "ancient astronaut" theorists this indicates that alien visitors played a pivotal role in ancient human history. To sceptics it indicates that UFOs are a modern interpretation of an ancient tradition.

✓ UFO reports often involve technology that is only one step ahead of contemporary limits.

✓ Medieval and Victorian UFO sightings took the form of sky ships and mystery airships.

✓ 1940s' America was primed for the UFO mystery by science fiction and Cold War tension.

✓ The 1947 Arnold sighting was prefigured by the foo fighters of World War II.

✓ UFO sightings tend to come in waves.

✓ The period between 1947 and the early 1970s was the Golden Age of ufology, marked by the growth of civilian UFO organizations.

✓ From the 1970s onwards, ufology became weirder and more paranoid. It developed ugly elements including alien abduction and cattle mutilation, culminating in the "Dark Side" hypothesis of alien-government conspiracy and hybridization/ colonization programmes.

Chapter 18

Classic Close Encounters

AT THE HEART OF UFOLOGY is the actual sighting or encounter. In this chapter we take a look at five classic UFO cases. These aren't necessarily the most famous cases of all time, but each is significant in its own way. Above all, they show how often in ufology a promising case becomes a tangled web of claims and counterclaims, where the truth is hard to find.

In this chapter...

- ✓ **Roswell (1947)**
- ✓ **The Valentich incident (1978)**
- ✓ **The Cash-Landrum case (1980)**
- ✓ **Rendlesham Forest (1980)**
- ✓ **The Mexican wave (1991)**

A CLASSIC CLOSE ENCOUNTER OF THE CINEMATIC KIND

Roswell (1947)

PROBABLY THE MOST FAMOUS and controversial UFO incident of all time happened in July 1947, near the town of Roswell, New Mexico.

On the morning of 8 July, the Roswell* Daily Record *carried this explosive headline: "Roswell Army Air Field Captures Flying Saucer on Ranch in Roswell Region".

Based on an official military press release the newspaper article revealed that the wreckage of a saucer that had crashed on a ranch in Lincoln County the previous week had been retrieved and taken to Roswell Army Air Field.

That same afternoon a military press conference announced that the "saucer" wreckage was nothing more than a downed weather balloon. The mystery was apparently over as quickly as it had begun.

A Roswell official *poses with remains of the downed weather balloon. Was this part of a cover up?*

Case reopened

In 1980 Charles Berlitz (a major proponent of the Bermuda Triangle mystery) and William Moore published *The Roswell Incident*, in which they claimed that the "balloon story" was part of an official cover-up.

Contemporary witnesses told of crash debris composed of strange lightweight metals and, even more incredibly, the bodies of the saucer's crew.

As more investigators entered the fray and dug up more testimony, an amazing story emerged. The government had spirited the wreckage and alien bodies away for secret research, storing them at the notorious Area 51 top secret military testing ground in Nevada, where it was using them to ***reverse engineer*** advanced technologies of its own.

DEFINITION

Reverse engineering *is the process of working backwards from super-advanced alien technology to arrive at technology that humans can understand and use.*

Even more fantastic details were unearthed. Apparently Area 51 was now the site of a secret alien base, buried beneath the Nevada desert, and was a centre for UFO testing and hybridization experiments. There has even been a film purporting to show army doctors performing an autopsy on an alien corpse.

Trivia...

In 1947, Roswell Army Air Field was the home of the world's only nuclear bomb squadron, the 509th Bomb Group. This was the squadron that had bombed Hiroshima and Nagasaki.

A tangled web

As the Roswell story became ever more fantastic, large holes began to appear. The government admitted that it had been testing secret high-altitude radar balloons at Roswell in 1947, and reports of the wreckage match this story. In 1997 an Air Force press release blamed stories about alien bodies on confused memories of human-shaped dummies used in crash tests (although admittedly such testing only began in 1954).

A nurse said to have passed on vital secret information was proved never to have existed. The alien autopsy film was widely derided – the alien almost exactly resembled a model made for a film about Roswell.

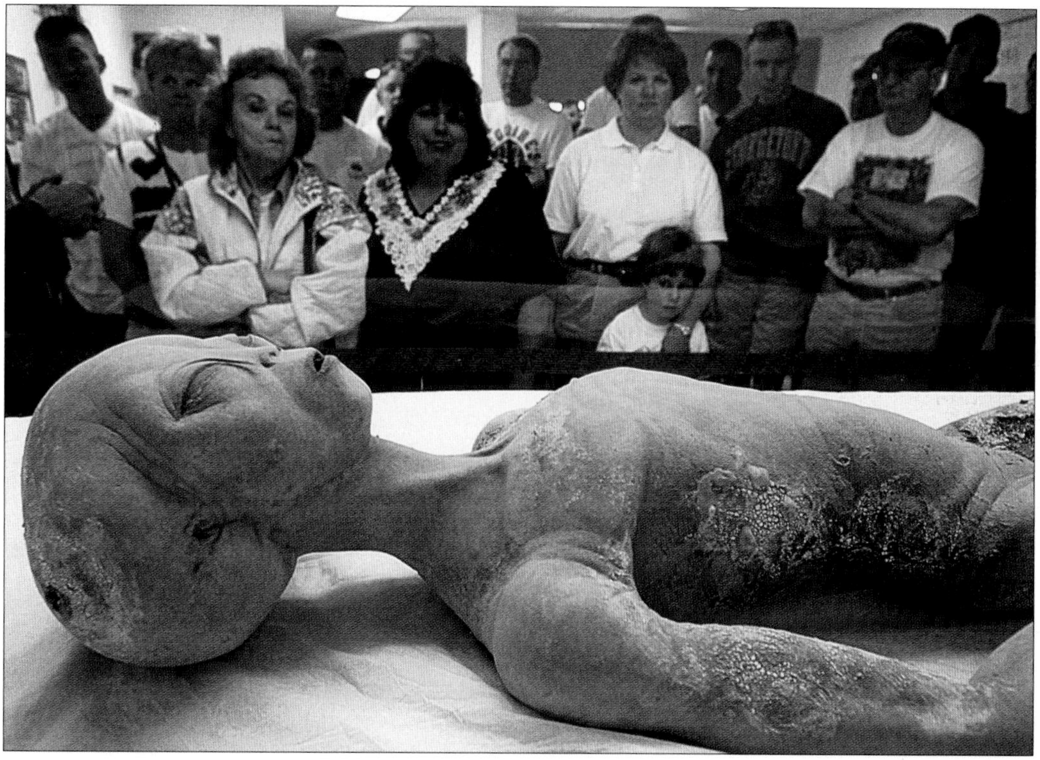

Visitors to the International UFO Museum and Research Center *in Roswell, New Mexico, can view a replica of an alien made for the 1994 TV movie* Roswell.

Declassified

Perhaps most damagingly, documents declassified in 1996 reveal that in 1948 a senior Air Force intelligence officer, Colonel H. McCoy, writing in a secret memorandum, reports that no "physical evidence of the existence [of UFOs] has been obtained". In another memo McCoy moans, "I can't even tell you how much we would give to have one of those crash in an area so we could recover whatever they are."

INTERNET

www.af.mil/lib/roswell

Go to this site to read the official USAF report on the Roswell Incident, optimistically entitled "Case Closed".

In conclusion, the most plausible explanation for the Roswell incident is probably the Air Force one, while the UFO story is too full of holes and totally unsupported by any hard evidence.

The circus-like air of recent 50th anniversary celebrations at the site did nothing to dispel this concern. There are now six possible crash sites around Roswell competing for tourist dollars.

For many ufologists the Roswell incident has come to embody the tacky side of ufology.

The Valentich incident (1978)

GIVEN THE ALLEGEDLY HOSTILE intent of the aliens who are believed to be piloting the UFO spaceships, there have been remarkably few fatalities in the history of ufology. One such incident happened on 21 October, 1978, when Australian pilot Frederich Valentich disappeared while flying over the Bass Strait off the coast of Victoria, Australia.

Valentich's last message

Shortly after 7 p.m. Valentich reported to the radio operator in Melbourne that a large UFO had appeared above him, and that his single-engined Cessna 182 was experiencing engine trouble. In the ensuing conversation the operator confirmed that there were no known aircraft at that height in the area, and Valentich described how the object seemed to be "playing some sort of game. He's flying over me two to three times … at speeds I could not identify." He went on to describe a long shape with a green light and a shiny, metallic exterior.

An artist's impression *shows the unidentified craft over Valentich's Cessna shortly before his disappearance.*

Frederich Valentich's chilling last words from his plane – "that strange aircraft is hovering on top of me again. It is hovering, and it's not an aircraft" – were followed by 17 seconds of metallic scraping sounds, and then silence.

The disappearing Cessna

When Valentich failed to show up at his destination, a series of searches were begun. None of them ever found so much as a scrap of debris, and the official investigation was unable to draw any conclusions.

Witnesses on the mainland described a number of UFO sightings in the area from the same day. Speculation about the disappearance flourished, and many theories were proposed. To ufologists it looked as if Valentich and his aircraft had been abducted by a giant UFO.

The aviation authorities favoured the theory that Valentich had become disoriented while also developing engine problems, and then crashed and sank.

Other theories blamed lightning, dirigibles used by drug smugglers, suicide, a faked disappearance (that is, Valentich was still alive), and even a meteorite. In 1982 a TV producer claimed that some divers had approached him with photos of a crashed Cessna on the Bass Strait seabed, but this was never verified. The Valentich disappearance remains unsolved.

The Cash–Landrum case (1980)

ON THE NIGHT of 29 December, 1980, Vickie Landrum, her grandson Colby, and friend Betty Cash were driving in woods near Huffman, Texas, when they saw a diamond-shaped UFO ahead of them. Unable to turn around on the narrow road, they stopped the car and Cash got out to have a look. The object was extremely bright and seemed to be giving off an intense heat.

White heat

All three could feel themselves burning, and the car grew so hot that when Vickie Landrum put her hand on the dashboard her fingers sank into it, leaving a handprint. As the UFO flew off, a fleet of helicopters suddenly appeared and surrounded it – Cash counted 23 in all.

INTERNET

www.skiesare.demon.co.uk/c-l.html

Go to this site for a detailed online account of the Cash–Landrum case.

Within hours the three witnesses developed severe burns and other symptoms of intense exposure to radiation, including nausea, headaches, hair loss, and damage to eyesight. Cash was so seriously affected that she had to be hospitalized and never fully recovered – later she was diagnosed with cancer. In fact, she was hospitalized 25 times after the incident.

The Cash–Landrum case promised to be the best instance yet of a close encounter of the second kind (in which a UFO physically affects the environment and/or human beings).

There was concrete physical evidence in the form of the witnesses' injuries and the marks on the dashboard, and independent corroboration of their story about the helicopters.

The untraceable helicopters

The best lead seemed to be the fleet of helicopters. Such a large number of aircraft should have been easy to trace. However, every civil and military authority, including the Army, Air Force, National Guard, and all airfields in the area, disclaimed all knowledge of the helicopters.

With no other leads to go on, the case petered out and remains unsolved. Sceptics point out that no one knows for sure what the state of the health of the witnesses was before the alleged incident.

Cash and the Landrums launched a $20 million civil suit against the US government, but the case was thrown out because there was no record that the government possessed anything like the UFO.

This illustration *shows the "diamond of fire" moving out of sight and the fleet of helicopters moving in on Betty Cash and the Landrums. "The helicopters seemed to rush in from all directions", claimed Cash.*

Rendlesham Forest (1980)

THE STRANGE EVENTS that took place around a now deserted American air base in the English county of Suffolk in late December 1980, have led to this case being called "the British Roswell". It's a story of dramatic close encounters, secret nuclear weapons, and official cover-ups.

If you go down to the woods

Early in the morning of 26 December, 1980, security officers at RAF Woodbridge, part of a two-base complex in Rendlesham Forest, Suffolk, run by the US Air Force, were called out to investigate some strange lights in the woods outside the base.

Three patrolmen reported encountering a glowing, metallic, triangular object in the woods. The UFO moved off, leaving three holes in the shape of a triangle – readings seemed to indicate high levels of radiation. The shaken patrolmen returned to the base, and their encounter was entered into the log, but this was just the beginning.

Two nights later Deputy Base Commander Lieutenant-Colonel Charles Halt reported seeing more strange lights in the woods. Halt submitted a report to the British Ministry of Defence, but no one got back to him. His superiors insisted that it was a matter for the British police, and refused to investigate further.

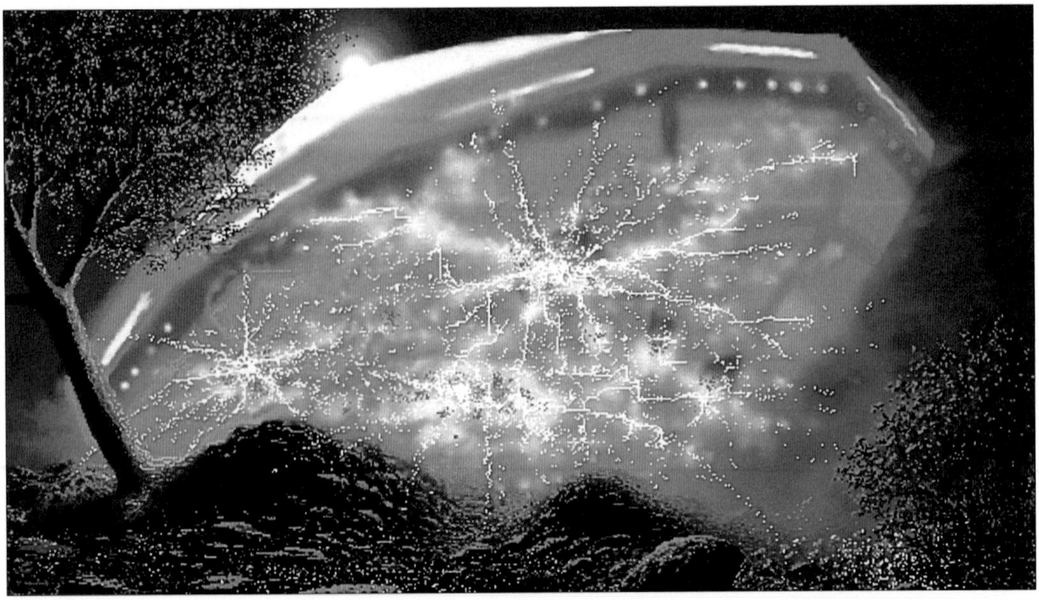

An artist's impression of the "strange lights" *in Rendlesham Forest – did the security officers see an unidentified flying object, or did they simply misinterpret the beacon from the nearby lighthouse?*

The plot thickens

British ufologists were beside themselves with excitement, and the story got better and better. As the various witnesses were interviewed, new details emerged. One of the three patrolmen described the UFO in detail, including strange markings on its side that he touched and sketched. A roll of film he had shot did not come back from the base pharmacist. Other rolls were fogged.

Halt described how lights set up after the first incident mysteriously failed, and how radio communication was impossible due to interference. He had made a tape recording of the whole incident that seemed to provide concrete confirmation of his story. Radar Command had tracked unidentified objects in the area. Nuclear weapons were stored in bunkers at the air bases, and Halt described how the beams of light from the UFO seemed to be aimed at these.

INTERNET

www.ufoworld.co.uk/ rendlshm.htm

Check out this site for the inside story on the whole Rendlesham incident.

Several of the witnesses claimed to have been harassed and intimidated by the authorities since the incident. The Rendlesham Forest case was shaping up to be one of the best UFO cases of all time.

Rabbit holes and lighthouses

As so often happens in ufology, a potentially landmark case collapsed under detailed investigation. Doubts first began to surface when investigators at the scene noticed that a nearby lighthouse was visible from Rendlesham Forest. Could this have been the source of the strange lights? The discovery of the original witness statements from the nights in question suggested so.

Trivia...

On the same nights as the Rendlesham Forest incident occurred, a meteor shower and a Russian satellite re-entered the Earth's atmosphere, breaking up spectacularly in the skies over Britain.

According to the statements, the three patrolmen never got closer than 50 m (150 ft) to the purported object, and were unable to make out any details at all. After pursuing strange lights through the woods they realized they had been looking at the nearby lighthouse all along.

There were also large holes in Halt's story. The timing and description reported on his tape showed that he too had almost certainly been looking at the lighthouse. His radio had never stopped working, and there was nothing strange about the broken lights – they frequently malfunctioned. The "landing marks" were probably rabbit holes, and the radiation readings were not significantly higher than normal. Most serious ufologists consider the case solved, but others insist that something strange was seen that night, and that the government is trying to cover it up.

The Mexican wave (1991)

"MASS HYSTERIA" IS OFTEN GIVEN as an explanation for strange phenomena witnessed by many people, but this concept itself is poorly understood. Nonetheless, it is possible for large numbers of people to convince themselves that something strange is going on when the evidence suggests otherwise. The 1991 wave of UFO sightings above Mexico City is a prime example, and a powerful illustration of both the unreliability of modern technology and the power of the media to shape people's perceptions.

UFOs of the eclipse

At 1.29 p.m. on 11 July, 1991, the residents of the world's largest city, Mexico City, watched a solar eclipse. Even before the sun dimmed bright lights were visible in the sky, and were recorded by many of the people videotaping the eclipse. To many people's eyes the lights seemed to move about, and hundreds reported a UFO (in Spanish an OVNI) sighting.

Leading television journalist Jaime Maussan reported the sightings on the Mexican *60 Minutes*, and was soon inundated with tapes apparently showing one or more UFOs moving at incredible speeds and even changing shape. Further appeals for evidence led to a constant stream of such tapes over the next couple of years, and hundreds of eye witnesses.

Maussan insisted that technicians had ruled out camera artefacts – false images produced by the camera itself – as the source of the UFOs. Magnification of the images appeared to show UFOs with clear shadows, UFOs with clouds going behind them, and UFOs merging or "docking".

■ **It's likely that the "light show"** *during the 1991 eclipse was entirely natural in origin. Venus and many stars were especially visible, and the unusual appearance of the sun's corona added to the effect.*

Dance of the planets

Almost from the beginning there were significant doubts about the value of the video evidence. OVNIs were popular TV fodder in Mexico and dozens of documentaries and sell-through videos were based around the camcorder footage. In the UFO community outside Mexico, however, the sightings attracted limited interest.

Careful technical analysis by photographer Rob Irving has shown that the original camcorder footage almost certainly shows Venus or other planets or stars. It has also been shown that the apparent movement, shape changes, and other features of the "UFOs" are almost certainly due to rapid camera movement and the effects of magnifying very small images.

In summary, the Mexican UFO flap of 1991 and subsequent video evidence have been almost completely debunked. The case graphically illustrates the way that enthusiastic media coverage together with endorsements from "experts" can convince people that an, at best, ambiguous sighting is in fact a spaceship.

A simple summary

✓ Even the best UFO cases tend to be ambiguous, and what seems like a strong piece of evidence often doesn't hold up to scrutiny.

✓ The Roswell incident happened in July, 1947. ETH enthusiasts believe that a saucer and its crew crashed and were retrieved by the government, who subsequently became involved in a grand conspiracy with the aliens.

✓ On 21 October, 1978, pilot Frederich Valentich disappeared with his plane off the coast of Australia, after reporting a UFO above him. No sign of the plane has ever been found. The authorities say he probably became disoriented and crashed into the sea.

✓ In the Cash–Landrum case three witnesses apparently suffered radiation poisoning after seeing a UFO and a fleet of black helicopters. The helicopters have never been traced and the case remains unsolved.

✓ US Air Force personnel reported two UFO encounters in Rendlesham Forest, Suffolk, in late December, 1980, in what has been called the British Roswell. A lighthouse was probably the source of the lights.

✓ Hundreds of people saw and filmed UFOs over Mexico City in 1991, but were almost certainly seeing Venus and other planets or stars.

Chapter 19

Aliens

SOON AFTER it was first suggested that UFOs were alien spaceships, people began to wonder who was flying them. Ever since, the subject of aliens has divided the world of ufology. What is the likelihood of alien intelligence? If aliens do exist what do they look like, and more importantly what do they want?

In this chapter...

- ✓ **Is there anyone out there?**
- ✓ **Alien nation**
- ✓ **The Starchild controversy**
- ✓ **What do they want?**

THE CLASSIC "GREY" ALIEN FROM WHITLEY STREIBER'S *COMMUNION*

Is there anyone out there?

SCIENTISTS ARE DIVIDED into two camps on the question of extraterrestrial intelligence (ETI) – the existence of intelligent life on other worlds.

■ **The universe** *is boundless – can we be sure no intelligent life exists elsewhere?*

Some scientists believe there are many Earth-like planets in the universe, and that it's extremely probable that intelligent life has evolved on these planets.

The other camp believes that the Earth is extremely unusual and possibly unique, and that the right conditions for intelligent life to evolve are incredibly rare in the universe.

Over the last few decades scientific discoveries have tended to support the view that extraterrestrial intelligence is unlikely.

For instance, it now seems that Earth-like planets are probably very rare, and that Jupiter uniquely protects our planet from constant asteroid bombardment that would have prevented the evolution of higher life forms.

The searchers

It's likely that radio waves, travelling at the speed of light, would be the first sign of an alien civilization that we could detect on Earth.

SETI – the Search for Extraterrestrial Intelligence project that leads the hunt for ETI – uses radio telescopes to pick up radio waves from outer space.

These are then analyzed by computer to see whether they have come from natural sources, such as stars, or artificial sources (an alien civilization, for example). So far no evidence of ETI has been detected. Believers in the extraterrestrial hypothesis (ETH) of UFO origin say that SETI's lack of success is the result of either government conspiracy or a desire on the part of the aliens to remain hidden and secret.

SETI AT HOME

The SETI project has gathered an enormous amount of raw data that requires computer processing, but they don't have the computer power available to do it themselves. Instead they've turned to home computer users. SETI@home is a program that anyone can download from the Internet. It takes advantage of your computer's spare time, when it might be in screensaver mode, by using it to analyze raw data and send the results back to SETI. Thousands of people have now downloaded the program, massively increasing the processing capacity available to SETI.

INTERNET

www.setiathome.ssl.berkeley.edu/

Visit this site to download the SETI@home program and do your bit to find ET.

The SETI project collects data from all over the world. *This radio telescope in Parkes, New South Wales, Australia, observes wavelengths from 5–20 millimetres, and often contributes data to the project.*

Alien nation

HUNDREDS OF CLOSE ENCOUNTERS of the third kind (where witnesses see and/or meet the occupants of a spacecraft) have been reported over the years, and witnesses claim to have encountered dozens of different types of alien.

Little green men?

There has been a lot of discussion about what an alien might look like. Although reports of little green men are rare, most sightings do involve humanoid aliens. To sceptics this clearly shows that alien encounters have psychological and cultural sources (in film and TV, aliens are usually portrayed as humanoid in order to save money). However, according to some authorities, humanoid aliens are only to be expected. Some scientists believe that the rules of evolution favour the development of a similar body form to our own.

■ **"Take me to your special effects department."** *Because of low effects budgets, early film and TV aliens were nearly always humanoid, like this one in* The Outer Limits.

They expect that an alien would most likely be an oxygen-breather with legs and arms, something like hands for using tools, and a head containing eyes and a brain. Other scientists claim that this assumption is wrong, and that alien life might be so different from us that we could barely recognize it as a life form.

Rogue's gallery

Leading ufologist Jerome Clark says that most aliens seem to fit into one of a few categories, including human or near-human aliens, dwarf aliens, and non-human aliens.

Dwarf aliens often bear a strong resemblance to folkloric characters such as elves and goblins.

For instance, in August 1955 the Sutton family of Hopkinsville, Kentucky, had a celebrated encounter with a 1.2 m (4 ft) tall green alien with huge eyes, pointed ears, and long arms with claws. The Hopkinsville alien looks a lot like a Victorian illustration of a goblin.

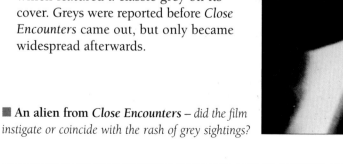

Regional variations in the distribution of types of alien have been noted. Small hairy dwarves and non-human aliens, for instance, are much more common in South America.

Since the 1980s, the most common type of alien has been the "grey". The grey is short and slim with pale grey skin, a large bald head, small nose, pointy ears, and large, dark eyes.

A key element of the Dark Side hypothesis (see pp. 263–64) is that the government is in league with the greys, possibly in an interstellar war with reptilian aliens known as reptoids. Proponents of the Dark Side hypothesis refer to aliens as extraterrestrial biological entities (EBEs).

Too many or too few?

The diversity of alien reports poses a problem to supporters of the ETH. It seems too far-fetched to suppose that dozens of different alien species are visiting the Earth, which means that at least some of the witnesses must be mistaken. But which ones, and if one why not all of them?

Supporters of the ETH point to the consensus of the 1980s and 90s, when the grey emerged as almost the only type of alien sighted. But to sceptics this is even more suspicious.

Sceptics argue that widespread reports of greys simply reflect their appearance in some key UFO sources – for instance the 1977 film *Close Encounters of the Third Kind* and the influential 1987 Whitley Strieber book *Communion*, which featured a classic grey on its cover. Greys were reported before *Close Encounters* came out, but only became widespread afterwards.

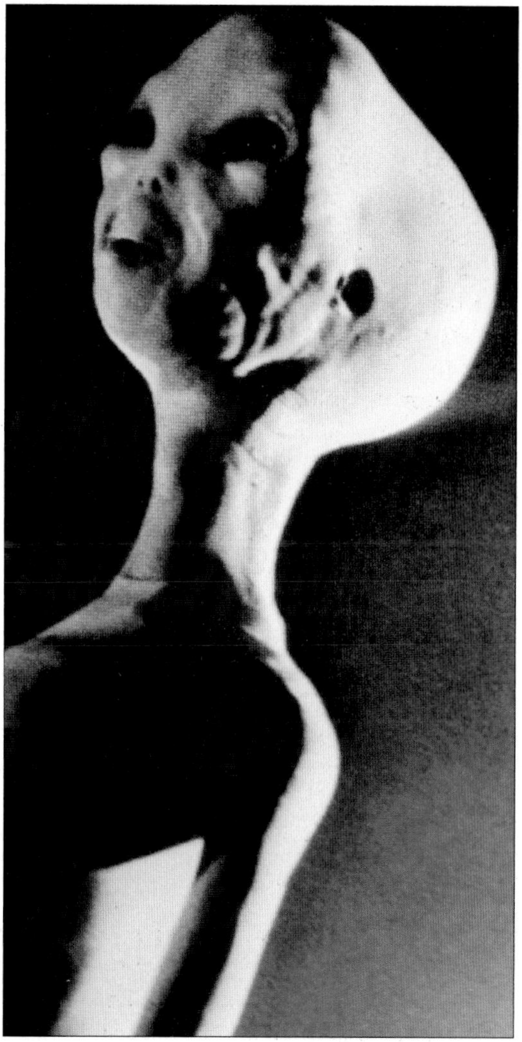

■ **An alien from *Close Encounters*** – *did the film instigate or coincide with the rash of grey sightings?*

The Starchild controversy

SINCE FEBRUARY 1999 a bizarre looking skull, known as the Starchild skull, has been exhibited at UFO conferences and heavily discussed in UFO journals.

***The Starchild skull is alleged to be the remains of an alien-human* hybrid.**

Legend of the Star People

According to the Starchild Project, an organization that wants to arrange DNA testing of the skull to prove an incredible origin, the skull was discovered in the mountains of northern Mexico. Indian tribes from the region have legends of Star People – beings from the sky who visit Earth to impregnate local women before returning years later to retrieve the hybrid infants.

DEFINITION

A **hybrid** *is a cross between two different breeds or species. Only closely related species can interbreed or "hybridize", and it seems unlikely that humans and aliens would be similar enough.*

Big head

The skull has several strange features that suggest it is not human. It has a massive brain capacity, flattened rear, shallow eye sockets, and is missing the front sinuses.

The Starchild Project claims to have consulted over 50 experts, the vast majority of whom argue that the skull is that of a deformed human child.

Most experts say that the Starchild skull is that of a child suffering from hydrocephaly, a disease in which fluid builds up on the brain and makes the skull swell.

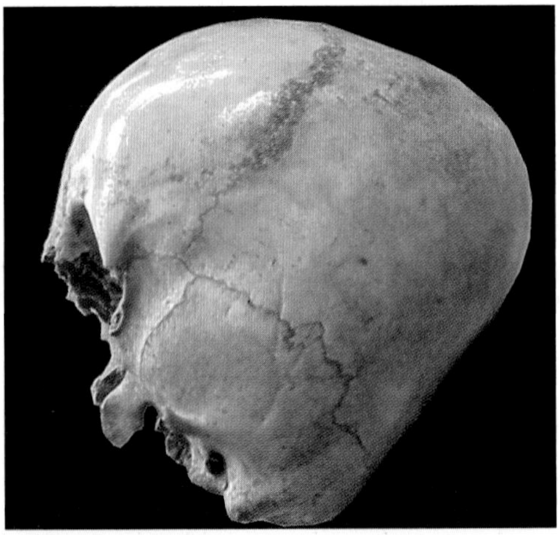

■ **The Starchild skull** *is far from normal. But is it from an abnormal or cradle-boarded human infant, or perhaps an alien–human hybrid?*

It is also widely thought that the skull has been cradle-boarded. Cradle-boarding is the practice of strapping an infant's head to a board and causes flattening of the back of the skull. It was practised in the area of Mexico where the skull comes from. The Starchild Project argues that close examination of the skull rules out this explanation, and is attempting to raise funds to pay for DNA testing – the only way to be certain of the skull's origins.

What do they want?

IF ALIENS WANTED TO ESTABLISH normal relations with the people of Earth they would surely have made themselves known to us a long time ago. So what do they want? People who encounter aliens (contactees and abductees) report varying motives – usually either good or evil.

The Day the Earth Stood Still

This is the title of an influential 1951 movie in which a humanoid alien and his robotic companion land on the White House lawn, and then warn humanity of the dangers of nuclear weapons.

During the 1950s many contactees claimed that the aliens were here to warn us of impending nuclear doom.

In later decades contactees claimed that aliens were now more concerned about impending environmental catastrophe. Sceptics ask why the aliens seem to choose only crackpots and eccentrics as the bearers of such important news.

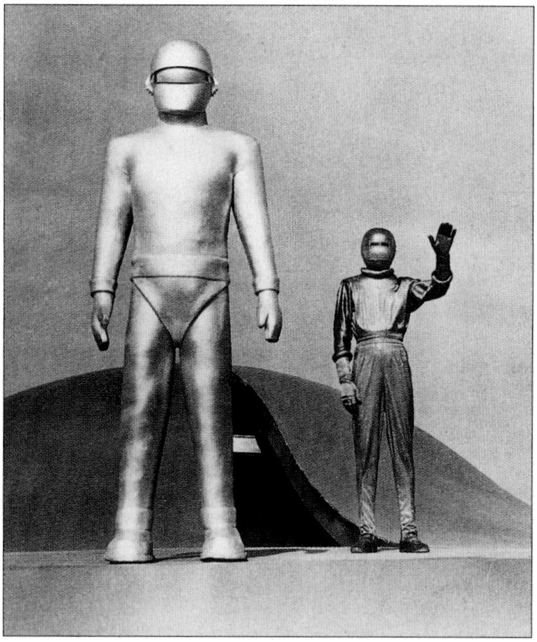

In the early UFO film, The Day the Earth Stood Still, *aliens visit Earth to tell us that we must live peacefully or be destroyed as a danger to other planets.*

THE RETREATING ALIENS

Ufologists have noted that the more recent the report of alien contact, the further away the home planet of the aliens involved. The contactees of the 1950s claimed that their alien Space Brothers came from Venus, Mars, Uranus, Saturn, and even the Moon. When scientists established that life could not survive on the planets of our Solar System, the aliens moved further afield. Nowadays their origins are either vague, or they claim to hail from distant star systems such as Zeta Reticuli or Sirius.

Under the microscope

Since the 1970s aliens seem to have become a lot less friendly. Many UFO enthusiasts believe that aliens carry out cattle mutilations and abductions as part of a programme of experiments.

According to this view, the aliens are retrieving Earth DNA and even body parts, semen, and fetuses to use in hybridization experiments, to rejuvenate their ailing species, or simply in order to study mankind. Sceptics point out that alien and human (or cattle) DNA would not be compatible, and ask why the aliens seem to need so much of it, and why they are apparently so clumsy about collecting it.

Sex and death

Dark Siders take the alien experimenter theory a step further.

Dark Siders believe that the "greys" are here to take over the world, possibly by colonizing it with alien–human hybrids.

■ **This alien** *from the tongue-in-cheek 1989 film* Earth Girls Are Easy, *although not a grey, nonetheless represents the darkest fears of Dark Siders everywhere.*

Their motive may be to escape from their dying home world, to rejuvenate their dying species, or simply to meet Earth women. The governments of the Earth are usually supposed to be involved to some extent. Eventually ordinary humans will be enslaved or destroyed, possibly by an evil plague being developed by alien and government scientists. Dark Siders sometimes claim that HIV is just such a plague.

Needless to say most people dismiss the Dark Siders as lunatics, but unfortunately some believe this wild paranoid fantasy and live in heavily armed fear as a result.

Trivia...

According to unconventional psychic and self-proclaimed messiah David Icke, the British Royal Family are shape-shifting reptilian aliens who regularly eat humans.

Signs of the times

Sceptics and supporters of the psychosocial hypothesis (PSH) argue that the motives attributed to aliens tell us about the concerns and fears of those who encounter aliens and the societies they come from. For example, during the Cold War anxieties of the 1950s the aliens brought anti-nuclear messages. During the eco-conscious 1980s and 90s they were preaching environmental awareness. The fears of the Dark Siders reflect a growing sense of alienation, disenfranchisement, and anxiety about faceless government and big business, primarily, but not only, in the US.

A simple summary

- ✓ Scientists are divided over the existence of extraterrestrial intelligence (ETI). The anti-ETI camp is gaining ground.
- ✓ The Search for ETI (SETI) uses radio telescopes to look for radio waves from alien civilizations, but so far hasn't found any.
- ✓ Many different types of alien have been reported, although in recent years most encounters involve "greys" – slim grey aliens with large heads and large eyes.
- ✓ Sceptics argue that both the diversity of early reports and the uniformity of recent years indicate a cultural source for images of aliens.
- ✓ The Starchild skull is alleged to be that of an alien-human hybrid. Most experts think it is the skull of a deformed child.
- ✓ Aliens have changed their motives for visiting and their point of origin over the years. Earlier aliens were friendly and wanted to warn humanity about nuclear and environmental danger.
- ✓ Dark Siders believe that the greys are using human DNA to create a race of hybrids to take over the Earth.
- ✓ Sceptics and supporters of the psychosocial hypothesis (PSH) believe that the motivations of the aliens reflect human concerns and anxieties.
- ✓ In general, reports of alien encounters have tended to weaken the case for the extraterrestrial hypothesis (ETH), because there are so many contradictions and problems in the stories of contactees and abductees.

Chapter 20

Abductions and Abductees

ALIEN ABDUCTION is the capture of a human, known as an abductee, who is taken on board a ship, subjected to experiments, and then returned, usually with missing memories. To believers the abduction phenomenon is horribly real; to sceptics it is one of the most extraordinary examples of mass delusion in history.

In this chapter...

- ✓ **The abduction experience**
- ✓ **How many?!**
- ✓ **Up close and personal**
- ✓ **Implants**
- ✓ **Truth and lies**

THEY COME IN A BLAZE OF LIGHT

The abduction experience

ALMOST ALL ABDUCTION experiences follow the same pattern. The details may vary, but the core experience is usually the same.

There are four key stages in the majority of abduction experiences – abduction, examination, return, and aftermath.

They come by night

Abductees have been abducted from all sorts of places, but in the majority of cases they are taken from their bedrooms or from their cars while driving in lonely places. Most abductions happen at night and often the person is asleep to start with.

The abduction experience starts when the person sees a strange light, which often comes streaming through the windows. This is accompanied by a growing sense of unreality, as if entering a dream, and a loss of mental and physical control.

The abductee may become paralysed, feel drugged or dozy, or under the control of another will. The abductee may see, or may simply feel, a presence. He or she is escorted to a spaceship, although the details of the transfer are often cloudy – abductees sometimes pass through walls or closed windows. A floating sensation is often reported.

Many abductees report *waking to a sight similar to this one.*

On the slab

Once inside the spacecraft the abductee finds himself on an examination table or bed, surrounded by aliens – usually "greys" or very similar creatures. Sometimes humans are present. The aliens then examine the abductee.

The examination usually involves inspection with a strange device followed by probing with needles. Sometimes microscopic devices are implanted into the abductee. The reproductive organs are normally the focus of interest. Abductees often report that the aliens seem to extract semen or eggs, or use needles to implant or extract things from the womb.

Trivia...

Abductees who report being abducted as children claim that the aliens were friendly or playful, only becoming abusive after the children had reached puberty. It is rare for a first abduction to occur after the age of 35.

This is the scene described *by four men who claim to have had experiments performed on them by a group of grey aliens in a spacecraft, after being abducted from a canoeing trip in Maine in 1976.*

Added extras

At this point the stories of abductees start to diverge, and a variety of elements are introduced.

Common post-examination story elements include telepathic conversation with the aliens, a tour of the spaceship or testing facility, seeing other abductees, or being introduced to hybrid children.

Conversation with the aliens, known as the "conference" stage, often involves warnings about the future of humankind or information about the origin and purpose of the aliens. Some abductees get to explore – the aliens often seem strangely relaxed about them wandering around. Common sights include rooms full of fetuses or bizarre hybrids in jars (known as incubatoriums), glimpses of otherworldly alien environments, or strange alien rituals. Some abductees are introduced to hybrid babies or children, which are usually sickly and subdued.

Missing time

Abductees are returned in the same fashion they were taken, and many report feelings of sadness about leaving mixed with joy about the experience (even though it was unpleasant). The abductee may be told to forget what has happened, and fall asleep.

On awakening or coming to his or her senses, the abductee usually has no conscious memory of the events, but is left with a vague feeling of unease. Abductions usually take 1–3 hours. If the abductee was conscious when taken he or she may notice that some time has elapsed but will have no memory of it. This is called "missing time", and is regarded by abduction researchers as a sure sign of abduction.

Following their experience many abductees complain of sleep problems (including nightmares) and headaches and other illnesses, or discover strange scars on their bodies. Some abductees claim that their abduction is followed up by a visit from the Men in Black. Others claim to develop psychic powers.

Most abductees do not know they've been abducted until they meet an abduction researcher or other abductees. Their full stories only emerge after hypnosis. The vast majority of abduction narratives are recovered through ***hypnotic regression***.

Abduction researchers argue that the extreme similarities between reports are proof that abductees are describing a real experience.

DEFINITION

Hypnotic regression *is the recovery of memories through the use of hypnotic trance. The subject is told to imagine himself at a time in the past and then asked to describe what is happening.*

How many?!

THE ABDUCTION PHENOMENON has divided the UFO community. Many ufologists who believe the ETH are nonetheless bitterly opposed to the abduction researchers, as they feel that the abduction phenomenon undermines the credibility of the subject.

The Roper survey

Nothing embodies this divide like the debate over the number of people abducted. If the abduction researchers are right, as many as 22 million abductions take place every year! This extraordinary statistic comes from a 1991 survey conducted by the Roper polling organization. They sampled almost 6,000 people with a carefully devised questionnaire.

The 1991 Roper survey didn't ask people directly if they'd been abducted – after all, they should have no memory of it. Instead they were asked about experiences that abduction researchers claim are clear indicators of having been abducted.

The abduction experiences included: seeing unusual lights in a room; having missing time; experience of floating or flying in the air without knowing why; paralysis in the presence of strange figures; and finding strange scars on the body.

According to abduction researchers any one of these experiences suggests abduction. For the purposes of the survey, anyone who answered positively to four of these five questions was considered to have been abducted.

A nation of abductees?

The results of the survey were astonishing. Two per cent of the sample had had experiences that suggested they had been abducted. Extrapolated to the wider US population this means there are 5 million abductees in America – 1 in every 50 Americans has been abducted! Incredible as they might sound, these figures match abductees' accounts of hundreds of people being processed simultaneously by the aliens.

Given that most abductees report multiple abductions over their lifetime – on average around ten – the Roper results suggest that 1 million abductions happen in the US every year – 2,740 per day!

Assuming that abduction is a global phenomenon, as believers assert, the Roper results mean that 22 million people worldwide are abducted every year.

UFO gridlock

Between them, ufologists Robert Durant, Patrick Huyghe, and Dennis Stacy attempted to work out exactly how many aliens would be needed to perform this number of abductions.

Following abduction reports, it seems that about six aliens are needed for an average 2-hour abduction.

Watching and waiting. *Some reports suggest that thousands of us are abducted every night by tens of thousands of aliens intent on research.*

Ufologists calculate that at least 33,000 aliens in hundreds or thousands of UFOs must be performing abductions around the clock, 365 days a year, to meet the demand.

If the statistics based on the Roper report are true, there must be thousands of UFOs permanently hovering over the world's cities. For all but the most hardened abduction enthusiast this is too much to swallow.

Up close and personal

TODAY THE ABDUCTION PHENOMENON is the central issue in ufology, but until 1980 there were only a handful of abduction reports in UFO literature, and abduction was regarded as nothing more than a curious offshoot of the UFO mystery. At the centre of the phenomenon and its increasing popularity are a number of key cases.

Setting the pattern

The first abduction case took place in November 1957, when a young Brazilian, Antonio Villas-Boas, claimed that a number of small aliens had dragged him into a UFO and taken a blood sample, after which a humanoid female alien had sex with him. The few ufologists who knew of this case thought it too lurid and sensational to merit close attention.

The abduction phenomenon really began in September 1961, when New Hampshire couple Barney and Betty Hill reported seeing a saucer-shaped UFO with windows, which came close enough for Barney to make out the occupants. The next thing they knew it was 2 hours later.

Afterwards they suffered nightmares and health problems. It wasn't until they came to be hypnotized by psychiatrist Benjamin Simon that their full story emerged. Under hypnosis, the Hills recalled that small aliens, matching later descriptions of "greys", had taken them on board the UFO, examined and probed them (including their reproductive organs), and then instructed them to forget the experience before returning them to their car.

Trivia...

Two weeks before Barney Hill recalled, under hypnosis, the wraparound eyes of his alien abductors, an episode of The Outer Limits *was broadcast featuring just such an alien. Betty Hill claims that Barney did not see this episode.*

The case of Barney and Betty Hill *is one of the most influential in the history of alien abduction. This artist's impression shows the spacecraft and aliens who abducted the Hills in New Hampshire in 1961.*

The Hill case contains all the core elements of later abduction stories – capture, examination, conference, return, missing time, aftermath, and the use of hypnotic regression. To sceptics this is evidence that later abduction stories are based on this "classic" early case.

The woodsman and the writer

Other important cases include the 1975 Travis Walton case and the 1987 Whitley Strieber case. In November 1975, six woodcutters claimed that their colleague, Travis Walton, had disappeared after approaching a UFO. When he reappeared several days later, he told a lurid tale of greys, abduction, and a hangar full of UFOs.

It has been suggested that the Walton episode was invented to cover up the woodcutters' failure to meet their work quota.

Trivia...

Both the Walton and Strieber cases have been made into movies, respectively called Fire in the Sky *and* Communion, *the latter starring Christopher Walken.*

Whitley Strieber is a horror writer (a fact that immediately arouses the suspicion of sceptics) whose 1987 account of his abductions and brutal examinations, *Communion*, was a massive bestseller and helped to propel the abduction phenomenon to the forefront of ufology. Its cover image of a typical grey has become famous. Whitley Strieber's account of being anally probed by aliens echoes the same element in Barney Hill's story.

The holy trinity

Despite the high profile of the Hill case and others, the abduction phenomenon was still a minor element of the UFO mystery until the work of New York artist Budd Hopkins. Unlike most ufologists Hopkins did not believe that abductions like the Hills' were isolated incidents. Instead he believed that the aliens' ability to block memories meant that anyone could be an abductee, and that it might be happening on a far larger scale than previously imagined.

Budd Hopkins's 1981 book* Missing Time *brought together the stories of many abductees to suggest a sinister pattern of co-ordinated alien activity. His 1987 book* Intruders *introduced the idea of alien–human hybrids, providing a motive for the evil alien conspiracy.

INTERNET

www.intrudersfoundation.org

Check out the home page for Budd Hopkins's Intruders Foundation.

Together with two other abduction researchers, psychiatrist John Mack and historian David Jacobs, Hopkins became the driving force behind the growing phenomenon. The three have been referred to as "the holy trinity" of abduction research.

The Brooklyn Bridge mystery

Possibly the most sensational abduction case so far is the 1989 Linda Cortile "Brooklyn Bridge" abduction. Cortile claims that in November 1989 she was "beamed" out of her New York apartment, in a typical abduction scenario.

LINDA CORTILE WITH BUDD HOPKINS

In 1991 Hopkins received a mysterious letter from two police officers who explained that they saw Linda Cortile floating out of her window into a UFO, which then dived into the Hudson River near the Brooklyn Bridge. Hopkins suggests that another source of confirmation came from a woman driving across Brooklyn Bridge at the time. His research uncovered an increasingly fantastic story. Hopkins claims that the two "police officers" were Secret Service men escorting UN Secretary-General Javier Perez de Cuellar, who not only witnessed Cortile's abduction but was later abducted himself.

The case remains frustratingly, and typically, unresolved. Abduction researchers call it the "Case of the Century". Sceptics point to a tendency for UFO and abduction claims to become steadily more sensational, a pattern usually associated with entertainment media rather than true stories.

The Brooklyn Bridge *was the scene of the 1989 Linda Cortile abduction – the "Case of the Century".*

Implants

ONE OF THE MAIN PROBLEMS with the abduction phenomenon is that in most cases the only evidence is the abductee's story. As we've seen in previous chapters, anecdotal evidence is not always reliable.

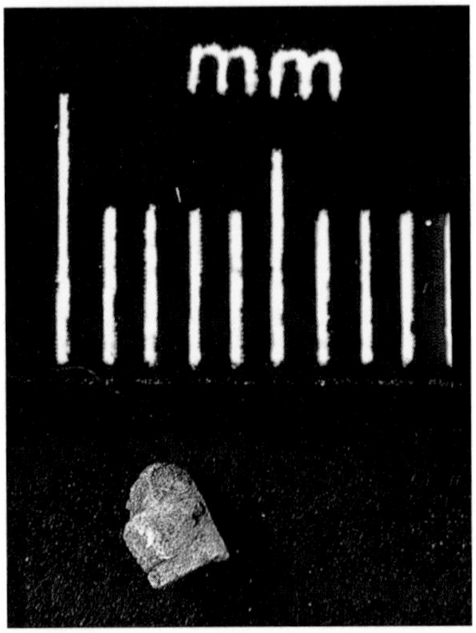

This "alien implant" *was removed from the roof of an abductee's mouth.*

Some abductees report that the aliens implant tiny devices in their heads or bodies. If these "implants" could be recovered and examined, they might provide physical evidence to back up the claims of the abductees.

In typical ufology fashion this has not proved straightforward. Budd Hopkins and others have attempted to arrange scans to look for implants in the heads of abductees. On the rare occasions that a possible implant has been detected by a scan, the device has failed to show up on subsequent scans. Abduction researchers claim that the aliens have removed them during the interval. Sceptics say they were simply scanning artefacts in the first place.

In a few rare cases suspected implants have been extracted from abductees, but analysis has failed to identify what they are. Sceptics point out that there is no way of proving that the devices weren't inserted by the abductees themselves.

THE CAMERA SHY ALIENS

Many abductees claim that they are regularly and repeatedly abducted from their bedrooms, which has inevitably led to the suggestion that they should be videotaped at night. Both Budd Hopkins and David Jacobs have attempted this without success. Either the aliens (understandably) avoid abductees when they are under video surveillance, or they use their mind control powers to make the abductee destroy the tape. An interesting, if not entirely ethical, experiment would be to videotape abductees without their knowledge, but as far as I am aware this has not been done.

Truth and lies

THE EXTRAORDINARY CLAIMS of the abduction researchers have aroused hostility and disbelief from sceptics and conservative ufologists alike. But if the abduction believers are wrong, how can we explain the mass of abduction reports from sincere, sane people? The sceptical position is that the true source of the abduction phenomenon are the abductees themselves. In other words the abduction experience comes from the mind of the abductee.

DEFINITION

When one person is subconsciously influenced by another, this is known as **folie à deux**. *The term is French for "madness of two".*

Psychological explanations for the abduction phenomenon include hypnotically induced fantasies, hypnagogic hallucinations, sleep paralysis and night terrors, temporal lobe epilepsy, and ***folie à deux***.

Hypnosis on trial

The abduction researcher's primary tool for obtaining reports from abductees is hypnosis. Abduction researchers argue that hypnosis is essential to overcome the memory blocks imposed by alien mind control, but the reliability and credibility of memories recovered under hypnosis is increasingly in doubt.

There is considerable evidence that memories recovered under hypnosis are not real memories, but fantasies based on scraps of actual memory, combined with other material to make a plausible story. Psychologists call this process "confabulation".

Confabulation is not the same as lying. People who confabulate under hypnosis are not consciously making up stories. They are unconsciously combining fact and fiction to produce a fantasy. But why would they do this?

■ **No-one knows** *if the information recovered under hypnosis is reliable fact or confabulation.*

The conformists

Psychologists have found that people in a hypnotic trance (known as subjects) are extremely susceptible to subtle mental pressures. These pressures include the desire to please the hypnotist, who is an authority figure – someone who has psychological authority over the subject.

Another mental pressure on potential abductees is the desire to conform – to go along with everyone else. All humans feel this pressure, but particularly people who are confused or troubled, as is the case with many abductees.

Psychologists believe that the pressure to please the hypnotist, combined with the pressure to conform to the group, can lead the subject to confabulate an abduction story. All of these processes are unconscious.

The fantasy-prone personality

What about abductees who don't need hypnosis to remember their abductions? Some sceptics argue that they probably have fantasy prone personalities. Fantasy-prone people are not mentally ill; they are simply more likely to experience rich fantasies than others, and may have greater difficulty distinguishing between fantasy and reality.

INTERNET

www.skeptic.com/archives29.html

Visit this site for the sceptic's position on recovered memory and hypnotic regression.

There is some evidence that the fantasy-prone personality type is common among abductees – according to one survey 87 per cent of abductees show signs of fantasy proneness. However, many psychologists argue that there is no such thing as a fantasy-prone personality.

The madness of crowds

Many abduction researchers are aware of the shortcomings of individual witness testimony. They point to abduction reports that seem to be confirmed by another witness, who may have been abducted as well, or simply have seen a UFO.

Sceptical psychologists say that multiple witness abduction reports are the result of one person subconsciously influencing another – the folie à deux phenomenon.

Without consciously realizing it, one person follows the other's lead in making decisions and interpreting what they see. They may even unconsciously invent memories that coincide with the other person's. For instance, some sceptics argue that Barney Hill's abduction account was unconsciously influenced by his wife's own recollections. He invented a fantasy that agreed with hers, and soon came to believe that this was his own memory.

Folie à deux is a very controversial explanation for shared abduction reports. Even many sceptics think it is nonsense, and it is very difficult to prove.

Folie à deux usually only happens with two people who are strongly emotionally linked. But even strangers can influence each other's stories under the right conditions – for instance, in abductee groups. Sceptics consider that a witness's testimony will always be suspect unless it is given completely independently.

In almost every recorded abduction report involving more than one person, the witnesses either know or have spoken to one another.

The source

Most abductees tell their stories before they've met other abductees, so if they're making the story up, where does the fantasy come from?

Sceptics and supporters of the psychosocial hypothesis claim that abduction fantasies draw material from popular culture, including recent sources like science fiction and abduction literature, together with older sources such as folklore and fairy tales.

For instance, almost all abductions reported since the 1980s are very similar to the experiences of the Hills. Sceptics also point out that all the elements of the typical abduction story can be found in science fiction from the end of the 19th century onwards.

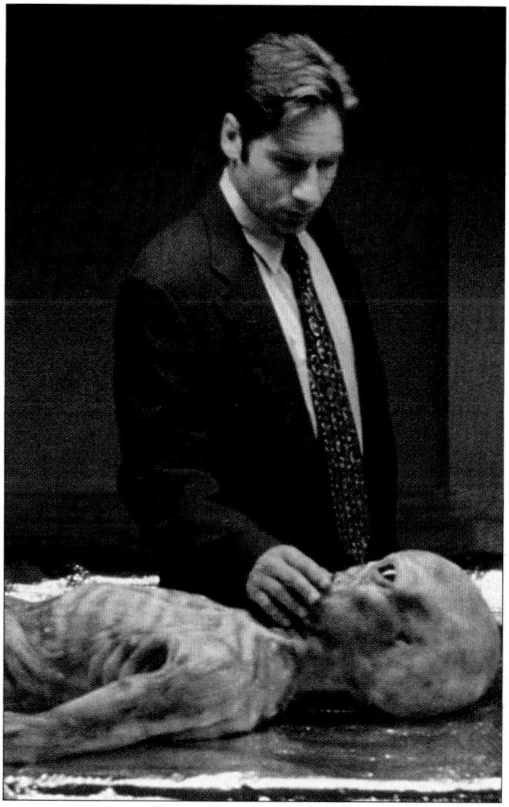

■ ***The X-Files*** *has provided alien enthusiasts and abduction fantasists with ample fodder since 1993.*

ALIENS AND FAIRIES

Alien abduction stories have many similarities to folk tales about fairies. Stories of encounters with fairies tell of small creatures with big eyes and pointy ears that appear surrounded by bright lights. These creatures sometimes come from the sky, and can lift humans into the air with them. Others come from fairy mounds, which resemble some descriptions of flying saucers. Humans who are abducted by fairies and then returned experience missing time, and a common motive for fairy abduction is to help provide the fairies with children, often fairy–human hybrids, in order to help rejuvenate their dying race. These are all classic elements of the alien abduction experience as well.

Fairy folklore *has many features in common with alien abduction literature.*

Monsters of the id

What could make someone begin to think they've been abducted in the first place? Most people accept that abductees have experienced something, even if their subsequent description of the experience is shaped by cultural and psychological influences.

Some forms of hallucination cause experiences similar to those described by abductees.

Sleep paralysis, also known as "night terrors", gives rise to sensations of loss of mental and physical control, and is often accompanied by the feeling that a strange or menacing presence is nearby. Sleep paralysis is closely related to hypnagogic hallucinations, which can take many forms, including strange creatures and places. Vivid dreams can also be reinterpreted as real memories under the influence of hypnosis. A little known but potentially quite common medical condition, temporal lobe epilepsy can cause vivid hallucinations without any other symptoms.

In summary, the human mind can produce an incredible range of bizarre and disturbing sensations without the help of aliens.

The true source of the alien abduction experience is more likely to be inner space than outer space.

■ **The stuff of nightmares:** *experiences in the unconscious realm of sleep and dreams can blend with real-life occurrences to create fantastic fabrications.*

A simple summary

✓ In alien abduction a human (abductee) is captured by aliens, taken on board a UFO, examined and probed, and then returned with no memory of the experience.

✓ According to one survey, 2 per cent of the US population has been abducted.

✓ The most important abduction case is the 1961 abduction of Betty and Barney Hill while driving through woods in New Hampshire. Their story contains all the elements found in later abduction stories.

✓ The most important abduction researcher is Budd Hopkins. He uses hypnosis to uncover blocked memories of abduction, and believes that the greys are using humans to create human–alien hybrids.

✓ Sceptics believe that the abduction experience is a fantasy, created under hypnosis or by a fantasy prone personality, by mixing together a real experience, such as a hallucination or dream, with elements from folklore, science fiction, and other abduction stories.

Chapter 21

Conspiracies and UFOs

ACCORDING TO ONE SURVEY, 80 per cent of Americans think that their government is hiding evidence of UFOs. This level of suspicion is the result of decades of official secrecy and lack of interest in UFOs. Are the world's governments responsible simply for mishandling the UFO issue, or are they hiding real secrets?

In this chapter...

- ✓ The official investigation
- ✓ Conspiracy theory
- ✓ Men in black
- ✓ Cover-up
- ✓ Back to the future

CLOAKED IN MYSTERY – A MAN IN BLACK

The official investigation

THE OFFICIAL RESPONSE to the UFO problem has sometimes been contradictory and confusing. For some decades now there has been no concerted official effort, or interest, in investigating UFOs, but during the first 20 years of the UFO mystery it was the military who took the lead in collection and investigation of UFO reports.

Project Blue Book

Obviously no one was more interested in unidentified craft in American airspace than the US Air Force. At first, reports were gathered haphazardly by local officers, but soon the Air Force began a series of official projects to investigate UFO reports.

The first official Air Force UFO investigation was Project Sign (1948), which was replaced by Project Grudge (1948–52), which was in turn replaced by Project Blue Book (1952–69).

Initially there was disagreement within the Air Force over the identity of the UFOs. In September 1948, senior Project Sign officers wrote an "estimate of the situation" in which they concluded that UFOs were interplanetary spacecraft. This "estimate" caused a storm in the Pentagon, where senior officials disagreed with the Project Sign assessment. As a result, Project Sign was quickly replaced with the more sceptical Project Grudge.

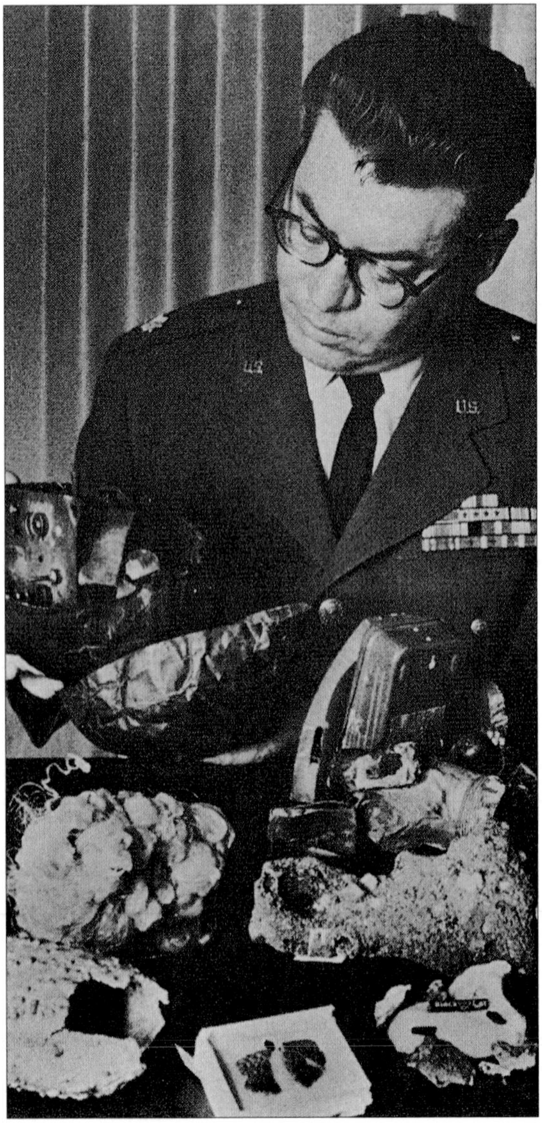

Project Blue Book *chief Hector Quintanilla with some items of interest to his investigation team.*

The cover-up begins

After a "flap" in 1952, when UFO sightings over Washington threatened to cause mass panic, the CIA decided that the public must be persuaded that there was no UFO mystery. Project Blue Book's new aim was to explain away UFO sightings – the military cover-up of the UFO mystery had begun. Unfortunately for the government, this new direction was at odds with the growing public belief that flying saucers were real alien spaceships.

Project Blue Book's increasingly unconvincing explanations only served to irritate public opinion, and led to widespread calls for congressional hearings into the UFO mystery. The Air Force seized its chance to dump the responsibility for UFO investigation altogether.

Trivia...

The French agency GEPAN (Study Group into Novel Atmospheric or Aerospatial Phenomena) is the only governmental UFO investigation agency in the world.

In 1966 the Air Force commissioned a deliberately sceptical review of the UFO evidence, known as the Condon Report. Its damning conclusions led to the closure of Project Blue Book in 1969.

Since 1969 there has been no official body responsible for investigating UFO reports, although the Air Force Office of Special Investigations (AFOSI) may look into individual incidents.

Officially the US Government is no longer involved in active UFO investigation. Many ufologists believe that the truth is very different.

Conspiracy theory

DURING THE 1980s a very different story about UFOs and the government emerged. This story has come to be known as the Dark Side hypothesis.

The Dark Side in full

The full Dark Side hypothesis goes something like this:

The US government started the cover-up almost from the very beginning, after retrieving the wreckage of a flying saucer and the bodies of its occupants from Roswell in 1947. Following the retrieval, President Truman set up a top-secret council of 12 leading scientists, military men, and politicians as a policy-making body to deal with the UFO question. This council was known as MJ-12.

The "MJ" stands for "Majestic" or "Majority", depending on the story teller. Associated with MJ-12 was Project Aquarius; an umbrella project covering smaller projects such as Project Plato and Project Sigma, which deal with communications with the aliens.

INTERNET

www.majesticdocuments.com

Go to this site to check out the MJ-12 documents for yourself.

At a 1954 meeting with the US Government at Holloman Air Force Base, a race of aliens called the greys revealed that they were just one of nine alien races visiting the Earth. They had come from Zeta Reticuli 25,000 years ago to influence human evolution through genetic engineering, and now they wanted government help for a scheme to rejuvenate their dying race.

The two sides signed a treaty. The government helped the aliens abduct cattle and humans, (for extraction of body parts and DNA, and for food), and to create hybrids and cyborgs – creatures that were part flesh, part machine. The aliens worked out of secret bases in the US Midwest. Meanwhile, the government was using alien technology to create its own advanced technologies at secret research centres such as Area 51.

MJ-12 operated as a secret government within the government, using experimental mind-control techniques and alien implants to control and subjugate the human race in preparation for conquest and colonization.

By this time the secret government included the leaders of Russia and other world powers. With alien technology they had established bases on Mars and the dark side of the Moon (hence the name "Dark Side"). The UN is just a front for their activities.

In order to fund their activities MJ-12 started trading in drugs. JFK was assassinated when he threatened to blow the whistle. Using drugs, guns, and genetically engineered diseases such as HIV, the secret powers seek to eradicate troublesome humans and prepare the population for martial law.

■ **The Dark Side:** *what do the shadows hide?*

Eventually a ***New World Order (NWO)*** will rule the Earth, using humans as slaves while alien hybrids and cyborgs settle the planet.

In the wilder versions of the Dark Side myth, the aliens have used time travel to foresee an imminent apocalypse on Earth, and the NWO is preparing to save a chosen few in vast underground bases until the Second Coming.

DEFINITION

In conspiracy circles, the **New World Order (NWO)** *is a secret global government that is using the UN as a front to take over the world.*

The disinformants

Incredibly, the origins of this lurid tale can be traced back to the Air Force. The Dark Side hypothesis first appeared in about 1980 after mentally unstable ufologist Paul Bennewitz started asking questions about strange lights near an air force base.

With the help of another ufologist, William Moore (co-author of the first Roswell book), an AFOSI officer named Richard Doty fed Bennewitz a stream of ***disinformation***.

Although Bennewitz became increasingly paranoid and eventually suffered a breakdown, he influenced other ufologists, including Linda Howe (producer of a celebrated documentary on cattle mutilation), John Lear, and Milton Cooper, some of whom also had dealings with Doty. Fake documents appeared, apparently confirming the existence of MJ-12 and other elements of the story, and the Dark Siders gained enormous popularity on the lecture circuit.

DEFINITION

Disinformation *is deliberately misleading information, which may be a mixture of truths, half-truths, and lies, given out with the intention of confusing or discrediting a person or point of view.*

Eventually Moore came clean about the disinformation campaign, but questions still remain. Why did the government go to so much effort to create the Dark Side movement unless it really had something to hide? Was Doty acting on his own (his military career ended in ignominy)?

Bad company

The Dark Side hypothesis is closely related to a number of other conspiracy theories that are popular and influential, especially in the US. Many of them are fascist or anti-Semitic.

The Dark Side hypothesis contains elements of the JFK and "fake moon landings" conspiracy, Christian fundamentalist warnings of the Apocalypse, and anti-Semitic conspiracy theories dating back to the 18th century, which accuse the Jews of setting up a secret government to control the world. It also overlaps with the theories of American anti-government militia/survivalists who believe that the UN is a front for the NWO.

Men in black

MEN IN BLACK (MIBs) are mysterious, possibly governmental, possibly alien, figures who act to conceal UFO evidence and threaten people into silence. Typically MIBs appear at the home of a witness shortly after an alien sighting, often before he has told anyone about it, and question him, despite seeming to know more about it than he does. They remove vital physical evidence and then warn the witness to keep quiet about the incident.

Encounters with MIBs date back to the beginning of the UFO mystery, but during the 1960s influential ufologist John Keel popularized the notion that MIBs had supernatural powers and were not of this world.

The MIBs introduced several elements that have now become staples of the UFO mystery – mysterious and menacing government involvement, unmarked black cars and vans, the convenient disappearance of supposedly conclusive UFO evidence, and the tendency of vital witnesses to change their stories or never materialize.

Considering their popularity in UFO literature, there is surprisingly little evidence that the MIBs actually exist.

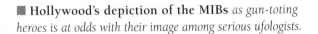

Hollywood's depiction of the MIBs *as gun-toting heroes is at odds with their image among serious ufologists.*

Cover-up

THE DARK SIDE HYPOTHESIS might be a paranoid delusion, but there is little doubt that governments and the military routinely spend billions on secret programmes, and go to great lengths to keep them secret.

The Manhattan Project

There have been several genuine secret military programmes in the last 60 years. These were shrouded in secrecy to start with, and in many cases the governments in question still haven't come clean.

In the 1940s the US Manhattan Project developed the atom bomb. This was a huge undertaking that was mostly kept quiet until the bomb was actually dropped on Hiroshima. Ufologists often cite the successful cover-up of the Manhattan Project as proof that the government could be keeping a huge UFO project secret.

The Manchurian Candidate

During the Korean War, communist forces shocked America by successfully brainwashing captured US soldiers. The hit 1962 film, *The Manchurian Candidate*, starring Frank Sinatra, dramatized the potential of this distressing new psychological technology. As a result, the CIA and other US agencies did attempt to develop mind-control techniques of their own, trying drugs and hypnotism.

Area 51

Some of the staples of UFO myth have a basis in fact. Agencies like the American CIA and National Security Agency (which deals with domestic security), or Britain's MI5, do sometimes use plain, black, or unmarked vehicles, while Secret Service men traditionally wear dark suits.

Area 51, where, according to Roswell enthusiasts and Dark Siders, the government researches alien technology above a huge underground alien base, is a real place. Part of the USAF Nevada Test Site, Area 51 is the home of genuine top-secret military research, including perhaps the development of the Stealth Bomber.

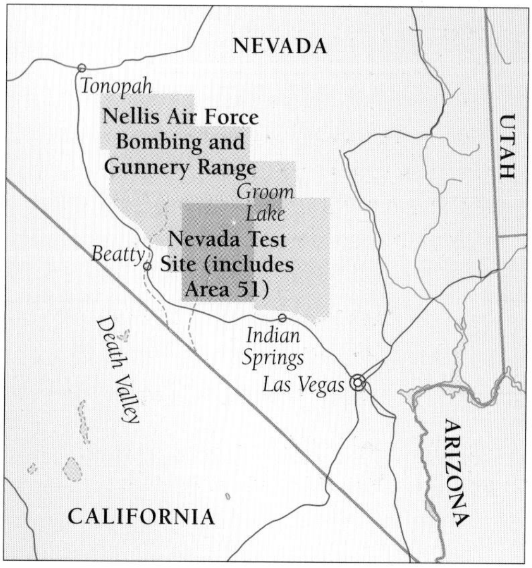

■ **Area 51 is located** *deep in the Nevada desert.*

Back to the future

A CENTRAL FEATURE of the Dark Side hypothesis is that the US government is using alien technology as the basis for advanced technology of its own, through reverse engineering. Dark Siders even claim that the USAF has working flying saucers of its own.

The federal hypothesis

This theory is close to one of the earliest and most popular theories about the origin of UFOs.

Most early UFO enthusiasts believed that some sort of advanced secret human technology was behind UFO sightings.

It was Kenneth Arnold's concern that his UFOs might be some form of Russian technology that prompted him to report his 1947 sighting. If advanced technologies were responsible for some UFO sightings it would explain the secrecy of the military.

OPERATION PAPERCLIP

America was indeed involved in a secret conspiracy with "alien" scientists to develop space flight technology – Operation Paperclip. The US government spirited away most of the top Nazi rocket scientists, who had developed the V2 rocket, bringing them to America immediately after the war. There they worked on missiles and rockets, helping the US develop inter-continental ballistic missiles (ICBMs) and the NASA space programme.

■ **Werner von Braun**, *ex-Nazi rocket scientist, proposed a variety of designs for interplanetary spacecraft (illustrated here) in his post-war position as head of the US space programme.*

Secret weapons?

Encouraging belief in UFOs might actually help the military, by providing a cover for testing of new technologies – the so-called "federal hypothesis". There have been a number of craft that might fit the bill.

One of the strongest contenders is also the earliest – the Air Force's top secret Skyhook balloon. It was used to detect traces of nuclear testing in the atmosphere, and was essentially a spying device.

Since then the military has developed several secret aircraft, including spy planes, pilotless drones (small remote-controlled aircraft equipped with cameras and even weapons), as well as "stealth" technology, which makes vehicles invisible to radar.

Project Y

Even more suggestively, there have been a number of attempts to build real flying saucers. In 1962, Jean Grimaldi of Normandy, France, built a propeller-powered, saucer-shaped airship. He claimed it could fly at 160 kph (100 mph). In 1986 American engineer Paul Moller successfully reached a height of 10 m (35 ft) in his propeller-powered mini-saucer, the Moller 200X.

■ **Skyhook** *high-altitude atmospheric-testing balloons were used in the 1950s and 60s by the US armed forces. Is it possible that civilian observers mistook these strange craft for alien UFOs?*

■ **The Avrocar** *was developed in Canada under the sponsorship of the US Army and Air Force, and was unveiled by the Pentagon in 1960. It was propelled by three gas turbine engines located in the centre of the vehicle.*

The most UFO-like aircraft built by humans was probably the USAF Avrocar, a sort of hovercraft built in the late 1950s. Originally designed by a British engineer in Canada for the company AV Roe, the Avrocar project – known as Project Y – was taken over by the US military in 1953. Stability problems eventually killed the project.

Project Y also tried to develop the Avroplane – a remarkable Vertical Take Off and Landing (VTOL) plane that was decades ahead of its time. The Avroplane incorporated many design features later found in the Stealth Bomber, and was supposed to reach speeds of up to 4,000 kph (2,500 mph).

Trivia...

The remains of the Avrocar are stored in a Maryland warehouse belonging to the National Air and Space Museum.

Some ufologists argue that confused memories of these strange aircraft, or perhaps even just their pictures, are responsible for some of the stories about secret UFO-storage hangars and reverse engineering.

A simple summary

✓ The first ufologists were USAF personnel, working for the official UFO investigation projects – Project Sign, Project Grudge, and Project Blue Book.

✓ Project Blue Book was closed down in 1969, by which time most ufologists believed the government was involved in a cover-up.

✓ Dark Side conspiracy theorists have constructed an elaborate story linking UFOs and abductions to secret government conspiracies to take over the world.

✓ The Dark Side theories may be based on government disinformation, suggesting that the government has something to cover up.

✓ Men in Black (MIBs) are popular figures in modern-day UFO stories, but there is no evidence that they really exist.

✓ True-life government and military activities, such as the Manhattan Project, and the development of secret advanced weapons or vehicle technology, may provide some basis in fact for many elements of the UFO mystery.

Further resources

Books

Ablaze! The Mysterious Fires of Spontaneous Human Combustion
by Larry Arnold, M. Evans & Co, 1995

The Bermuda Triangle Mystery Solved
by Lawrence Kusche, New English Library, 1975

Book of the Damned
by Charles Fort, John Brown, 1995

Borderlands
by Mike Dash, Arrow Books, 1997

The Complete Books of Charles Fort
by Charles Fort, Dover Books, 1974

Dark White
by Jim Schnabel, Penguin, 1995

Encyclopaedia of Hoaxes
by Gordon Stein, Gale Research, 1993

The Encyclopaedia of Mind, Magic and Mysteries
Francis X. King, Dorling Kindersley, 1991

The Ghost Hunter's Guide Book
Troy Taylor, Whitechapel Productions Press, 1999

In Search of Ghosts
by Ian Wilson, Headline, 1995

A Natural History of the Unnatural World
by Joel Levy, Carroll & Brown, 2000

The Occult
by Colin Wilson, Grafton, 1971

The Old Straight Track
by Alfred Watkins, Abacus, 1974

On the Track of Unknown Animals
by Bernard Heuvelmans, Kegan Paul, 1995

The Oxford Companion to the Mind
by Richard Gregory (Ed), OUP, 1987

The Paranormal Source Book
by Jenny Randles, Piatkus, 1999

The Prophecies of Nostradamus
by Erika Cheetham, Perigee Books, 1973

Psychics and Other Mysteries
by Joe Nickell, Prometheus Books, 1992

Quest for the Unknown Series
Reader's Digest, 1991

The Serpent and the Rainbow
by Wade Davis, Collins, 1986

Test Your Psychic Powers
by Susan Blackmore and Adam Hart-Davis, Thorsons, 1995

Turin Shroud: In Whose Image?
by Lynn Picknett and Clive Prince, Bloomsbury, 1997

The UFO Book
by Jerome Clark, Visible Ink Press, 1998

The UFO Mystery
by Hilary Evans and Dennis Stacy (Eds), Fortean Times, 1998

The Unexplained
by Karl Shuker, Carlton, 1996

Unexplained Phenomena: A Rough Guide Special
by Bob Rickard and John Michell, Rough Guides, 2000

Magazines

Fate
PO Box 1940
170 Future Way,
Marion, OH 43305-1940,
USA
www.fatemag.com

Fortean Times
IFG LTD
9 Dallington St
London EC1V OBQ
UK
www.forteantimes.com

Strange Magazine
PO Box 2246
Rockville, MD 20847
USA
www.strangemag.com

Skeptical Inquirer
PO Box 229
Buffalo, NY 14215
USA
www.csicop.org/si/

Organizations

The Charles Fort Institute
BCM Forteana,
London,
WC1N 3XX
UK
Research institute that studies strange experiences and anomalous phenomena.

Committee for Scientific Investigation of Claims Of the Paranormal
Box 703
Amherst, NY 14226
USA
716-636-1425
CSICOP encourages the critical investigation of paranormal and fringe-science claims.

Intruders Foundation
PO Box 30233
New York
NY 10011
USA
212-645 5278
An organization set up to research abduction phenomenon as well as provide support and understanding to those who have undergone a UFO abduction.

Society for Psychical Research (SPR)
49 Marloes Road, Kensington,
London W8 6LA ,
UK
020 7937 8984
An organization whose aim is to advance the understanding of psychic or paranormal events in a scientific way.

The Unexplained on the Web

THE INTERNET is an inexhaustable source of information on paranormal phenomena, where you can find web sites ranging from scientific research into UFOs to sites through which you can hire real-life ghost busters to rid your home of unfriendly spirits. This list is a starting point for your browsing.

www.apbonline.com/media/gfiles/cattle/
Read the official FBI investigations into the cattle mutilation phenomenon.

www.aspr.com
The official web site of the American Society for Psychical Research – one of the original paranormal investigation societies.

www.assap.org
The Association for the Scientific Study of Anomalous Phenomena can offer help and information concerning all sorts of supernatural and religious phenomena.

www.bfro.net
The Bigfoot Field Researchers Organization claims to be the only scientific body probing the Bigfoot mystery.

www.bigcats.org/
A whole site dedicated to big cats in the Scottish countryside.

www.britannia.com/wonder/wonder.html
A good introduction to a range of earth mysteries and mysterious sites from a travel company, so you can book a visit to the weirdest places in the UK.

www.britishdowsers.org
Home page of the British Society of Dowsers that tells you all you need to know about this subject.

www.castleofspirits.com/shc.html
Excellent coverage of Spontaneous Human Combustion basics and a list of cases, together with a sceptical review of the evidence.

www.cropcircleresearch.com/database/
A database of crop formations, with links to other sites.

www.csicop.org
The home page of the world's leading sceptical organization – the Committee for the Scientific Investigation of Claims of the Paranormal – contains lots of features, including electronic versions of some articles from the *Skeptical Inquirer* magazine.

www.cufos.org
Home page of the J. Allen Hynek Center for UFO Studies, which is dedicated to the scientific study of UFO phenomenon.

www.daniken.com
Enter Erich von Däniken's World of Mysteries.

www.encyclopedia-titanica.org/
The Encyclopedia Titanica provides detailed and ongoing discussions on everything connected with the ill-fated liner.

www.enterprise.net/apf/
Click here for everything you need to know about porphyria.

www.fatemag.com

This is the online version of *Fate*, started by Palmer as a UFO-centred sister publication to *Amazing Stories*.

www.feb.se/

The home page of the Swedish Association for the Electrosensitive (in English).

www.fiji.to/legends/firebeqa.htm

Learn more about Fijian fire-walking legends, and the specifics of an actual fire walk on the island of Beqa.

www.forteana.org

Home page of the recently founded Charles Fort Institute.

www.forteantimes.com

The web site of the journal of record for all things unexplained.

www.ghostclub.org.uk

The site of the UK Ghost Club, the oldest psychical investigation society in the world, provides a wealth of national and international information on cyclical, re-enactment and all other types of ghost.

www.ghostweb.com

The International Ghost Hunters Society web site has loads of convincing pictures to test your scepticism.

www.globalpsychics.com

Visit this web site and link to "Animals Talk" to meet Laura Simpson, a real life Dr Doolittle (or Animal Communicator), who telepathically communes with the animal world.

www.hauntings.com

The home page of the International Society for Paranormal Research, where you can hire some professional ghost busters.

www.hypnos.co.uk/

This site lets you download recorded hypnosis sessions to help treat a range of problems, including stopping smoking, asthma, and weight control.

www.kabbalah.com

Flashy, ultra-modern Kabbalah web site.

www.kirlianlab.com

Craig Bratcher, "Kirlian engineer", has set up a site where you can buy your own Kirlian apparatus, incorporating all the latest digital technology.

www.lobster-magazine.co.uk

Lobster magazine is one of the leading conspiracy journals.

www.lochness.co.uk

Keep an eye on Loch Ness in real time and try your hand at monster spotting.

www.magonia.demon.co.uk/

Leading advocates of the psychosocial school of ufology.

www.majesticdocuments.com/

Check out the MJ-12 documents for yourself.

www.marfalights.com

Official home page for America's premier earth lights.

www.mcn.org/1/miracles

The Miracles Page is an excellent online guide to all types of religious phenomena.

moebius.psy.ed.ac.uk/js_index.html

Visit the Koestler Parapsychology unit – the working department that's at the forefront of serious parapsychological research.

www.mysterylights.com

Good overview of the whole subject.

www.near-death.com/origen.html

Learn about Christian attitudes to reincarnation.

newage.about.com/religion/newage/msub134exp.htm

This site suggests experiments you can do with pyramids, where you can buy one, and how to build your own.

www.nostradamususa.com

The web site of the Nostradamus Society of America.

www.nsac.org

The web site of the American National Spiritualist Association of Churches gives links to other spiritualist associations.

ourworld.compuserve.com/homepages/AndyPage/

The Ultimate Ufologists web page provides an excellent launching point for UFO beginners.

paranormal.about.com/science/paranormal/cs/earthmysteries/

Overview of a variety of earth mysteries for beginners.

physics.about.com/science/physics/cs/quantumphysics

An easy-to-read guide to quantum physics – a decent introduction to a difficult subject.

www.princeton.edu/~accion/chupa.html

A *chupacabras* folklore site, set up by Princeton University students.

www.psici.force9.co.uk

The web site of the Scole Group gives their side of the story.

www.psiexplorer.com

This web site provides a simple, illustrated introduction to the auto-Ganzfeld experiment.

www.rael.org

The home page of the neo-fascist Raelian saucer cult outlines their aims to clone human beings (for the bargain price of US$200,000 [£140,000] a time).

www.raingod.com/angus/Gallery/Photos/SouthAmerica/Peru/Nazca.html

A gallery of aerial photographs of the amazing giant pictures.

www.religioustolerance.org/voodoo.htm

This web site contains lots of interesting background information and detail on the history and practice of voodoo.

www.rendlesham.com

Get the inside story on the whole Rendlesham incident.

saints.catholic.org/stsindex.html

An index of nearly every saint, which provides all the information on them that you could possibly need.

www.sciam.com/askexpert/physics/physics30.html

This *Scientific American* web page explains all about ball lightning.

www.setiathome.ssl.berkeley.edu/

Visit this site to download the SETI@home program and do your bit to find ET.

www.shroud.com

Keep up to date with the latest research and news about the shroud.

skepdic.com
The *Skeptic's Dictionary* provides in-depth investigation of a wide range of supernatural subjects.

skepdic.com/pphotog.html
A useful entry on thoughtography from the *Skeptic's Dictionary*, an online paranormal reference source.

skepdic.com/stigmata.html
This page from Robert Carroll's *Skeptic's Dictionary* makes a convincing argument that (almost) all stigmata are self-inflicted.

www.skiesare.demon.co.uk/c-l.html
Detailed online account of the Cash-Landrum case.

www.snu.org.uk
The home page of the UK's Spiritualist' National Union.

www.starchildproject.com
This web site has more information about the skull and attempts to have it properly analysed.

www.strangemag.com
This is the web site of *Strange* magazine, one of the leading fortean journals in the US.

www.themystica.com
On-line encyclopaedia of all things occult.

www.tmeg.com/artifacts/tunguska/tunguska.htm
Extremely detailed exploration of every aspect of the Tunguska mystery.

www.ufomind.com
As good a place to start as any, providing resources and links to the ocean of UFO material on the web.

www.uri-geller.com
Meet the great man himself on his official web site.

www.war-of-the-worlds.org
A comprehensive guide to the original Welles broadcast and the panic it set off.

www.wicca.com
A web site that sells Wiccan and pagan supplies, including stuff you might need for casting a spell.

www.wired.com/wired/archive/7.11/persinger.html
Fascinating article from *Wired* magazine about a machine built by Michael Persigner, which can induce paranormal experiences.

yaron.clever.net/precog
Yaron Mayer, former member of the Israeli Parapsychology Association, has set up his own Central Premonitions Registry, where you can officially log any premonitions or prophetic dreams that you have.

A simple glossary

AAP Anomalous aerial phenomena – another name for UFOs.

ABC Alien Big Cat – panther-like cat foreign to area where it is sighted.

Abductee Someone who has been abducted by an alien.

AFOSI Air Force Office of Special Investigations – US body that sometimes looks into UFO incidents.

Alchemy Magical and philosophical quest for spiritual and material transformation.

Alien abduction A CE4, where the subject is kidnapped, taken on board a UFO, experimented on, and returned with all memories of the event erased.

Ancient astronauts Theory that ancient peoples were visited by advanced spacemen who taught them the wonders of civilization.

Anecdotal evidence Evidence from stories or personal recollections, rather than from laboratory studies.

Angel hair Mysterious thread-like substance from the sky – probably spiders' webs.

Animal magnetism Invisible force, similar to electricity, which was believed to flow through all living things.

Animism Belief in nature spirits.

Anomaly Something that is out of place or not as expected.

Anspi Animal psi – ESP abilities in animals.

Apports Objects that materialize out of thin air during a séance.

Ascendant Sign of the zodiac that was rising on the eastern horizon when you were born.

Astral body Spirit or soul-like form that can leave the body, according to spiritualists and magicians.

Astral projection The ability of the soul to leave the body and travel on the astral plane.

Astral travel Journey made by the astral body.

Aura A glowing outline that surrounds people or objects, not visible to the naked eye.

Automatic writing Writing produced by someone in a trance state (e.g., under hypnosis or possessed by spirits).

Autoscopy Medical condition that causes people to hallucinate a transparent mirror image of themselves.

Ball lightning Highly charged, spherical ball of fire created by storms.

Bermuda Triangle Area of the Atlantic Ocean in which a large number of ships and aeroplanes have mysteriously vanished.

Bilocation Appearing in two places at once.

Bioelectricity Electrical energy in living things.

Bird parliament Gathering of birds apparently trying another bird, which is then executed by the assembly.

Camera artefacts False images produced by a camera or camcorder.

Cartomancy Divination using cards.

Cattle mutilation Phenomenon mainly found in the American mid-west, associated with sightings of black helicopters and UFOs.

CE1 Close encounter of the first kind – sighting of a UFO.

CE2 Close encounter of the second kind – encounter with a UFO that leaves physical traces such as landing marks.

CE3 Close encounter of the third kind – sighting of or contact with the occupants of a UFO.

CE4 Close encounter of the fourth kind – encounter where the witness enters a UFO.

CE5 Close encounter of the fifth kind – encounter with paranormal elements such as telepathy.

Cereology The study of crop circles.

Channelling The ability to allow another spirit or consciousness to act or speak through you.

Charismatics Faith-healing preachers of great emotional power who often perform dramatic cures as part of large prayer meetings.

Chupacabras Bat-winged kangaroo-like creature that drains the blood out of goats, chickens, and other livestock in Latin America.

Circle maker Someone who makes crop circles.

Clairvoyance The ability to perceive information about objects, places, and events without the use of normal senses.

Confabulation The process of unconsciously combining fact and fiction to produce a plausible story.

Contactee Person who claims to have been given special knowledge or powers by aliens.

Correlation A relation between two things. If two factors correlate, they are not necessarily directly linked but a causative link is implied.

Crisis apparition Ghost of a living person experiencing or approaching a crisis.

Crop circle Pattern in a field, formed by flattened plants.

Cropwatcher Cereologist.

Cryptomnesia Hidden memory – memories stored in the brain that cannot be consciously recalled.

Cryptozoology The study of strange creatures.

Cultural source hypothesis Theory that supernatural experiences are derived from the cultural background (the myths, legends, folklore, superstitions, etc) of the people who have them.

Cyborg Creature that is part flesh, part machine.

Cyclops One-eyed giant of Greek myth.
***Daoine sidhe* ["theena shee"]** Gaelic name for original fairy inhabitants of Ireland.
Dark Side hypothesis Theory that world governments and aliens are in conspiracy to create a race of human–alien hybrids to take over the world.
Daylight disc Apparently metallic, structured UFO seen in daylight.
Disinformation Deliberately misleading information given out with the intention of confusing or discrediting a person or point of view.
Divining rod *See* Dowsing rod
Doppelganger A double – an apparition that looks exactly like the witness.
Dowsing Ability to find hidden water or other substances using a dowsing rod or similar tool.
Dowsing rod Forked rod made out of wood or other material, used to find hidden water or other substances.
Earth lights Lights seen emanating from or disappearing into the ground, or which are associated with other aspects of earth mysteries, such as crop circles or standing stones.
EBE Extraterrestrial biological entity, or alien.
Ectoplasm Matter from the spirit world, produced from the body of a medium.
Electromagnetism Combination of electrical energy and magnetic force.
Electrosensitivity Adverse health reaction to electromagnetic forces.
Electrostatic field A field generated by static charge.
Endorphins Substances produced by the brain and other nervous tissue in response to pain or strong emotions.
Epicentre The focus of a poltergeist haunting – commonly a child or adolescent.
ESP Extra-Sensory Perception – the ability to perceive information without the use of the senses known to science.
ETH Extraterrestrial hypothesis – theory that UFOs are alien spacecraft.
Ether Originally believed to be the medium through which electricity moved, now believed by spiritualists to be the medium in which the spirits reside.
ETI Extraterrestrial intelligence – the existence of intelligent life on other worlds.
EVP Electronic Voice Phenomena – messages received from the dead by means of electronic media.
Exorcism Driving out a ghost or evil spirit by means of prayer and holy ritual.
Expectant attention A state of mind where you are expecting to see something and thus more likely to interpret information accordingly.
Faith healing Healing produced by divine power, channelled through an intermediary.
Fakir Indian holy men trained in the mystic arts, from the Arab meaning "poor man".
False memory Memories unwittingly "implanted" by a hypnotist in the mind of a subject.
Fantasy prone personality Someone who is more likely to experience rich fantasies than others.
Fire-walking Ritual practice of walking barefoot across hot coals, embers, stones, or other material.
Firestarters People with a form of PK that allows them to start fires without using any apparent means of ignition, often without conscious control.
Folie à deux Psychological phenomenon where one person is subconsciously influenced by another, resulting in shared perceptions.
Foo fighters Allied nickname for UFOs seen by airmen during World War II.
Forteana Events, occurrences, or things that are strange, unexpected, or inexplicable. People who study such things are called forteans.
Ganzfeld "Uniform field" of light and sound that minimizes distractions from the outside world and helps focus attention inwards.
Gauquelin effect Statistical finding that scientists are more likely to have been born with Saturn in the ascendant, and soldiers and athletes with Mars in the ascendant.
Geomancy Earth magic – magic involving use of geography or landscape.
Ghost rockets Mystery missile-like UFOs seen over Scandinavia during 1946.
Glossolalia Babbling gibberish or in a foreign language, brought on by religious ecstasy.
Grey Since the 1980s most commonly reported type of alien – short and slim with pale grey skin, a large bald head, small nose, pointy ears, and wraparound eyes.
Hallucination Experience that seems real but happens entirely in the mind.
Hybridization Interbreeding between two different races or closely related species. Believed to be the aim of alien abductors.
Hypertrichosis Genetic disorder that causes sufferers to grow hair all over their skin, including face and hands.
Hypnagogia Slightly altered state of consciousness experienced on going to sleep, during which intense, bizarre, and vivid hallucinations may be experienced.
Hypnopompia Slightly altered state of consciousness experienced on waking up (*see* hypnagogia).
Hypnosis State of consciousness somewhere between sleep and full alertness.
Hypnotic regression Recovery of memories through the use of a hypnotic trance.
IFO Identified flying object.
Implant Tiny device inserted by aliens into the head or body of abductee.

Initiate Someone who has been introduced to secret knowledge – usually by being admitted, or initiated, into a secret society.

Kabbalah Jewish mystical/magical system.

Kirlian photograph An image produced by passing a high voltage electric current through an object on a photographic plate.

Laying a ghost Performing whatever ritual or process is necessary to let a ghost rest in peace.

Laying on hands Healing by means of placing hands on the sick person.

Leidenfrost effect Phenomenon where an insulating, protective boundary sheet of vapour forms over a liquid exposed to extreme heat.

Ley hunter Someone who searches for ley lines on a map or in the countryside.

Ley line A line across the landscape between points of historical or cultural significance.

Lung mei Channels of earth energy in landscape, named after the Chinese term for "dragon path".

Lycanthropy Psychological disorder that leads people to believe that they are wolves. Some sufferers even attack people.

Magonia Mythical or folkloric land in the clouds, which was the home of medieval sky ships.

Medium Person who can summon and communicate with the spirits of the dead.

Mesmerism Early term for hypnosis – Anton Mesmer's ability to put people into a trance.

MIB Men in black – mysterious, possibly governmental, possibly alien, figures who act to conceal UFO evidence and threaten people into silence.

Missing time Time that has elapsed of which an abductee has no conscious memory.

MJ-12 Majestic or Majority 12 – the secret council that controls US government policy on UFOs, according to the Dark Side hypothesis.

NDE Near-death experience – sensation of leaving the body and travelling down a tunnel towards a light.

New Age Holistic, mystical fusion of belief systems.

New World Order (NWO) In conspiracy circles, a secret global government that is using the UN as a front to take over the world.

NICAP National Investigations Committee on Aerial Phenomena – first and largest civilian UFO organization.

Night terror Another name for sleep paralysis.

Nuts and bolts School of ufology that favours the Extra-Terrestrial Hypothesis.

OBE Out-of-body experience – where a person's consciousness seems to leave his body and look about independently.

OOP Out Of Place animal – creature sighted or encountered someplace where it doesn't belong.

Oracle Both something that gives prophecies or advice and the actual answers given.

Orthoteny The idea that ley lines are flight routes for alien spaceships.

Ouija board A board marked with letters, numbers, and words that can be indicated by a pointer.

Paranormal Phenomena that are usually believed to be the result of some sort of natural power that is not yet known, but which will fit into the natural universe once we understand it better.

Parapsychology Study of the paranormal using psychological methods.

Pareidolia Tendency for the brain to impose meaning or patterns on random sensory input.

Pendulum A weight that can swing freely on the end of a string – can be used for dowsing.

Pentacle A five-pointed star; a potent symbol in magic.

Philosopher's Stone Substance or artefact that allows lead to be turned into gold.

Placebo effect Any therapeutic effect produced by treatment that has no actual medicinal value.

Plasma vortex Whirlwind of hot, charged gas that might create crop circles.

Poltergeist An invisible ghost or force that manifests through physical phenomena, such as making loud noises or throwing items around.

Porphyria Genetic disorder that can cause insanity and/or extreme sensitivity to sunlight.

Precognition Ability to perceive information about the future.

Project Blue Book USAF project that replaced Project Grudge. Ran until 1969.

Project Grudge USAF project that replaced Project Sign.

Project Sign First USAF project to investigate UFOs.

Psi A force, a type of energy that gives the human mind control over matter, space, and even time.

Psychic One who possesses strong psi abilities, whether they involve seeing through walls or lifting objects.

Psychic healing Healing produced by the power of one person's mind on another person's body.

Psychic rhetoric Language tricks used by psychics to make it sound as if they are more accurate than they really are.

Psychic surgery Form of psychic healing where the "surgeon" cures the patient by apparently physically removing diseased tissue without leaving a scar or wound.

Psychoneuroimmunology The study of how the mind can affect the body's natural defence systems.

Psychosocial hypothesis (PSH) Theory that UFO sightings result from a psychological source, interpreted according to social and cultural background.

Pyramid power Effect on objects placed inside a pyramid.
Pyramidology Study of the secret wisdom that could be encoded within the structure of the pyramids.
Quantum physics Branch of science that deals with the world of subatomic particles and events.
Radiesthesia Dowsing with a pendulum.
Recovered memory Suppressed memories recovered through hypnosis.
Religious ecstasy Altered state of consciousness produced by religious fervour, excitement, or prolonged contemplation, sometimes with the help of drugs or fasting.
Remote viewing Type of clairvoyance, where a psychic is apparently able to mentally travel to a distant and/or unknown location and observe what is going on there.
Reptoids Reptilian aliens, possibly at war with the greys.
Reverse engineering Process of working backwards from super-advanced alien technology to arrive at technology that humans can understand and use.
Roc Giant bird of Arabian legend. Preyed on elephants.
Royal touch The belief that kings, queens, and emperors can heal simply by touch.
RSPK Recurrent spontaneous psychokinesis – believed by many to be the real cause of poltergeist phenomena.
Satanism Worship of the Devil and use of black magic.
Saucer cult Religion based on alien contact and secret wisdom gained from the aliens.
Scepticism Open-mindedness; suspicion of dogmatic thinking.
Séance A group of people gathered together to summon the spirits and watch a medium perform.
Shaman Holy man of Eastern Siberian tribes such as the Tungus. Combination of priest, healer, wise man, and magician.
SHC Spontaneous human combustion.
Sindologist Someone who believes that the Turin Shroud is a genuine image of Jesus.
Sitters Guests at a séance.
Sleep paralysis Phenomenon related to hypnagogia, where the subject is conscious but paralysed and experiences feelings of menace, sometimes associated with hallucinations.
Spell Set of actions and/or words that produce a result through magical means.
Spirit rapping Noise used by spirits in order to communicate.
Spiritual healing Healing produced by a supernatural force – a person's spirit or soul, or a higher power that is being channelled by the healer.
Spiritualism A new form of religion based on the belief that it is possible to communicate with the dead.
Spontaneous human combustion The reduction to ashes of some or all of a human body by a fire of unknown origin, which damages only the body and areas in immediate contact with it.
Stalk-stomper A plank with rope attachments for making crop circles.
Stigmata Marks on the body that correspond to the wounds Christ received during his crucifixion.
Supernatural Involving powers or spirits that do not belong to the natural world – ones that are literally "above nature".
Table turning Spiritualist practice where spirits answer questions by rapping, knocking, or moving a table.
Tachyon An imaginary particle predicted by theories of quantum physics, which travels faster than the speed of light and could therefore travel back in time.
Tarot Deck of 78 cards used in divination.
Tectonic strain theory (TST) Theory of earth light generation, which says that tectonic strain generates electrical energy that is discharged into the atmosphere, causing the lights.
Telekinesis The ability to exert physical force using only the power of the mind.
Telepathy The ability to receive and sometimes communicate information between two minds, without the use of normal senses.
Teleportation Travelling between two places instantaneously – disappearing from one place and reappearing in another without physically travelling over the intervening distance.
Therapeutic touch A diagnostic method that involves passing the hands over the body without touching it, and sensing the illness within.
Thoughtography Ability to project images onto surfaces, usually photographic film, using only the power of the mind.
Trance State of consciousness where someone does not respond normally to the outside world, acting as if they are not fully awake or aware.
Transmutation The transformation of lead (or other base metals) into gold.
Tunguska Body (TB) Object, probably asteroid, which detonated like an atomic bomb over Siberia in 1908.
UFO Unidentified flying object.
Ufology Study of UFOs.
Vampire Undead humans who feed off human blood and live only by night.
Voodoo Haitian magical religion based on the fusion of African religions and Catholicism.
Will o' the wisp Ghostly lights found in marshes and swamps.
Werewolf Humans who transform into savage wolves or half-wolf creatures.
Working Magical ritual.
Zener cards Cards printed with a set of five symbols and used in early parapsychology experiments.

Index

T

U

V

W

Y

Z

Acknowledgments

Publisher's acknowledgments

Dorling Kindersley would like to thank Simon Murrell for design assistance, Barry Robson for the design of the dogs, Katy Wall for jacket design, Beth Apple for jacket text, Jennifer Lane for editorial assistance, Hayley Smith for DK picture library research, and Hilary Bird for the index.

Picture credits

The publisher would like to thank the following for their kind permission to reproduce their photographs: (Abbreviations key: t=top, b=bottom, r=right, l=left, c=centre)

Bridgeman Art Library, London / New York: 42tl, 119tr, 133tr, 136b, 137b. **Corbis**: 56c, 162c; Tony Amuza 68br; Craig Aumess 165c; Bettman 53bc; Bettmann 53bc, 57c, 80cr, 213br, 270c; Marilyn Bridges 166bl; Brian Cencura 84c; Christie's Images 139c; Cathy Crawford 105br; Darren Gulin 122br; Josette Lenars 58tr; Walter Lopez 150c; Caroline Penn 127tr; Digital Art 40br; Galen Rowell 244c; George Hall 62c; So Hing-Keung 114br; Joe Sachs 116c; Joseph Sohm/ Chromo Sohm inc 29bl; Paul A Souders 68br; David & Peter Tumley 58c; Jeff Vanuga 188c; Bill Varie 156cl; Kennan Ward 204br; Ralph White 54bc; Bob Witkowski 144cr. **Mary Evans Picture Library**: 44br, 52br, 86cr, 87br, 108cr, 109br, 126br, 134br, 141br, 154br, 220br, 224tr, 227t, 247t, 249br, 258tr, 268br; Guy Lyon Playfair 76br; Harry Price Collection 22br. **Werner Forman Archive**: 208. **Fortean Picture Library**: 3tr, 5tr, 45tr, 47r, 88br, 91bl, 95bl, 98cr, 102tr, 102tr, 107br, 110bl, 131tr, 140br, 141tr, 142br, 149tr, 172tr, 173c, 176, 178t, 183br, 184br, 185b, 190b, 192cr, 194r, 195br, 197b, 199br, 200br, 204cr, 206br, 207tr, 212tl, 214c, 215cr, 215br, 217tl, 219c, 229b, 230b, 251t, 252cr, 254cr, 260, 262r, 269r; Klaus Aarsleff 23br; Larry E. Arnold 152r; Dr Susan Blackmore 37t; Janet and Colin Bord 164br, 171bc; Paul Broadhurst 157bl; Robert A Ferguson 70c; Dr Elmar R. Gruber 64; Dr Thomas J. Larson 66bl; Tony O'Rahilly 78r. Derek Stafford 2; Andreas Trottman 210br; R.K Wilson 193br; **Tim Graham**: 222. **Ronald Grant Archive**: 60br, 94c, 184tr, 198cl, 217cr, 234, 238cr, 239br, 241cr, 242cr, 266r. **Hulton Archive**: 104bc. **The Image Bank / Getty Images**: 120br, 121bc, 253c; Rob Atkins 6-7, 8-9; Thomas del Brase 103tc; Bob Elsdale 123tr; Garry Gay 118cl; Inc. archive photo royalty 03RI archive holding 27tr; Pete Pacifica 34bl; Antonio M. Rosario 246cr; Laurie Rubin 35c; Randy Wells 100c; Corey Wolfe 132cr; **Masterfile UK**: Daryl Benson 170tr. **Moviestore Collection**: 257br. **Photodisc**: Lawrence Lawry 32c, Johnnie Miles 128c. **Photonica**: 15br; Michael Gesinger 112c; Louise Wheatley 106bc; **The Picture Desk**: The Art Archive/Egyptian Museum Cairo 43tr. **Popperfoto**: 21b. **Rex Features**: 46tr. **Scala Group S.p.A.**: 89b. **Science & Society Picture Library**: Jim Grace 205tr. **Science Photo Library**: 72r, 73br, 147bl, 169cr, 182t, 202r, 232cr, 255bl, 264l; Garion Hutchings 12r, 75cr; Peter Menzel 225b, Dr Seth Shostak 237b; Frank Zullo 41c; **Stone / Getty Images**: 18; Christopher Bissell 259tr; Robert Earnest 16tr; Reza Estakhrian 113cr; Robert Holmgren 82tr. **Telegraph Colour Library / Getty Images**: FPG International 39br; FPG International/Kamil Vojnar 48br; FPG international/Ken Chernus 31tl; FPG International/Stephen Simpson 50. **Topham Picturepoint**: 93cl. **Charles Walker Collection**: 24br, 25tr, 28tr, 186bc.